Roger Symonds,

Tai'rmynydd.

1982.

BRITISH FOREIGN SECRETARIES SINCE 1945

Avi Shlaim, Peter Jones, Keith Sainsbury

DAVID & CHARLES
Newton Abbot   London   North Pomfret (Vt)   Vancouver

ISBN 0 7153 7381 1

Printed in Great Britain
by A. Wheaton & Co., Exeter
for David & Charles (Publishers) Limited
Brunel House   Newton Abbot   Devon

Published in the United States of America
by David & Charles Inc
North Pomfret   Vermont 05053   USA

Published in Canada
by Douglas David & Charles Limited
1875 Welch Street   North Vancouver   BC

CONTENTS

Foreword by Lord Sherfield   6

Preface   9

List of Foreign Secretaries Since 1945   11

1   The Foreign Secretary and the Making of
    British Foreign Policy   13

2   Ernest Bevin   27

3   Herbert Morrison   70

4   Anthony Eden   81

5   Harold Macmillan   110

6   Selwyn Lloyd   117

7   Lord Home   144

8   R.A.Butler   174

9   Patrick Gordon-Walker   181

10 Michael Stewart   191

11 George Brown   205

    Postcript   221

    Notes   226

    Index   260

FOREWORD

I am glad to write a foreword to this volume of essays on
the British foreign secretaries from 1945-1972. First,
because it is the product of the Department of Politics
at the University of Reading, which is bringing out a
number of interesting studies in contemporary history,
and secondly because I have myself, at one time or
another, served and worked with seven out of the ten
Secretaries of State included in this volume.

I do not myself subscribe to a number of the judgements
which are delivered in these pages. It would be unusual
if I did. In particular I find the assessment of my
former Chief, Lord Avon, (Anthony Eden) unduly harsh.
But each of these essays is a serious contribution, based
on personal interviews and correspondence as well as
available documents, to the history of a period still too
close for a final evaluation of the policies which were
followed, and of the men who bore the main responsibility
for them.

It is probably right to regard Ernest Bevin as the outstanding foreign secretary of the epoch. He rose above
the handicaps of his early life, his inexperience of
national politics, and later his ill-health. His parliamentary and public appearances remained a problem for his
advisers to the end. He would acknowledge the merits of
a draft speech and say "But it isn't me" adding on one
celebrated occasion "Give it to me and I'll degrammatise
it". Innumerable episodes of this kind endeared him to
his staff, but were irrelevant in relation to the magni-
tude of his performance.

Ernest Bevin had the elusive quality of flair, the
intuitive ability to assess a political situation and the
people involved in it, and to act accordingly. Anthony
Eden and Harold Macmillan, and occasionally George Brown,

also displayed this invaluable asset in a high degree,
though Harold Macmillan did not stay long enough at the
Foreign Office to exploit it. At the other end of the
scale Herbert Morrison appeared to be totally deficient
in it.

For me, several important points emerge from these
essays. First, the importance of a close relationship
and a good understanding between the foreign secretary
and the prime minister is clearly brought out. Here
there is a close correspondence with the relationship
between an American Secretary of State and his President.
Secondly, it is a significant and reassuring fact that
only in isolated cases has there been anything but a
close and intimate working relationship between successive
foreign secretaries and the officials of the Foreign
Office. Thirdly, the essentially bipartisan character of
British foreign policy in the period under review emerges
very clearly. It is a fortunate circumstance that party
politics have rarely affected major policy decisions,
except in the case of two or three countries of which
successive Labour governments have never been able to
take an objective view.

There is bound to be some question about the merits of
attempting, in retrospect, to apportion praise or blame
for specific decisions on this or that aspect of foreign
policy. In practice the making of policy is a continuous
process, with decisions in different fields interacting
on one another. Nor need it be a matter for surprise or
criticism, in an essentially bipartisan field, that one
foreign secretary should carry forward the policies of
his predecessor. The idea that the process of decision
making on foreign policy can be systematized is in my
opinion rightly rejected. A decision on a foreign policy
matter is usually the product of many minds and often has
to be taken in circumstances which could not have been
foreseen.

The foreign secretaries of this book were dealt
progressively weaker hands as the process of decolonisa-
tion diminished the British strategic position, and
British economic performance and strength declined, at a
rate beyond reasonable expectation, in relation to that
of other major industrialised countries. In these

circumstances the achievement of successive governments in the conduct of foreign policy has on the whole been creditable.

It is easy, even after a relatively short time, to under-estimate the effect of the climate of opinion in which foreign policy is made. This is particularly true of the European policy. There was virtually no support, in the early fifties, for British membership of a European federation, either in the two main political parties or from the public; and while it is the responsibility of Governments to give a lead to public opinion, they had in this period no help, and a good deal of hindrance from their European neighbours. In the end membership of the European Community was achieved, as almost all "historic" steps are achieved, only after deep and bitter controversy.

Now that the decision has finally been taken and ratified, British foreign policy has entered a new phase and acquired another dimension in which new perspectives and techniques will be needed. In this sense the conclusion of this book marks the end of an era. But in the new phase there will be no lack of scope for British initiative, and no dimi-nution of the burden of responsibility on the foreign secretary and his advisers for the protection of British interests and the deployment of British experience and influence in world affairs.

Sherfield
September 1976

PREFACE

We should like to record our thanks to the following
people who have spared the time to give us interviews,
answer questions, or comment on parts of the earlier
drafts: Lord Butler of Saffron Walden; Lord Caccia of
Abernant; Mr Robin Cecil; Sir Douglas Dodds-Parker;
Lord Duncan-Sandys; Lord George-Brown; Lord Gladwyn;
Mr J.E.Godber, MP; Lord Gordon-Walker; Lord Gore-Booth;
Lord Greenhill; Lord Harlech; Lord Home of the Hirsel;
Lord Inchyra; Lord Selwyn Lloyd; Professor F.S.Northedge;
Mr J.D.Profumo; Lord Sherfield; Mr Michael Stewart, MP;
Sir Douglas Wass; and Sir Kenneth Younger.

In addition we should like to thank the following for
their help in preparing the manuscript: Mrs R.B.Atton;
Mrs D.Duckmanton; Mrs M.R.McNamara; Mrs.R.Richards;
and Mrs.S.Simpson

Finally we should like to thank those innumerable
people who have given us help and encouragement – knowingly
or not – over the last few months during the research for
this volume.

Although this book is a co-operative venture, each of
us took general responsibility for writing individual
chapters: Avi Shlaim is responsible for the Introduction
and the chapters on Ernest Bevin and Anthony Eden: Keith
Sainsbury for those on Harold Macmillan, Selwyn Lloyd,
Lord Home and R.A.Butler; and Peter Jones for those on
Herbert Morrison, Patrick Gordon-Walker, George Brown
and Michael Stewart.

The manuscript was completed before James Callaghan left
the Foreign Office to become Prime Minister, hence he is
not included in the volume. The general reader need not
linger over the Introduction which is concerned mainly

9

with the theoretical approach adopted by the authors.
Those foreign secretaries who had two terms of office
(Michael Stewart and Lord Home) are placed in accordance
with their first term and the chapter on them covers both
periods in office. We should like to point out that,
unless directly attributed, all opinions expressed in the
chapters are those of the authors and do not reflect, in
any way, the opinions of others. We therefore take full
responsibility for the opinions expressed and for any
factual errors.

Reading, March 1976   A.S.
                                             P.M.J.
                                             K.A.F.S.

LIST OF FOREIGN SECRETARIES SINCE 1945

Ernest Bevin   July   1945 - March   1951
                              (Chapter 2)

Herbert Morrison   March   1951 - October   1951
                              (Chapter 3)

Sir Anthony Eden   October   1951 - April   1955
                              (Chapter 4)

Harold Macmillan   April   1955 - December 1955
                              (Chapter 5)

Selwyn Lloyd   December 1955 - July   1960
                              (Chapter 6)

Lord Home   July   1960 - October   1963
                              (Chapter 7)

R.A.Butler   October   1963 - October   1964
                              (Chapter 8)

Patrick Gordon-Walker   October   1964 - January   1965
                              (Chapter 9)

Michael Stewart   January   1965 - August   1966
                              (Chapter 10)

George Brown   August   1966 - March   1968
                              (Chapter 11)

Michael Stewart   March   1968 - June   1970
                              (Chapter 10)

Sir Alec Douglas-Home   June   1970 - March   1974
(Lord Home)   (Chapter 7)

CHAPTER 1

THE FOREIGN SECRETARY AND THE MAKING OF FOREIGN POLICY

Whereas diplomatic historians are open to the charge of giving undue predominance to the role of individuals in the sphere of foreign policy and sometimes writing international history almost wholly in terms of the great personalities involved, political scientists are apt to exaggerate the institutional elements of policy-making. The former rarely explain the premises by which their work is guided or provide a framework in terms of which the multitudinous factors which affect the actor's behaviour can be handled in a structured and coherent manner. The latter tend to emphasise political systems, social processes, and institutional patterns almost to the exclusion of any personal influences. Both fail to provide us with a meaningful account of the relationship between leading individual actors and underlying political structures. Yet it is only in terms of this relationship, that is, the interaction between individuals and the environment in which they operate, that a meaningful analysis of foreign policy is feasible.

The explanation of the sources of foreign policy and the motivation of a nation's international behaviour have traditionally been made in terms of the concept of national interest. Analysts of the 'realist' school have particularly tended to use the national interest as a central concept for organising their thinking about foreign policy as well as advocating it as the only rational basis for political action in the sphere of foreign relations. Thus, according to Hans Morgenthau, the 'objectives of a foreign policy must be defined in terms of the national interest'.[1] Interest he defines in terms of power which allows nations to follow 'one guiding star, one standard for thought, one rule for action: the national interest'.[2]

But the existence of a fixed and immutable set of foreign policy goals which can be objectively determined and which constitute the national interest, may be doubted. The criteria of power on which this concept hinges are rarely defined with adequate precision. To the analyst the concept of the national interest is too value-laden and has too many emotional connotations to be of much help in the process of systematic enquiry just as it is too vague and nebulous to be of any real operational value to the practitioner.[3] But even if these objections are over-looked and the existence of such a thing as the national interest is admitted, it can scarcely be denied that the interpretation it is given at any given point in time is influenced by the subjective values, ideological orien-tations and ambitions of the decision-makers in charge of the country's foreign policy.

It is this fundamental belief that foreign policy is made by specific agents in particular circumstances which leads us to prefer the decision-making approach to foreign policy. This approach, which was pioneered by Snyder, Bruck and Sapin, starts with the premise that 'state action is the action taken by those acting in the name of the state. Hence the state is the decision-makers'.[4] Thus, to all intents and purposes, the national interest becomes not something which can be objectively determined but what the decision-makers perceive it to be. The great advantage of this approach is that it provides the investigator with some leverage for analysing the generally elusive process of state behaviour. We shall not seek to apply the elaborate conceptual scheme developed by Snyder and his associates – a scheme particularly suited for research on specific major decision cases. We single out this approach because it helps to focus attention on the importance of individual actors and hence the importance of subjective, and in some cases idiosyncratic influences in the formulation of state policy. It reminds us that the impact of the external environment on the process of policy-making is not direct but is reflected through the prism of the decision-makers' minds. In the words of Snyder et al, 'the external setting is constantly changing and will be composed of what the decision-makers decide is important'.[5] The key to the explanation of why the state behaves the way it does lies in the way its decision-makers define the

situation. And in order to understand this 'definition of
the situation' from which action flows, we must attempt to
view the world from the perspective of those decision-
makers.

In this study we are concerned not with the whole group
of official decision-makers who are responsible for making
British foreign policy, but with one specific decision-
maker, namely, the foreign secretary. For it is the
foreign secretary who is responsible for laying down the
broad lines of British foreign policy. He is not simply
the most influential member of the foreign-policy-making
elite but he also stands, constitutionally, at the apex
of the pyramid of that section of the central government
machinery which is responsible for the management of
Britain's external relations. As a senior cabinet minister
his impact on policy can be crucial and he frequently
imprints on it his own personal stamp. No account of
British foreign policy would be complete unless it paid
sufficient attention to the role played by the foreign
secretary.

It is not our intention, however, to provide simply a
series of biographical sketches of the various holders of
the office, nor is it to contribute another diplomatic
history to an already crowded field.[6] The task we have
set ourselves is rather to look at British foreign policy
since 1945 from the individual vantage points of the
successive foreign secretaries themselves, as a preliminary
to explaining not simply how they reacted but why they
adopted certain policies in preference to others. An
account of the main lines of their policies can thus be
meaningfully followed by an assessment of their record in
the light of the scope and functions of the office.

The particular approach we have adopted leads us to pay
special attention to the foreign secretary as an individual;
his political status; the organisational context; the
domestic setting from which his policies spring; and the
international environment in which he operates.[7] We shall
now elucidate the meaning of these different variables.

The individual

In order to understand a foreign secretary as an individual

it is necessary to probe into his past not so much to
glean disparate data about his background, childhood,
education and career but rather to single out the
formative influences which account for his psychological
make-up and the salient factors which have moulded his
political evolution. His career prior to becoming foreign
secretary need not be examined in detail; only those
aspects of it which have a strong bearing on his subsequent behaviour need to be high-lighted and analysed.

   Foreign policy involves an element of choice, albeit a
limited one. It is for this reason that explanation of
specific goals and particular policies and to a lesser
extent the general orientations of British foreign policy
must take account of the beliefs and images of the
foreign secretary and his view of the world. The belief
system is composed of all the accumulated organised
knowledge that the individual has about himself and the
world outside. It may be thought of as a set of lenses
through which information concerning the outside environment is received. It orients the individual to his
environment, defining it for him, and identifying for
him its salient characteristics. Images are a crucial
component of the belief system and, therefore, have a
decisive effect on foreign policy since decision-makers
act in accordance with their perception of reality, not
in response to reality itself. As Kenneth Boulding
emphasised, 'We must recognise that the people whose
decisions determine the policies and actions of nations
do not respond to the "objective" facts of the situation
whatever that may mean, but to their "image" of the
situation. It is what we think the world is like, not
what it is really like that determines our behaviour'.[8]

   The subjective beliefs and images of decision-makers
are no less important in the analysis of policy when they
flow from instinctive judgements and unexamined premises
than when they are based on carefully thought-out
assumptions about the world. In both cases these beliefs
and images colour the decision-makers' perception of the
information they receive and condition their response to
it. And a great deal of confusion can be avoided by
distinguishing clearly between the psychological environment of the decision-makers and their operational
environment. As Margaret and Harold Sprout have argued,

16

while the outcome of state behaviour can be understood in terms of the decision-makers' operational environment – the capabilities and intentions of relevant actors – the decisions themselves must be understood in terms of the decision-makers' psychological environment – their beliefs about the world and other actors.[9]

Political status

The political status of the foreign secretary to a considerable extent affects his ability to secure the adoption of his chosen policies. Here one must distinguish between standing within the party and standing within the Cabinet. A broad popular base within the party would help a foreign secretary to sustain his conception of what British foreign policy should be in the competitive struggle between the various pluralist groupings which characterise modern political parties. In this respect Ernest Bevin's command of extensive trade-union support was a great asset to him in party conferences, just as Selwyn Lloyd's lack of a wide popular base severely limited his political influence.

Similarly, the seniority of a foreign minister, his place within the Cabinet hierarchy and the degree of respect which he commands in the counsels of the inner Cabinet will be reflected in the degree of influence he will be able to exert on the formulation of policy. The ability to inspire confidence in his colleagues is particularly important for the function with which he is frequently, but not invariably, entrusted, namely, to act as the co-ordinator of the country's policies in the external sphere. Until the merger of the Commonwealth Office and the Foreign Office in 1968 this involved overview of Commonwealth affairs apart from regular liaison with the departments responsible for economics and defence. But the traditional supremacy of the foreign secretary in the co-ordination of policies at Cabinet level has been eroded by the long-term trend towards the blurring of the division between foreign and domestic policy. Today, according to David Vital, 'if there is a single characteristic of the process of British foreign policy making that deserves special emphasis it is the manner and degree to which the handling of foreign affairs is liable to be integrated at the policy making level with all the other business of the nation'.[10] Membership of the European Economic Community has, in recent years, lent a powerful impetus to this process of integration.

The importance of the relationship between the foreign secretary and the prime minister for British foreign policy can hardly be exaggerated. The prime minister not only selects the foreign secretary, but also sets the parameters within which the latter should operate; to a large extent he defines the functions of the office and determines the precise responsibilities of the various ministers in the sphere of external relations. In his capacity as head of the government the prime minister exercises a general overview of the main policies in domestic as well as foreign affairs. In addition, he participates directly in the conduct of foreign policy. All recent developments such as regular meetings between heads of states, 'summit' conferences, frequent meetings with foreign diplomats and visits abroad, have led prime ministers to play an increasingly active and important role in the making of foreign policy and in the diplomacy by which it is carried out. Today the pace of events and the speed of communications, particularly in times of crisis, is such that important decisions sometimes have to be made as a result of a direct consultation between the foreign secretary and the prime minister without discussion in a full cabinet meeting. It is not surprising, there-fore, as one former prime minister has pointed out, that 'every foreign secretary must accept a great measure of interest, or even interference, from the prime minister of the day'.[11]

For all these reasons a foreign secretary can hardly expect to be able to pursue a firm and coherent policy unless he enjoys the confidence and support of his premier. The intimate partnership and mutual trust between Bevin and Attlee on the one hand and Eden and Churchill on the other, have been commented upon fre-quently. George Brown, by his own account, is an example of a foreign secretary whose performance was impaired and whose credibility was undermined by the troubled and stormy relationship between himself and Harold Wilson.

The organisational context.

Policy formulation by the foreign secretary cannot be
separated from the organisational setting in which he
operates. The machinery of which he is in charge is not
a passive piece of apparatus but has its own traditions,
preferences, functions, rules and patterns of interaction,
all of which play an important role in the decision-making
process. It can limit or widen his options; it can hinder
or enhance his policies. 'Policy', as William Wallace
observed, 'evolves in a continuing dialogue between the
responsible ministers and their civil servants, a continuing interaction between political direction and the
pressures of established practice and administrative
interests. Where political direction is clear, it is able
to carry the administrative machine with it; in the absence
of firm political pressures, however, administrative
politics prevail'.[12]

The structure of the policy-making machinery affects the
direction and substance of foreign policy in all states.
In western democracies of the British type where foreign
policy is made by relatively large groups and involves
liaison with elaborate intelligence, defence and economic
agencies, the institutional aspects of policy-making
deserve an added attention.[13] For it is largely their
complexity which accounts for the rigidity of foreign
policy in technologically advanced states.

In Britain, once decisions are reached there is usually
little difficulty in securing their ratification. The
Executive is given a virtual monopoly in the field of
foreign affairs. Parliamentary criticisms are voiced,
questions are asked and back-bench rebellions occur from
time to time, but in normal circumstances the government
can rely on a steady backing from its members which is
reinforced by the party machine. Generally, Parliament
plays only a marginal role in the making of foreign policy.
In contrast to the American system where Congress inter-
venes at all stages of policy formulation, in Britain
Parliament is usually presented with the final programme
which leaves little scope for changes.[14]

Consequently it is on the executive level that observation and analysis must focus. The relationship between

the foreign secretary and his top officials then becomes
of the utmost importance, for it is they who supply him
with information, interpretation and guidance. This
advice, as a rule, emphasises the need for caution and
continuity. Both Conservative and Labour politicians
have criticised the Foreign Office for its innate conservatism, organisational inertia and imperviousness to
political direction. This resistance to change is partly
the product of the self-image of officials as servants of
the Crown and not merely of a transient government.
Partly it is the natural result of policy-making within
a large organisation. Concentration on immediate and
pressing tasks leaves officials little time or energy for
fundamental re-evaluation of existing policies. Adjustments tend to be marginal and painfully slow. The
prospect of an agonising and protracted reformulation of
policy works in favour of preserving the status quo,
unless the latter is demonstrably unsatisfactory.
'Success', as Henry Kissinger pointed out, 'consists of
moving the administrative machinery to the point of
decision, leaving relatively little energy for analysing
the decision's merit. The modern bureaucratic state
widens the range of technical choices while limiting the
capacity to make them.'[15]

   In Britain the civil service does respond to leadership,
as Winston Churchill clearly demonstrated. On becoming
prime minister in 1940 he galvanised this slow-moving,
cumbersome and ponderous machine into a sudden and
vigorous spate of activity. But the average foreign
secretary in normal times needs a high degree of firmness
in order to overcome the inherent conservatism of his
office and its commitment to the status quo. Only mastery
of his field and single-minded determination would enable
him to replace the 'departmental view' by a policy which
is genuinely his own. George Brown has written that 'the
Foreign Office is equipped to give the best information,
the best briefing on any international issue ... But
what bothered me ... was ... that it was they who were
deciding the areas I should be briefed about, and I
quickly became aware that, unless I was very determined,
I would inevitably become the purveyor of views already
formed in the office'.[16] Furthermore, if the foreign
secretary were to achieve a significant and lasting re-
orientation in the central direction of British foreign

policy he would need to remain in office for a substantial
period of time. It is not entirely a coincidence that
Bevin, who had the greatest impact in this respect, held
power for six years, whereas Herbert Morrison and
R.A.Butler, whose tenure of office was less than a year,
made hardly any impression at all.

   Generally speaking, relations between British foreign
secretaries and their top civil servants are characterised
by a remarkable degree of co-operation and mutual trust.
In addition, the permanence of the civil servants partially
offsets the effects of regular ministerial changes on the
course of British foreign policy. The constitutional
position is that the civil servants have to present to the
minister the various options open to him; they may warn
him against a policy which they consider ill-conceived;
they may forcefully advocate a particular course; but the
last word always lies with the minister, and once he has
reached a decision it is their duty to carry it out to
the best of their ability. In practice, of course, this
relationship is affected by the strength of the minister's
character, his knowledge and experience in the field and
his political standing as well as the personalities of
his advisers.

The domestic setting

If the organisational context is relevant to the study of
foreign policy, the broader domestic setting in which
foreign policy is shaped is scarcely less so. For in a
sense foreign policy is only one aspect of domestic
politics; it is an integral part of the internal political
process of the country. Among the inexhaustible range of
domestic factors which potentially have a bearing on
Britain's international posture, the following would
appear to be of particular salience: political culture,
public opinion, political parties, and the policy-
influencing elites.

   Political culture is the most pervasive of these factors,
but it is also the most difficult to define. It normally
refers to national characteristics as moulded by historical
traditions, to the ethos which informs political activity
and to the way the society is organised and functions, all
of which are reflected in the characteristic modes of

political behaviour. In the conduct of external affairs
one can certainly speak of a typically British diplomatic
style which is emperical, pragmatic and practical. It
consciously eschews the polemical ferocity of revolutionary
states and the strong ideological components encountered
in the foreign policies of communist states, in a belief
that co-operation is preferable to conflict and that
compromise can be reached by rational discussion between
reasonable and frank men.

Public opinion rarely has a direct and positive effect
on foreign policy issues, partly because it is inchoate,
lacking effective organisation and leadership, partly
because of the public's general lack of interest in external policy, and partly because in this country the control
of foreign policy is more oligarchic than the control of
home policy. Consequently the foreign secretary and his
advisers do not have to constantly trim their sails to
the shifting winds of public opinion. Reflecting on his
experience as minister of state as the Foreign Office,
Kenneth Younger could not immediately recollect any
occasion when he or his superiors had been 'greatly
affected by public opinion in reaching important
decisions'.[17] But, as he himself recognised, 'the Government tends to identify itself almost unconsciously with a
vaguely sensed general will'.[18] In other words, public
opinion sets the limits beyond which governments can only
venture by risking their survival, and in this sense 'the
(foreign) minister is there to tell his officials what
the public would not stand'.

Pressure groups which lend organisation and weight to
the views of particular segments of the public and which
promote sectional interests by acting as lobbies in
Parliament appear to play a minor role in the shaping of
foreign policy compared with the role they play in
domestic politics. But the paucity of the evidence
available makes it difficult to generalise about the
patterns of their activity and the degree of influence
they wield or to account for their direct impact on
particular policies of specific ministers.

More tangible and better researched is the link between
the party system and British foreign policy. The main
political parties act as channels for the expression of

public opinion as well as agencies for influencing policy. International issues, therefore, can and do get caught up in the cut-and-thrust of inter-party rivalry. The question of whether or not to join Europe, for instance, has been the plaything of British party politics for most of the post-war period. On the whole, however, the British two-party system encourages responsible opposition and reduces friction between Parliament and the Executive. The behaviour of both parties and particularly of their leaders is significantly influenced by the pattern of British government with its bias in favour of a strong Executive unhindered by partisan obstruction. Indeed its bi-partisan nature is one of the most striking features of post-war British foreign policy. With the exception of the Suez crisis and EEC entry, over which the Conservative governments came under heavy fire from the Labour oppositions, disagreement on foreign policy issues has tended to be on emphasis, timing and detail, and has not extended to the main principles of British foreign policy on which there has been a solid consensus. In so far as bitter controversies over fundamental issues have occurred (for instance, over unilateral nuclear disarmament), they have normally taken place not along party lines but within the Labour Party between the left wing, the idealists and the pacifists of the party, who demand the replacement of power politics by a 'socialist foreign policy', and the earthbound leadership.

The basic agreement between the Labour and Conservative parties on foreign policy is paralleled by a remarkable similarity of outlook on the part of the policy-making and policy-influencing elites. This is the product of the educational and social homogeneity which unites the political leaders, the top civil servants, the diplomatic service, the leading members of the armed forces, the controllers of the mass media and the directors of the academic and research establishments. Although the single-mindedness of these various official and unofficial elites which are sometimes referred to collectively as "the Establishment" is sometimes exaggerated, they undoubtedly exercise a major influence on policy-making in the relatively insulated sphere of external affairs.

The domestic environment can thus be clearly seen to affect external policy through its impact on the foreign

secretary. He not only shares the common beliefs and
values of the nation and its political culture, but also
plays an active role in the internal political process.
As a politician and party leader he cannot remain imper-
vious for long to the currents of public opinion, to the
wishes of major interest groups and to the implications
of his policies for the electoral fortunes of his party.
Nor is he immune to the informal pressures of the cluster
of elites which is concerned with foreign policy and of
which he is a prominent member. Both his desire to
retain power and his concern for the success of his
policies, which require a broad dependable domestic
consensus to sustain them converge to make him suscep-
tible to pressure from the welter of conflicting domestic
forces.

The international environment

The impact of domestic pressures on the making of foreign
policy is, however, limited and mild compared with the
compelling power of the external environment. For in no
other sphere is the freedom of government more limited by
forces over which it has little or no control. This
situation results from the structure of the international
system which, in the absence of one effective and authoritative centre of power, leaves states as the sovereign
entities. Consequently, whereas in the domestic sphere
sovereignty means supremacy, in the external sphere
sovereignty signifies the legal equality of all states.

   British foreign secretaries do not operate in a vacuum;
their actions and policies are subject to the inescapable
constraints imposed by the international environment.
Though not of their own making, this environment imposes
on them some of the main lines of their policy and
severely limits their area of real choice. 'Effective
freedom in foreign affairs', writes Professor Northedge,
'is capacity to choose between relatively few options.'19
The global balance of power, Britain's status in the
international hierarchy, the relations between and the
polities of the super-powers and the changing configuration of power between rival alliance systems are among
the abiding concerns of British foreign secretaries. At
the same time, Britain's limited military capability, her
intractable economic shackles and a general decline in her

power position relative to the other major centres of power, have significantly reduced her capacity to influence international events. She is no longer a first-class power but, in the words of the Duncan Report, 'a major power of the second order'.[20]

The limits imposed by external pressures on Britain's margin of choice raise the question of whether British foreign policy consists simply of passive, defensive responses to the harsh facts of international life or whether it is a purposive and goal-orientated foreign policy based on firmly held values and clear long-term aims. The latter is a rare phenomenon in a world deminated by power politics where most foreign policies fall between these two opposing poles. It is, therefore, more meaningful to distinguish between sullen submission leading to an aimless drift on the currents of world politics and an active and dynamic policy of adjustment designed to direct these currents, as far as circumstances would permit, to the nation's advantage. Among post-war British foreign secretaries Bevin stands out as an example of someone who practised the second type of reaction. Starting with a clear conception of long-term objectives he pursued a firm and positive policy aiming to extract the maximum advantage from a difficult situation. His successor, Herbert Morrison, by contract, does not appear to have had a clear notion of British objectives and his policy was not free from muddle and indecision.

The five variables we have been considering do not constitute an exhaustive list of factors with universal validity or a perfect scheme of categories whose relations are constant and between which there is no overlap. They should be regarded rather as the main components of a systematic investigation of the record of post-war British foreign secretaries. They should not constitute a strait-jacket on analysis but act as general guidelines for selecting the most relevant facts and exploring the relations between them. Even as such they cannot always be followed adequately because of lack of detailed evidence, particularly in the case of the more recent holders of the office.

Essentially this framework of analysis consists in seeing the foreign secretary as standing at the point of

confluence between two streams of pressures: one stream
emanates from the domestic environment and the other from
the external. The latter is clearly more powerful, but
the manner in which he reacts to both is conditioned by
subjective factors such as background, personality, style,
values, images and perceptions. The policies which are
the concrete expression of his reactions are shaped by the
organisational context in which they are formulated, and
his success in securing the adoption of these policies is
contingent on his political status and influence.

CHAPTER 2

ERNEST BEVIN

I

Ernest Bevin (1881-1951) stands out among post-war British
foreign secretaries by reason of his unusual career, his
unique character and the strong personal imprint which he
made on British foreign policy. He was the first Labour
foreign secretary to be supported by an overall majority
in the House of Commons. His tenure of office (1945-51)
was not only longer than any single term of any of his
successors, but coincided with a crucial phase in British
foreign policy, and his actions and policies during these
six eventful years laid the foundations for post-war
British foreign policy. For all these reasons, Bevin not
only calls for extended treatment, but offers an interesting and rewarding case study.

Bevin's roots were solidly working-class and he never
lost sight of the welfare of the working-man.[1] The qualities of realism, drive, resourcefulness and ability to
take a broad view of the interests of the Labour movement
as a whole, carried Bevin to the forefront of the trade
union movement. His career as a Labour leader helped to
produce a tough and self-reliant individual, preferring
organisation to empty rhetoric and able to take bold
decisions and stand by them. Above all, it taught him
the overriding importance of power. And it was the
profound conviction of the need to negotiate from strength
which was later to characterise his whole conduct of
British foreign policy. Yet there was always a touch of
the visionary in Bevin. While concentrating on the
immediate tasks, he always kept his long-term aims before
him. At the 1927 Trades Union Congress, for example, he
moved the surprisingly far-sighted motion in favour of a
European economic union.

Bevin distrusted the Right instinctively, but after he
began to play an active part in Labour Party politics in
the 1930s, he also learnt to distruct sections of the
Left, especially the Communists. Profoundly intolerant
of the idealists, pacifists and intellectuals of his own
party, Bevin helped to bring about the resignation of
George Lansbury from the leadership by a savage attack at
the 1935 Party Conference. He used all the influence of
the trade union movement to inculcate a measure of realism
into Labour's foreign policy and in 1937 succeeded in
reversing its opposition to rearmament.

With the formation of Winston Churchill's coalition
government in 1940, Bevin became Minister of Labour.
Although he was on the threshold of his sixtieth year
and had had no previous ministerial experience, he soon
emerged as one of the toughest members of Churchill's War
Cabinet, displaying remarkable organisational ability in
mobilising the nation's manpower and industrial resources
and immense political courage in introducing the unpopular
anti-strike legislation. Bevin also showed a keen interest in foreign policy during the war, criticising the
narrow social base of British diplomacy and emphasising
the possibilities of using foreign policy as a means of
promoting the welfare of ordinary people everywhere.

For Bevin, as for the other Labour members, the long
service during the war was not simply a useful prelude to
office, but a major formative experience. The training
they received in the rough Churchillian school of
realpolitik left a deep mark on their whole outlook. A
first-hand knowledge of the practical problems of con-
ducting a foreign policy in a world of power frequently
led Bevin to side with the Conservatives against members
of his own party, as he did towards the end of the war
over the support of the royalist regime in Greece by
armed intervention. The wartime foreign secretary,
Anthony Eden, told the Commons that throughout their
service in the coalition there was never a disagreement
between them on a major issue. For his part, Bevin was
evidently predisposed to continue along the main lines of
the common policy after the coalition government came to
an end.

When the Labour Party was returned to power by the
general election of July 1945, few people could have
expected Bevin to become foreign secretary. Asked by
Clement Attlee for his preference in the new adminis-
tration, Bevin said that finance and taxation had been
a special interest of his since his service in the
Macmillan Committee of 1931 and asked to go to the
Treasury, recommending Hugh Dalton for the Foreign Office.
Attlee initially agreed, but later reversed the arrange-
ment. Two main considerations made him decide to send
Bevin to the Foreign Office. The first was his expecta-
tion, based on his experience at Potsdam, that the
Russians would be aggressive and uncooperative and that
Bevin would be the best man to deal with them. The
second was that since Attlee had invited Herbert Morrison
to become Lord President of the Council and Leader of the
House of Commons, he feared friction between him and
Bevin and decided to keep them as far apart as possible.[2]

Since Attlee chose Bevin as the most powerful of the
Labour leaders and for his independence of mind, it was
only natural that he should have left Bevin as much freedom as possible in determining the main lines of the
Government's foreign policy and complete control over the
execution of policy. Having a strong foreign secretary
suited Attlee who took the view that foreign affairs was
the province of the foreign secretary and made a point
of not intervening, except in moments of crisis or when
Bevin asked him to. '"If you have a good dog", he wrote
in his autobiography, "don't bark yourself", is a good
proverb, and in Mr.Bevin I had an exceptionally good
dog.'[3] Attlee's main interests lay in the domestic sphere
and this arrangement enabled him to concentrate on getting
through the Government's vast legislative programme.

Attlee and Bevin were probably closer than any other
two members of the Cabinet. By the time they took office,
their personal friendship had grown into a mature political partnership. Attlee was quite clear on this point:
'My relationship with Ernest Bevin was the deepest of my
life. I was fond of him and I understood that he was
fond of me ... we understood each other very well'.[4]
Temperamentally, they were well suited to work together:
Attlee was quiet, unassuming, practical and detached,
and tended to remain in the background; Bevin was

exuberant, full of ideas and enjoyed the exercise of power and the responsibility that went with office. He had a high regard for Attlee's critical judgement and formed the habit of thinking aloud in his presence so as to clarify his own thoughts, and of sounding him out before cabinet meetings. The initiative always lay with Bevin, but his formulation of policy benefitted from Attlee's common-sense approach and there is no evidence that they ever disagreed on any major issue.[5]

Bevin not only enjoyed the confidence of the prime minister to an exceptional degree, but also commanded the respect and trust of his cabinet colleagues. As the leading trade unionist in the Cabinet his personal position was unassailable. As a senior member of the 'Inner Cabinet', which included Attlee, Herbert Morrison, Sir Stafford Cripps and Hugh Dalton, Bevin was not only in charge of the Foreign Office,[6] but was co-ordinator of overseas affairs generally. His eminent position also ensured that the Foreign Office point of view was seriously considered by the Cabinet in the formulation of foreign economic policy.[7] The absence of a standing cabinet committee on foreign affairs enhanced Bevin's freedom of action and unchallenged dominance in this field. He worked in close contact with the chancellor of the exchequer and the president of the board of trade, and when he made up his mind to get a policy adopted, provided he had Attlee on his side, he rarely failed to carry the Cabinet with him.

The wide industrial base on which his influence rested, coupled with an assertive personality which commanded attention to his views on a wide range of matters made Bevin the strongest member of the Cabinet next to the prime minister. In the first year there were many references to 'Government by Triumvirate' (Bevin, Morrison and Attlee) and one commentator observed that 'Attlee is called Prime Minister, Morrison thinks he is Prime Minister and Bevin is Prime Minister'.[8] Whenever doubts arose about Attlee's capacity for leading the party and the Cabinet, it was usually Bevin who was thought of as the best replacement. Repeated attempts were made to organise a palace revolution. In September 1947, Cripps told Dalton: 'we must now shift Attlee and replace him by Bevin, otherwise the Government, the Party and the country are all sunk'.[9]

But Bevin threw his weight against a change, compared Attlee to Campbell-Bannerman in his gift of holding a team of clever men together, and asserted that the party did not need personal leadership. Consequently, as George Brown noted, 'whatever personal ambitions there were in the rest of the team more or less cancelled each other out. Attlee was hoist on Bevin's shoulders and as long as Bevin kept him firmly there nothing could break'.[10]

Bevin's ascendancy in the party was partly the result of his capacity for energetic leadership. His trade-union experience taught him that leaders must be prepared to lead and not simply to follow. His skill in ensuring that he had the support of the majority gave him confidence in asserting the rightness of his policies. But more important than his personal qualities was the solid and unswerving support he received from the trade unions. In party conferences he could always rely on their massive bloc vote to rout his opponents.

In exercising leadership and control over the Labour Party generally, and in directing without losing the support of the party conference in particular, the Attlee-Bevin partnership was as effective as it was in other spheres. Attlee posed as the impartial, unspectacular, almost self-effacing party chairman, always ready to bow to the will of the majority and a model of integrity and high principles. Bevin's impact was unmistakably that of a working-class leader, forceful and blunt, direct in argument and unsparing in his attacks on opponents, particularly when he found them guilty of the deadly sin of disloyalty to the party. Using to the full his powers as an orator, wooing and cajoling his hearers, he rarely failed to elicit the anticipated majority in support of government policies.

In the House of Commons, Bevin was far less effective as a speaker. He was fifty-nine when he first entered Parliament in 1940 and he was probably too old to adapt his style to the new setting. He was much more at home in the tougher atmosphere of the Trades Union Congress and in informal gatherings, where he usually established spontaneous rapport with his audience and where his cavalier treatment of syntax was overshadowed by the force and conviction of his oratory. In the House of Commons his surveys were dry and long-winded, and he was unable to make a smooth speech or answer interruptions effectively. When asked how he dealt with parliamentary procedure, he replied: 'I stand up when they nudge me, I sit down when they pull my coat'.

Bevin's difficulties as a parliamentarian were increased by the almost unremitting hostility which the left wing of his own party displayed towards him. The Foreign Affairs group of the Parliamentary Labour Party included many intellectuals, pacifists and fellow travellers who spent much of their time drafting critical resolutions and argumentative papers which infuriated Bevin. For this state of affairs he was partly himself to blame, because he was out of touch with parliamentary opinion and took little trouble to get to know his critics and explain the reasons for his decisions. In-as-much as any explaining was done, it was by Dennis Healey who took it upon himself to interpret Ernie to the party. Bevin did things. Healey provided the intellectual rationalisation.[11] Bevin himself was savagely intolerant of minorities. What in his philosophy was unforgivable was any attempt to change policy by critics who did not share his burden of responsibility. This was the cause of his hatred of intellectuals who criticised the official policy from the sidelines or sought to modify it from the back benches.[12]

II

In contrast to his failure as a parliamentarian, as the head of a government department Bevin was an almost unqualified success. The news of his appointment was received at the Foreign Office with some misgivings. It was feared that the man who had warned in 1940 that 'the limited Court Circular Society of the Chancelleries will never return'[13] would set out to overhaul the diplomatic service. But no wholesale changes in personnel took place and Bevin soon became attached to his staff by a bond of mutual respect and affection. Many of them retained a sense of having worked with a great man with a powerful intellect and an inspiring vision. 'He radiated determination and personal force', writes Sir William Hayter. 'He was substantially the ablest and most powerful Foreign Secretary of my time.'[14] A no

less warm tribute was paid by Lord Strang who became permanent under-secretary at the Foreign Office in 1949: 'it
is difficult to think of a Foreign Secretary who inspired
more whole-hearted devotion in the members of the Foreign
Office at home and abroad than, by his qualities as a man
and as a stateman, this member of the unskilled working
classes and trade union leader was able to do.'[15]

Bevin made a deep impression on the Foreign Service as
a whole, and even those in distant parts who never had any
dealings with him were conscious of his impact. It was not
only that they felt he cared for their welfare and wished
to improve their conditions, or that he had shown his
readiness to stand up for members of the Service against
any criticism. As Bevin's private secretary pointed out,
morale was also boosted by the knowledge that 'foreign'
policy was now made in the Foreign Office - not at No 10
or elsewhere - and that once the foreign secretary was
convinced of the rightness of a given course it was unlikely that he would fail to get it endorsed by the
Cabinet. There was, furthermore, throughout the service,
great confidence in the basic soundness of his judgement
and admiration for the way in which he defended essential
British interests.[16]

It was sometimes alleged in the Labour Party that Bevin
was the victim of a successful bureaucratic conspiracy to
maintain the old order and prevent the promulgation of a
Socialist foreign policy.[17] There was little in Bevin's
personality to support the idea that he was an unwitting
puppet in the hands of wily and reactionary civil servants,
nor is there any evidence that his relations with his top
officials diverged from the normal constitutional pattern
in accordance with which their function was to advise and
his was to decide. He had a very strong will, normally
knew just what he wanted and had very clear ideas about
ministerial responsibility. Sir Ivone Kirkpatrick, who
succeeded Lord Strang as permanent under-secretary, has
emphatically rejected the claim that Bevin 'fell completely
within the hands of the permanent officials of the Foreign
Office ... He never allowed himself to be bounced into
doing something against his better judgement'.[18] 'Nothing
could be further from the truth', concurs Sir William
Hayter. 'He would listen patiently to what we had to say,
but he was liable to ask penetrating questions and his
decisions were often not those we expected or wanted. He

could be quite critical, too; once, when Rex Leper, on
leave from Athens, was expounding to him his views on
Greek politics, he said scornfully, 'You sound to me like
'Erb Morrison trying to fix an election'.[19]

When Bevin became foreign secretary in 1945, he had no
direct experience of Foreign Office work. But he brought
to his new job a great fund of wide and varied experience.
He had a passion for knowledge, and, preferring conversation to reading, he picked up facts and ideas by talking
to people. With his prodigious memory went a lifelong
habit of distilling wisdom from experience and of rearrange-
ing disparate pieces of knowledge in new and unfamiliar
patterns which threw a fresh light on problems. He mis-
trusted abstract ideas and theories and was supremely
confident in the soundness of his own intuitive judgement
precisely because it was so firmly grounded in experience.
Nor did Bevin's lack of previous experience of Foreign
Office work in any way mean ignorance of foreign affairs.
As a trade union official, he was accustomed to attend
conferences and discuss international problems with his
foreign colleagues. He travelled extensively in Europe,
the dominions and America, and had accumulated an
impressive store of knowledge of foreign countries. In
conversations with his officials, he frequently referred
to his earlier experiences and contacts.[20]

As foreign secretary, two of Bevin's qualities were of
particular significance: his grasp of essentials and his
breadth of outlook. He had a gift for reducing complex
situations to their basic components and of getting
straight to the essence of problems. He took all the
important decisions himself without getting involved in
secondary problems. With this gift went an ability to
look at international relations as an unfragmented whole.
His decisions were not taken in isolation, but as an integral part of a general conception of Britain's foreign
relations. 'For him there were no watertight compartments
in foreign policy: the world was one.'[21]

Bevin's greatest contribution to the process of policy
formulation in the Foreign Office was his creation of a
committee composed of one of the junior ministers and the
deputy and assistant under-secretaries, with the task of
preparing studies on long-term aspects of policy. This

34

was beneficial in offsetting the related tendencies of too
rigid a division of labour and losing sight of long-term
goals through immersion in minutiae. This committee provided a kind of planning machinery; it forced top officials
to think about problems other than their own and provided
the Foreign Office with an agreed set of goals and a sense
of direction.[22]

Though never a dreamer or a utopian, Bevin was endowed
with a rich imagination, with foresight and vision. For
all his practical hardheadedness, he was the creator in
politics. Attlee once noted that 'Ernest looked and
indeed was the embodiment of common-sense. Yet I have
never met a man in politics with as much imagination as
he had, with the exception of Winston'. Comparing Bevin
with Cripps, Attlee wrote that both men were tremendous
egotists but 'Cripps had the egoism of the altruist,
Bevin the egoism of the artist'.[23]

Fortunately for Bevin's assistants, his fertile imagination and the unsystematic quality of his mind did not
impair his skill in keeping short-term and long-term
goals constantly and simultaneously in mind. There was
a sense of purpose in everything he did, and once he made
up his mind he would not budge. This gave his policies a
certain steadiness and consistency. It also enabled his
subordinates, in acting on his behalf without troubling
him with every decision they made, to feel reasonably sure
that they were acting as he would wish them to act. They
learnt to know the way the Secretary of State's mind
worked and many of the senior members of the Foreign
Office became remarkably adept at producing very quickly
a document that correctly represented his ideas.

Another quality which must have endeared Bevin to his
advisers was his indifference to the whole range of
domestic pressures which frequently deflect less determined ministers from their chosen courses. Confident in
his ability to maintain Cabinet backing for his policies,
he experienced none of the normal anxieties of ministers
about the public reactions to their policies. He talked
about British foreign policy as his policy; about negotiations as his negotiations. According to Sir Ivone
Kirkpatrick, he was singularly little perturbed by warnings
that his policy might be unpopular in Parliament, in the

press, or in the trade unions.[24] Once, when someone mur-
mured to him that what he wanted to do might not be welcome
to the chancellor of the exchequer, he retorted, 'I'll
swing that Dalton round my 'ead'. Brought up in a tough
world, the prospect of opposition never daunted Bevin.
'He would square up to anyone,' wrote Attlee, 'physically
or morally, with relish.'[25]

Bevin had boundless confidence in himself, in his ability
to marshal the evidence and reach the right conclusion, as
well as in his powers of persuading others to share his
point of view. Nor was he likely to be deterred from
action by the fear of responsibility. To quote Attlee
again:

   Because of his own genius for organisation and his
   confidence in his own strength, he did not fear — he
   embraced — power. Lord Acton's famous dictum on
   power probably never occurred to him. If he agreed
   that power corrupts, he would have said that it
   corrupted only the men not big enough to use it. And
   power was given to Ernest. Men recognised in him a
   national leader, someone to lean on. He attracted
   power. At a time when the Labour Movement had all
   the hopes, aspirations, ideas and saints necessary
   for Utopia, Ernest helped bring its feet to the
   ground by insisting that these things without power
   were useless. [26]

A keen appreciation of the importance of power was the
main quality which Bevin carried from the trade union
movement to the Foreign Office. He knew from experience
that the highest ideals and noblest intentions were as
useless in diplomatic negotiations as they were in industrial bargaining unless they were backed by force. Believing that Britain's influence was a positive and constructive force, he concluded that only by surviving as
a world power could she continue to play an effective
role in a world dominated by power politics.

As an actual practitioner of the art of diplomatic negotiations, Bevin's tactical ability was as impressive as
his grasp of the underlying dynamics. He mastered the
whole spectrum of diplomatic technique, ranging from complete intransigence to whole-hearted collaboration. The

36

particular technique he chose to deploy depended on the
setting, on the relative power positions and on his estimate of the other party's intentions, strengths and weaknesses. In dealing with the Russians, he was unyielding
and abrasive and never pulled his punches. In dealing
with his western and commonwealth colleagues, he could be
patient, helpful and accommodating. His forthright and
candid approach was a great asset in reaching agreement
and he frequently gained not only the confidence but the
affection of foreign statesmen.[27]

Bevin was subtle and resourceful in employing a variety
of expedients, making the most of his strong points, ex-
posing the weakness of his opponents, never conceding an
issue of substance unless he received a comparable concession. He usually prepared his hand in advance, but
rarely showed it too soon, keeping his trump cards to the
end. Acting swiftly when speed was called for, he was
equally capable of patient and painstaking work, consoli-
dating his position after every step, retreating in one
sector in order to advance better in another, gradually
gaining support and allies and isolating his opponents.

Once Bevin entered into an agreement, he observed it
scrupulously. He had a firm belief in the sanctity of
agreements and it was a point of honour with him to keep
his promises. The resulting confidence which the other
side could feel in any commitment into which Bevin had
entered was part of his strength as a negotiator.

Another feature of Bevin's approach to diplomatic negotiations was his emphasis on the economic factors. A
foreign secretary negotiating from a position of economic
weakness was, in his view, in the same difficulty as a
trade union official who was bargaining with employers
when the coffers of his union were empty. Britain's
acute economic weakness put him at a severe disadvantage
in dealing with foreign powers. He often said that a few
million tons of coal at his disposal would have made all
the difference to the outcome of some of his negotiations.

III

Bevin took control of Britain's foreign policy at a time
when the foundations of her former international pre-

eminence had been swept away by a revolution in the global distribution of power. The outcome of this revolution, which was completed by the Second World War, was the emergence of two non-European giants, Russia and America, which between them dominated the world scene and completely overshadowed the old centre of power in Western Europe. Britain's own decline was temporarily masked by the glamour of victory. But she emerged out of the war economically exhausted, militarily over-extended and with her political influence dangerously reduced. Her position as the leader of a world-wide empire was under stress and subjected to challenges everywhere. Britain retained the commitments, but not the capabilities of a great power.

At the same time, the British nation and the British political elite maintained a high degree of psychological involvement in world affairs; only an insignificant minority favoured a withdrawal into 'Little England'. Bevin's own faith that Britain was and should remain a major force on the international stage was stated in no uncertain terms:

> His Majesty's Government do not accept the view ...
> that we have ceased to be a Great Power, or the con-
> tention that we have ceased to play that role. We
> regard outselves as one of the Powers most vital to
> the peace of the world and we still have our historic
> part to play. The very fact that we have fought so
> hard for liberty, and paid such a price, warrants our
> retaining that position; and indeed it places a duty
> upon us to continue to retain it. I am not aware of
> any suggestion, seriously advanced, that by a sudden
> stroke of fate, as it were, we have overnight ceased
> to be a Great Power.[28]

The main hope for a stable world order lay in the continuation of the wartime alliance between the Big Three, Russia, America and Britain. The election slogan 'Left understands Left' not only expressed the Labour Party's traditional pro-Soviet policy but pledged the new foreign secretary to promote close collaboration with the Kremlin rulers. But these confident hopes were soon dashed by a rapidly deteriorating international situation. With the defeat of Germany, the wartime alliance began to break down. Instead of treating Germany as a single economic

unit to be administered by the allies jointly through the
Allied Control Council as stipulated in the Potsdam agreements, the occupying powers began to impose in their
respective zones their own social, economic and political
systems. Because of its central position in Europe,
Germany was the touchstone of relations between Russia and
the West and the deadlock here extended to most other
spheres. As the cleavage deepened, Britain became the
chief target of Soviet hostility. This took the form of
a sustained propaganda campaign in the United Nations
designed to isolate Britain by depicting her as a decadent
imperialist power, as well as direct pressure to tip the
scales against Britain in important strategic areas.

   Unlike some of his colleagues, Bevin, ever inclined to
expect the worst and not the best, entertained no extra-
vagant hopes of continuing East—West harmony when he came
into office. Having battled against communist infiltra-
tion in the trade union movement and having witnessed the
growing difficulty of maintaining a united front with
Russia over Poland towards the end of the war, Bevin was
not particularly surprised by the pattern of Russian
behaviour. Nor did he make any concessions, which might
smack of 'appeasement', to elicit Russian goodwill. On
the contrary, as the American Secretary of State observed
at Potsdam, 'his manner was so aggressive that both the
President (Truman) and I wondered how we would get along
with this new Foreign Minister.'[29] All subsequent Russian
moves were interpreted as evidence of her desire to undermine the regimes of Western Europe and take advantage of
Britain's post—war weakness to hasten the collapse of the
British Empire and move into the power vacuums which this
would create.

   Bevin did not think that the Russian leaders wanted war,
but he feared that they would not be able to control the
consequences of their policy of 'all mischief short of
war'. 'We are forced to recognise', he told a Commonwealth Prime Ministers' conference, 'that the Soviet
policy of expansion backed by her historic national ambitions and her Communist belief has engendered its own
dynamite which may prove too strong for Stalin despite his
shrewdness and his power. I don't think he is planning
for war, but he may be unable to control the forces he has
started. We have always got to be prepared for that'.[30]

Bevin made no allowances for Russia's own security fears arising out of her fearful losses during the Second World War and her consequent vulnerability. Soviet policy of imposing Stalinist regimes on Eastern Europe he rightly denounced as blatant violations of the Yalta agreements, but he ignored the defensive aspect of this policy prompted by fears of a resurgent Germany and 'capitalist encirclement'. He also assumed that Russian ambitions extended to Eastern Europe which the Russians regarded as their rightful sphere of influence.

Churchill got on much better with the Russians because he and Stalin spoke the same language of power-politics, as illustrated by the notorious percentages agreement. Churchill conceded that another country's vital national interests can sometimes override moral considerations. Bevin, to a certain extent, displayed the moralistic and self-righteous streak of British foreign policy which assumes all too readily that this country alone stands for justice and equity in international relations, whereas all others are selfish nationalists. Such an attitude did not make for smooth relations with foreigners, as is clear from Molotov's curious comment to Bevin at Potsdam: 'Churchill and Eden used to be friends of the Soviet Union, but you and Attlee are old-fashioned British imperialists'.[31] Most people would say Bevin's mistrust of the Russians was not unjustified and would also agree with him that 'You can never ... deal with the Russians if you lie down and let them walk all over you'.[32] But an understanding was not brought any nearer by Bevin's sanctimonious outpourings and his habit of addressing Soviet leaders as if they were representatives of a recalcitrant branch of the Transport and General Workers' Union. Thus, in what he called 'a heart-to-heart with Molotov' in December 1947, Bevin is reported to have said:

Now, Mr.Molotov, what is it that you want? What are you after? Do you want to get Austria behind your Iron Curtain? You can't do that. Do you want Turkey and the Straits? You can't have them. Do you want Korea? You can't have that. You are putting your neck out too far, and one day you will have it chopped off. We know much more about you than you imagine. We know that you cannot stand a war. But you are behaving in such a way that one day there will

be a show-down. And you will have to give way in
the end and lose your credit with your own people.
You cannot look on me as an enemy of Russia. Why,
when our Government was trying to stamp out your
Revolution, who was it that stopped it? It was I,
Ernest Bevin. I called out the transport workers
and they refused to load the ships. I wanted you
to have your Revolution in your own way and without
interference. Now again I am speaking as a friend.
You are playing a very dangerous game. And I can't
make out why. You don't really believe that any
American wants to go to war with you - or, at least,
no responsible American. We most certainly do not
want to. But you are playing with fire, Mr.Molotov,
and one day you will be badly burnt. And I don't
see the object of it all. If war comes between you
and America in the East, then we may be able to
remain neutral. But if war comes between you and
America in the West, then we shall be on America's
side. Make no mistake about that. That would be
the end of Russia and of your Revolution. So
please stop sticking out your neck in this way and
tell me what you are after. What do you want?[33]

Whether Bevin's suspicions of Russia were justified, or,
to put it differently, whether Russian conduct was motivated by expansionist ambitions or security fears, is
largely immaterial for understanding Bevin's policy. What
mattered was Bevin's perception of a Russian threat,
imagined or real, and his reaction to that perception.
For Bevin, Russian policy posed a threat not only to
British interests, but to the whole incipient structure
of world peace. Having witnessed the disastrous consequences of the collapse of the balance of power under the
weight of German ambitions in the inter-war period, he was
determined to frustrate what he saw as Russian designs to
undermine the precarious post-war balance. With her
meagre resources, Britain could not by herself check
Russian expansion; Bevin therefore had to look elsewhere
for a counterweight to Russian power.

This was not likely to be found in the United Nations,
the keystone of the Labour Party's foreign policy. At the
very first meeting the Security Council, designed as a
forum for international co-operation, degenerated into an

arena of political warfare. Bevin's manner caused the
Secretary-General some concern: 'He did not speak with
the traditional British moderation. At times, and particularly when outraged, he would descend to the Soviet
level of abuse; in the bitterness of his style and deli-
very, he competed freely with Mr Vychinsky ... Vychinsky's
calculated lunges maddened him: he was like a bull charg-
ing furiously at a red banner all over the field of
debate'.[34] The deep personal disenchantment which ensued
made Bevin uncooperative in his dealings with the new organisation.[35] While continuing to pay lip-service to the
idea of collective security, he began to look outside the
UN for a more robust regional instrument for ensuring the
safety of the British Isles and the protection of British
possessions and interests overseas.[36]

One solution which gained widespread popularity in the
period 1946-47, and which was urged on Bevin by many of
his own back-benchers with increasing force as the cold
war intensified, was the idea of the Third Force. The
third force would consist of Britain and the social democracies of Western Europe, standing ideologically half-way
between the rival systems of Russian totalitarianism and
American capitalism, balancing the two colossi on Europe's
flanks and acting as a neutral but positive force for
world peace. Bevin's biographer tells us that he considered this possibility seriously, and for a time was
inclined to favour it.[37] He rejected it, however, on the
grounds that the Continent and Britain could not, in the
time available, muster sufficient economic and military
strength to check the Russian threat. 'What remained of
Europe', recalled Attlee, 'wasn't strong enough to stand
up to Russia by itself. You had to have a world force
because you were up against a world force.'[38]

In reality the belief that democracy in Europe could not
survive without the closest support of the United States
pointed the way in the direction which Bevin now followed,
namely, an Anglo-American alliance. This was to become
the sheet-anchor of his foreign policy. In forging the
alliance with America, Bevin had to overcome the residual
friendship which the American public still felt for their
wartime partner in the east and the Roosevelt idea of
international brotherhood based on the great power concert
working through the UN as well as the age-old suspicions

of British imperialism, shared by many influential
Americans.

America's coolness towards Britain put Bevin in a predi-
cament. On the one hand he felt that, if the wartime
honeymoon between America and Russia continued, Britain
would be left out in the cold. On the other hand, to come
out openly against Russia could only serve to confirm
American suspicions of sinister British designs. He
resolved this by adopting a double-pronged policy which
aimed, diplomatically, at persuading the American leaders
that the Roosevelt idea was based on dangerous illusions
and, militarily, at holding the line against Russia,
until America was ready to step into the breach. The
eighteen months which followed the end of hostilities
were particularly grim in view of Russian encroachment on
northern Persia and Turkey and communist insurgency in
Greece, which could only be resisted at a heavy cost to
the British economy. After his famous 'Iron Curtain'
speech on 5 March 1946 which shook American public opinion, Churchill cabled Bevin that Russian expansion in the
Mediterranean had brought Truman and Byrnes to the British
point of view that some show of strength and resistance
was necessary to secure a good relationship with Russia.
He predicted that this would soon be the prevailing opinion
in the United States.[39]

Encouraging as this must have been to Bevin, his sense
of timing made him wait for the opportune moment to con-
front the American leaders with the choice of assuming
global responsibilities commensurate with their enormous
power or allowing the Russians to take over large areas
of vital strategic importance to the West. The head-on
collision between the communists and the pro-western
forces in the Greek arena provided Bevin with the clear
evidence of communist intentions which he had been waiting for.[40] At the end of February 1947, he sent a message
to the State Department saying that, from April, Britain
would not be able to bear the burden of aid to Greece and
Turkey. This message acted like a bomb-shell on the
American leaders. It in effect told them that Pax
Britannica was withdrawing from the eastern Mediterranean
and that, unless they filled the gap, it would be filled
by the Russians. The American Secretary of State, General
George Marshall, 'wired Bevin in strong language, protes-

ting against the British action ... He asked Douglas to
enquire whether this indicates a fundamental change in
British policy. Bevin replied in the negative.'[41]

The significance of the Truman Doctrine from Bevin's
point of view was that it committed American military
power to the defence of Europe and removed his worst fears
of an American return to isolation, but it offered no
solution to the problem of Western Europe's economic weakness. So, when George Marshall in his Harvard speech on
5 June 1947 made tentative proposals of American aid for
European economic reconstruction, Bevin 'grabbed them with
both hands'. They offered a splendid opportunity of building up stable European economies as a bulwark against
communist expansion. As Lord Franks later observed, 'the
keystone of Bevin's foreign policy swung into place'.[42]
Bevin's response to Marshall's offer was not, in fact, as
spontaneous as it was assumed to be. He had been given
an advance warning of the speech with an indication of
its importance.[43] But when his advisers suggested that
Marshall should be asked to clarify his intentions, Bevin
shrewdly refused and preferred to work on the assumption
that Marshall fully meant everything he said. Thus, to
quote Herbert Morrison, 'Ernest Bevin most adroitly mis-
interpreted what was in effect a "feeler" as a definite
proposal. His move to some extent turned a proposal into
a fait accompli and Marshall aid began.'[44]

Marshall's invitation extended to all European countries,
not only the western ones. The main condition was that
the programme for European construction must come not from
America but from Europe. Bevin took the lead in organising
the European response and gave the impulse to the formulation of the European Recovery Programme. He publicly welcomed the invitation to Eastern Europe as 'throwing a
bridge to link East and West', but privately he neither
expected nor desired Russia to use this bridge. When
Molotov arrived to the Paris conference on 27 June 1947
at the head of a large Soviet delegation, 'Bevin and
British Foreign Office (as well as some American) officials
were fearful that Stalin would agree and took no pains to
create a hospitable atmosphere at Paris for Molotov'.[45]
Bevin sternly resisted the Soviet proposals for aid without strings, insisted that there must be no delay and did
not conceal his satisfaction at the Soviet departure.[46]

The Truman Doctrine and the Marshall Plan, taken together, went a long way towards realising the immediate objective of Bevin's foreign policy which was the erection of a global balance of power. In underwriting Western Europe's security and committing vast resources to her economic recovery, the United States offset Soviet preponderance on that continent. Like his predecessor Canning, in the early nineteenth century, Bevin could congratulate himself on having called in the New World to redress the balance of the Old.

In Bevin's case, however, this was followed not by a period of stability and detente, but by the intensification of the cold war. Paradoxically, the Marshall offer of economic aid contributed to the crystallisation of the division of Europe into two hostile blocs. Attlee called the withdrawal by the Kremlin of the Eastern European acceptance of the invitations to participate in the joint programme 'the declaration of the cold war'.[47] One of Bevin's under-secretaries at the Foreign Office observed that 'from the middle of 1947 onwards, decisions were taken towards uniting the free world, at the expense of widening the gap with the Communist world ... From then on the objective changed from "one world" to "one free world"'.[48]

It was not until the failure of the Foreign Ministers' Conference in London in December 1947, however, that Bevin finally and openly abandoned even the appearance of co-operation with Russia. The conference proved decisive precisely because it decided nothing. It finally demonstrated that no understanding could be reached between Russia and the West. A particularly vitriolic attack by Molotov was the last straw. 'Now 'e's gone too bloody far', complained Bevin to his advisers in his customary unvarnished vernacular. On 12 December, Bevin told a sympathetic House of Commons the long story of the breakdown of relations with Russia and concluded that 'we cannot go on as we have been going on ... I do not know what is going to happen in the future'.[49]

With the hopes of great power unity not only hopelessly shattered but manifestly seen by the public to be so, Bevin turned with characteristic energy to the execution of the next phase of his foreign policy. The starting-

point of the new policy was the acceptance of the two
camps and its aim was the building up of a broadly based
anti-communist coalition backed by a powerful regional
system of Atlantic defence. The main components of this
policy were the Brussels Treaty Organisation and the
Atlantic Pact. Its basic premise was the necessity of
negotiating from strength. As Attlee explained, 'before
Russia would consider reasonable relations with the free
world, there must be a build-up of strength. Strength
was the only factor which the Russians considered'.[50]
This policy involved the pooling of the economic resources
of the West and undertaking definite military arrangements.
Britain was to abandon any notion of acting as an intermediary between the super-powers and throw her weight
decisively into the western side of the scales. Britain
also had no option but to accept American hegemony in the
new constellation but would hope to be, in Harold
Macmillan's phrase, 'the Greeks in the American Roman
Empire'. In other words, Britain's role in the new world
order would be on the one hand to harness America's vast
economic and military power to the defence of the 'free
world' so as to. maintain an equilibrium between the two
rival camps, and, on the other hand, to educate and
restrain America and temper the exercise of her world
power with British moderation, pragmatism and diplomatic
skill in order to prevent the virulent ideological dispute
between the two continental giants from escalating into
an armed clash and plunging the world into a third world
war. This dual role was to constitute the essence of
Britain's strategy in world politics for over a decade
after Bevin's death.

IV

If 1947 was the year in which the projected post-war
settlement collapsed, 1948 was the year in which Bevin
launched his alternative system. His new policy was un-
folded on 22 January 1948, in the 'Western Union' speech
which was perhaps the most momentous speech Bevin ever
made on foreign policy. He began with a broad survey
which was designed to demonstrate Russian responsibility
for the failure of the United Nations and of the policy
based on four-power agreement. He recalled events in the
Balkans, France and Turkey, Hungary and Poland. He described the futility of the various four-power conferences

and added that things were brought to a head in the negotiations on the Marshall Plan because the Russians thought
'they could wreck or intimidate Western Europe by political
upsets, economic chaos and even revolutionary methods'.
He stressed that Britain always wanted 'the widest conception of Europe, including, of course, Russia', and described
her efforts to keep Europe united 'and thus avoid the
necessity of crystallising Europe into separate blocs'.
But these hopes were in vain because 'in Eastern Europe we
are presented with a <u>fait</u> <u>accompli</u>'.

All these developments pointed to the conclusion 'that
the free nations of Western Europe must now draw closely
together', and 'the time is ripe for the consolidation of
Western Europe'. This, together with the declaration that
Britain would make it a major objective of her foreign
policy to join with the free democracies of Europe in
forming Western Union, was the crux of his message. He
hoped that treaties with France and the Benelux countries
would form 'an important nucleus in Western Europe'. This
could eventually be extended to include the overseas territories of the European states. The United States was not
specifically included, but her 'power and resources will
be needed if we are to create a solid, stable and healthy
world'. On the form which this Western Union would take,
Bevin confined himself to the vaguest generalities. He
pledged the Labour Government to foster 'both the spirit
and the machinery of co-operation' and added that 'unity
should be more of a brotherhood and less of a rigid
system'.[51]

The 'Western Union' speech was hailed as the great
turning-point in British foreign policy, which ended
Britain's traditional insularity and committed her to
active participation in the movement for European unity.
In fact, it was so deliberately ambiguous and so lacking
in any concrete proposals as to be open to almost any
interpretation, and hence the almost unanimous chorus of
praise with which it was greeted in the British press, by
the American Government and by the European allies.

In the negotiations which ensued, Bevin used the Anglo-
French Treaty as the nucleus for the new groupings. The
main clause of that treaty, which was signed at Dunkirk in
March 1947, dealt with action to be taken in the event of

47

German aggression.[52] Bevin now proposed the conclusion of a series of bilateral treaties similar to the Dunkirk Treaty, arguing that a premature conclusion of a multilateral defence agreement might be used by the Americans as a pretext for withdrawing their troops from Europe. But the Benelux representatives successfully pressed for a multilateral pact, with a system of regular consultation and provisions for economic, social and cultural collaboration to complement the military agreement.[53] The negotiations proceeded swiftly, with an added sense of urgency introduced by the communist coup in Czechoslovakia in February, culminating in the signature of the Brussels Treaty, on 17 March 1948, by the representatives of Britain, France, Belgium, the Netherlands and Luxembourg. The hub of this Treaty of Economic, Social and Cultural Collaboration and Collective Self-Defence was article 4. This carried the assurance of automatic assistance to any one of the contracting parties which became the victims of armed aggression in Europe.[54]

The turning-point which Bevin's Western Union policy was held to mark was more apparent than real. For Bevin, his speech and the organisation to which it gave birth were not conceived as part of a policy aiming at a united Europe. On the contrary, they were part of a scheme to commit America formally to the defence of Western Europe and thereby to underpin Britain's independent world role. By constructing a nucleus of self-defence in Europe, Bevin hoped to induce America to join in forming an Atlantic security system. He himself once admitted that Western Union was just 'a sprat to catch the mackerel'.[55]

Bevin's outlook was unreservedly Atlanticist, and any interest he may have shown in European unity sprang from his belief in the imperative necessity of obtaining an American commitment. All the available evidence suggests that from the beginning his policy was shaped towards this end. As early as 23 December 1947, Bevin informed Field-Marshal Montgomery that 'he had suggested to the Foreign Minister of France (M.Bidault) that the time had come to begin the formation of a Federation or Union in Western Europe, and if possible to bring the Americans into it'.[56] On 13 January 1948, Bevin informed Secretary of State Marshall that England was planning to approach France and the Benelux countries with a proposal for a series of

bilateral defence agreements and asked what the American
attitude would be to this new alliance. Marshall replied,
after consulting Truman, that this initiative would have
the administration's whole-hearted sympathy.[57] Encouraged
by this reply, but realising that the administration was
not prepared to face up to Congress at the time on the
question of a military commitment, Bevin emphasised the
'self-help' element in his Western Union speech to arouse
congressional sympathy. In this task he was helped by
the war panic caused by Russian pressure on Berlin in the
first week of March 1948. On 12 March, a few days before
the signature of the Brussels Treaty, Bevin made the
first explicit proposal for a North Atlantic pact. He
made three suggestions: '1 Build around the five nation
pact. 2 A plan for Atlantic security. 3 A Mediterranean
system of security'.[58] The idea presumably was that
Britain would be the focal point of these three interlocking security systems.

Shortly after the signature of the Brussels Treaty,
Bevin approached the Americans again (on 23 April 1948)
with a proposal for converting the newly born organisation into an Atlantic pact. This, he claimed, would be
the best way of deterring Russian aggression and the
only way of making the French agree to the rebuilding of
Germany. He concluded that 'it would be very difficult
for the British, or other free nations, to stand up to
new acts of aggression unless there was a definitely
worked out arrangement, which included the United States,
for collective resistance against aggression'.[59] Truman
agreed, and in July formal talks on Atlantic defence
began in Washington between the representatives of America,
Canada, Britain, France and the Benelux countries. In
October, the Brussels Treaty Powers were able to announce
'complete agreement on the principle of a defensive pact
for the North Atlantic and on the next steps to be taken
in that direction'.[60] After the signature of the North
Atlantic Treaty on 4 April, Bevin said to a friend: 'It
is given to few men to see their dreams fulfilled. Three
times in the last year I know I have nearly died, but I
kept myself alive because I wanted to see this North
Atlantic Alliance properly launched. This has been done
today'.[61]

The foregoing account of the origins of NATO reveals

that Bevin was the real architect of the new organisation
and that in the eighteen months preceding its formation he
systematically used the widespread support for the cause
of European unity to induce America to modify her policy
of eschewing entangling alliances and in order to promote
an Atlantic pact with full American guarantees. The importance of the Atlantic Treaty for Britain, he told the
House of Commons, was that 'the situation which we had in
1914 and 1939, and particularly 1940 and 1941, when we had
to hold the fort waiting and wondering when other nations
would realise the gravity of the aggressive menace, while
at the same time we were using up and exhausting our
resources – that situation would not be allowed to occur
again'.[62]

When he described the treaty as 'the biggest step in
collective security that has ever been taken in the
history of the world',[63] however, he was guilty of con-
fusing collective defence, which is a regional concept,
with collective security, which is a universal concept.
Forming a regional pact was precisely the type of traditional power-politics expedient which collective security
was intended to eliminate. But Bevin persistently confused
the two. In his Western Union speech, he claimed that one
of the principles of his foreign policy was the discarding
of the old-fashioned conception of the balance of power.
This was probably intended as a sop for the left wing of
the Labour Party and should not be allowed to obscure the
fact that balance-of-power considerations were of fundamental importance to his policy. As Attlee observed, 'the
Brussels Treaty and the Atlantic pact were both ... a
recognition of the fact of the changed balance of power in
the world'.[64] This suggests the key to the understanding
of Bevin's foreign policy. Fearing the consequences of
the imbalance which Soviet domination in Eastern Europe
created, he threw Britain's weight and drew America into
a countervailing coalition which would redress the
balance.

V

Bevin shared the Churchillian idea of Britain standing at
the centre of three interlocking circles: the Atlantic
circle, the Commonwealth and Western Europe. On 17 November 1949, Bevin told the House of Commons that these

'three great sectors of the free world' are interrelated
and that the United Kingdom 'not only now but always will
have to reconcile its responsibilities to all three; we
cannot isolate ourselves from any of them'.[65]

The problem of reconciling Britain's obligations to the
three different circles had, of course, been felt long
before 1949, and we have already seen that in Bevin's
order of priorities the American circle came first. Its
corollary was that Britain's continental commitments
should move in step with American ones and on no account
in advance of them.[66] This in turn constituted a very low
ceiling of European integration beyond which Bevin was not
prepared to advance. His attitude to Europe was coloured
by traditional British insularity and mistrust of foreigners and their unstable political systems. To this was
added the socialist fear that relinquishing control over
vital sectors of the economy would imperil full employment
at home and lower the standard of living of the British
worker. But much more fundamental was his belief that by
merging its identity with Western Europe, Britain would
destroy the foundations of her special relationship with
the United States which would be tantamount to sawing the
branch on which Britain was sitting. Nor did he see any
reason why Britain should sacrifice her leadership of the
Commonwealth and her world role on which Hugh Dalton
called ' the doctrinal altar of European Federalism'.

The emergence of a federation on the Continent, from
Bevin's point of view, had a number of serious drawbacks.
Firstly, it would present Britain with the painful dilemma
of either joining it and thus becoming 'just a bit of
Europe', or of staying out and thus running the risk of
becoming an offshore island increasingly relegated to the
sidelines of international politics. Secondly, if the
process of federating Europe proceeded too precipitately
and without due regard to the need for American support,
it might clash with the building of the wider Atlantic
community which he considered necessary for Europe's welfare and security and for a stable world order. Thirdly,
the federation of Europe, if successful, would create the
conditions and provide an excuse for American isolationism,
thereby realising his nightmare of American withdrawal
from Europe.

For all these reasons, Bevin drew a sharp distinction between the goals of a European federation to which he objected and the goal of European co-operation which he readily supported. This was reflected in his preference for organisations like NATO which involved no painful surrender of sovereignty nor reduction of Britain's freedom of action as a result of having to deal with America through the intermediary of a European grouping. It was also reflected in his strong preference for traditional methods of co-operation over supranational ones and for a slow and pragmatic approach. 'I feel that the intricacies of Western Union are such', he said, 'that we had better proceed ... on the same principle of association of nations that we have in the Commonwealth ... and I think that adopting the principle of an unwritten constitution, and the process of constant association step by step by treaty and agreement and by taking on certain things collectively instead of by ourselves is the right way to approach this Western Union problem'.[67]

Differences about the aims and method of European co-operation increasingly soured Bevin's relations with the proponents of integration on the Continent after 1947. The Europeans were disappointed when the speed and gusto of his response to the Marshall offer were not matched by equal enthusiasm for European economic integration. Initially, all he wanted was a temporary organisation to divide up the Marshall pie. 'We have no idea of setting up a permanent organisation to rival the United Nations', he told the Paris Conference on 12 July 1947, 'It is a piece of ad hoc machinery to grapple with this special problem'.[68] It was only European demands for a permanent organisation reinforced by American insistence on progress towards economic integration that made Bevin give way. Even then, the Organisation for European Economic Co-operation (OEEC) which eventually emerged in April 1948 conformed to Bevin's idea of a loose, consultative intergovernmental organisation rather than to the French idea of a centralised supranational organisation. To the frequent American suggestions for clothing the organisation with real powers and providing it with an effective central machinery, Bevin's unyielding reply was 'we are willing to consult, get advice, hear views and get opinions, but beyond that we cannot go'.[69] On the various policy areas his colleagues felt that, by resisting progress,

Britain was defaulting on implied obligations after securing the lion's share of Marshall funds.

Similarly, in the Brussels Treaty Organisation, misunderstanding arose because, for Bevin, Western Union was a
means to an end, whereas for his partners it was an end in
itself. They expected him to follow up his general idea
of co-operation by specific application of policy to particular areas and problems, but when one endeavours to
discover what the particular policies may be, 'the record
is one of disconcerting obscurity'.[70] His whole policy
after his Western Union speech can in fact be interpreted
as an attempt to restrain the powerful European currents
he had helped to release and to get the genie back into
the bottle.

The popular enthusiasm generated by the European Congress
at The Hague in May 1948, however, could not be easily contained, particularly after it engulfed official circles.
The congress's proposal for the setting up of a European
federal assembly was adopted by the French and Belgian
governments who placed it on the agenda of the Consultative
Council of the Brussels Treaty Organisation. The story
goes that when Bevin heard the news, he was heard muttering
'I don't like it. I don't like it. When you open that
Pandora's box, you will find it full of Trojan horses'.[71]
He felt that a political authority should come at the end
and not at the beginning of the process of co-operation.
'I do not think it will work', he warned, 'if we try to
put the roof on before we have built the building'.[72] He
saw no possible British gain from an organisation which
was not linked to America and which had no clearly defined
function, particularly since it was conceived as the first
step towards a European federation. He also feared that
a European assembly would be irresponsible and meddlesome,
that it would waste time on fruitless controversies about
federal constitutions and might clash with the responsible
governments ending in embitterment and frustration.[73]

When it became clear that Britain's partners were prepared to go ahead without her and a special committee was
appointed to examine proposals for a European assembly,
Bevin yielded at the last moment and in a grudging manner.
He advanced the idea of a council of ministers as a
counter-proposal to the idea of a popular assembly. The

statute which eventually constituted the Council of Europe embodied a compromise between the conflicting French and British positions. It consisted of a council of ministers with no executive powers and a consultative assembly with no legislative powers. Even the assembly's consultative capacity was hedged around with a thicket of restrictions. Bevin had to a large extent succeeded in his objective of making the Council of Europe 'as little embarrassing as possible'.[74] By locating it in Strasbourg, which was a difficult place to get to, Bevin may have secretly hoped that it would die a natural death.[75]

Having failed to prevent the birth of the Council of Europe, Bevin tried to limit its functions so as to reduce it to utter impotence. He used his considerable influence particularly with the Scandinavian delegates, and Britain's right of veto in the council of ministers to frustrate any proposal for modifying the statute which would infringe national sovereignty and to scotch any attempt to transform the assembly into 'a European political authority with limited functions but real powers'. His disenchantment with the Council of Europe became so deep that in January 1951 he seriously contemplated Britain's withdrawal from the organisation.[76]

The one constructive effect of the buckets of cold water poured by Bevin on successive federalists' initiatives in 1949-50 was to clinch their decision to go forward with Britain if possible, but without her if necessary. The new strategy which was elaborated by Jean Monnet for acting on 'one but decisive point' was reflected in Robert Schuman's historic call on 9 May 1950 for the pooling of Europe's coal and steel resources. This plan was conceived as a solution to the European crisis of over-production, as a framework for the solution of the German problem and as the first step towards an eventual European federation. But it also contained, as one French official admitted, 'the intention of forcing the hand of the British Government'.[77]

By failing to inform Bevin of his plans until the last moment and then confronting him with a fait accompli, Schuman aroused Bevin's anger and suspicion. Dean Acheson, who saw Bevin on the day of the French declaration, reported that he 'bristled with hostility to Schuman's whole

idea'.[78] The negotiations which followed had all the
appearances of a dialogue of the deaf between France's
cartesian insistence on the acceptance of the principle
of a supranational high authority and British diplomatic
pragmatism which would not countenance any prior commitments. Bevin's note of 25 May[79] proposing direct talks
between France, Germany and Britain without a preliminary
acceptance of the supranational principle suggests that he
may not have fully appreciated the nature and seriousness
of Schuman's proposals. French insistence on a supranational authority was not just 'a pedantic whim' as
Churchill suggested, but stemmed from the belief that
without it there would be no united Europe and the Schuman
plan would be doomed to failure.[80]

The French and British positions remained intransigent
and the gap between them could not be closed. On 3 June
France, Germany, Italy and the Benelux countries announced their intention of adopting the Schuman proposals as
the basis for negotiations. A British communique said
that Britain could not join the negotiations on that basis
and that the British Government was preparing its own
counter-proposals inspired by the French initiative.[81]
The publication on 13 June 1950 by the Labour Party's
National Executive of a pamphlet entitled European Unity
threw a spanner in the works of British diplomacy. Although Bevin agreed with the substance of its arguments
against the surrender of control over Britain's heavy
industries to a supranational authority, he was acutely
embarrassed by the tone and timing of this thunderbolt
which had fallen out of Transport House. But a more likely explanation of the British failure to publish any
counter-proposals is that Bevin, who was by now seriously
ill, was led to believe that the negotiations between the
Six would collapse without any British 'help' and that,
by putting forward her own proposals, Britain would only
incur the blame for the breakdown in discussions.[82] This
assumption must have been comforting for Bevin for whom
Schuman's proposals conjured up the spectre of a European
political federation. But Bevin's assumption was soon
shattered by the agreement of the Six to establish the
European Coal and Steel Community. Thus 'the first
European bus had started with Britain waving a limp hand
in farewell from the kerbstone'.[83]

The dangerous split between Britain and Europe which
started with the Schuman Plan was reinforced by the acri-
monious debate on German rearmament and the project of a
European army. The outbreak of the Korean War prompted
American demands for an immediate German contribution to
western defence. On 12 September 1951 at a meeting in New
York, Mr Acheson proposed to Bevin and Schuman the raising
of German divisions to serve in NATO. Bevin strongly
opposed this idea, but when the American demand was presented in the form of a package deal in which the sending
of American reinforcements to Europe and the appointment
of an American supreme commander were made contigent on
agreement to rearm Germany, Bevin rallied round to the
American position.[84]

Unable to accept the American proposal for the raising
of an independent German army, France proposed in October
1950 an ingenious formula for caging the German tiger.
This was the Pleven Plan for a European Defence Community
which would contain German units integrated at the lowest
possible level with other European units. Bevin's outright rejection of the French plan was dictated by his
hostility to the supranational formula on which it was
based, his reluctance to undertake any continental
commitment which was not shared by the United States, and,
above all, by his conviction that only an Atlantic framework could adequately guarantee Europe's defence. The
French plan, he told the House of Commons, 'will only
delay the building of Europe's defence ... we take the
view that the proposal for a European Army is too limited
in scope. We cherish our special ties with our old
European friends, but in our view, Europe is not enough;
it is not big enough; it is not strong enough and it is
not able to stand by itself. I understand the urge towards European unity and I sympathise with it, and, indeed,
I did much to help bring the Council of Europe into being.
But I also understand the New Paradox that European unity
is no longer possible within Europe alone but only within
the broader Atlantic Community'.[85] The controversy over
the European Defence Community raged for another four
years, but the British decision not to join it, taken
under Bevin and not modified subsequently, was probably
the single most important factor in its eventual defeat
in 1954.

In contrast to the negative policy which Bevin pursued in the European circle of British foreign policy, his policy in the Commonwealth circle was both imaginative and constructive. As in this sphere policy was not worked out by Bevin alone, but in close co-operation with successive colonial secretaries and the prime minister (who was a former dominions secretary and played an important part in Commonwealth affairs), we shall confine ourselves to the main lines of the Government's colonial policy and at the same time examine Bevin's policies in the Middle East and the Far East which do not neatly fall into any of the three circles.

Throughout the Empire, at the end of the war, the British Government was faced with nationalist stirrings and demands for self-rule. Britain had neither the forces nor the funds to retain the Empire by force, and such a course, in any case, had no appeal whatever to the Labour leaders whose party's traditions had always been so critical of imperial rule. So necessity and ideology coincided in encouraging them to guide the colonial peoples to self-government and gradually transfer the Empire into a multiracial Commonwealth of independent nations. It was hoped that by rebuilding the relations between Britain and her former colonies on a new footing of equality, it would be possible to maintain and even expand the economic and strategical links between them and thus provide a more viable forum for Britain's leadership and international influence.

This enlightened conception of self-interest accorded equally with Bevin's interest in colonial economic development and with his recognition of the need to scale down Britain's overseas commitments in order to bring them into line with Britain's reduced material resources so as to obviate the danger of over-extension and disproportion between means and ends. India and Pakistan were granted independence in 1947 and Burma and Ceylon in the following year.

Withdrawal from the Indian sub-continent, however, rendered inoperable an idea which dominated British military thinking at the time and which was accepted by the Cabinet's Defence Committee in April 1946. This was Field-Marshall Alanbrooke's conception of utilising the resources of the Commonwealth for defence in depth by means of a chain of inter-linked defence zones encircling the globe. As Alanbrooke recorded in his Autobiographical Notes: 'With the loss of India and Burma, the keystone of the arch of our Commonwealth Defence was lost, and our Imperial Defence crashed. Without the central strategic reserve of Indian troops ready to operate either east or west, we were left impotent and even the smallest of nations were at liberty to twist the lion's tail'.[86]

The resultant shift from the Empire to Europe as the first priority of Britain's strategy should have been accompanied by a reassessment of the value of the Middle East as the line of communication to India and an over-haul of the security arrangements in the area. It should have been apparent that any attempt to maintain physical control of the area would be of doubtful utility, would be costly and would exacerbate local hostility to British presence, and that Britain's remaining political and oil interests could be best protected by non-military means. Bevin to some extent realised this and one of his earliest acts in the Foreign Office was to circulate a memorandum on the theme of 'Peasants not Pashas', directing his officials' attention to the need to look at the problem of the Middle East from a new standpoint.[87]

But the pressure from within the Foreign Office and the War Office for continuing to uphold traditional British interests in the Middle East by traditional means was enormous. Whitehall remained firmly wedded to the view that the Arab states were essentially pro-British and, if properly handled, factors of stability in the area, where-as Zionism meant the intrusion of an alien and disruptive element which was bound to undermine Western influence in the Arab world. Bevin came to share the views of his advisers and he set out to secure a few viable bases in the Middle East from which the Suez and overland routes to the East and the Iraqi and Persian Gulf oil could be protected. This goal could be approached by a number of alternative routes, all of which were subject to two overriding constraints. In the first place, such bases could not be maintained, or at least could not be maintained at an acceptable level of cost, in the teeth of opposition from the host countries. Second, the consent of these countries could only be obtained by pursuing a policy in Palestine of which they approved.

The Labour Party was committed to abolishing the 1939 White Paper which restricted Jewish immigration into Palestine. In order to gain Arab goodwill, however, Bevin clung to the policy laid down in that White Paper. This was only one aspect of a wider policy of maintaining the status quo in Palestine until he could work out new agreements with the Arab regimes to safeguard British interests. But the situation in Palestine was far too volatile and explosive, and Bevin's attempt to freeze it not only intensified the Jewish campaign of defiance and violence, but also put Britian at loggerheads with America.

Pressure from President Truman on the British Government to issue 100,000 certificates for Jewish immigrants from Europe into Palestine led to the appointment of an Anglo-American Commission of Inquiry in April 1946. Of the commission's proposals Truman accepted only the admission of 100,000 people. Bevin insisted that the implementation of the commission's proposal for the dismantling of illegal forces must precede this, and also demanded American financial and military support to enforce the entire scheme. Bevin was enraged by what he regarded as Truman's cynical disregard for the fate of the Arabs in Palestine in his pursuit of American Jewish votes and funds for the Democratic Party. There was another committee, another plan, another conference, and a long series of embittered exchanges between British, Jews, Arabs and Americans, but it was obvious that the whole issue was getting nowhere. When Britain's final compromise plan of February 1947 for self-governing Jewish and Arab cantons was promptly turned down by both parties, Bevin, by now exasperated by the mounting tide of Jewish terrorism, announced his decision to drop this hot political potato into the lap of the United Nations.

When the United Nations came up with its partition plan, Bevin refused to accept any British responsibility for enforcing it and used the last few months of the British mandate to gain Arab goodwill. The manner of British withdrawal made chaos and war inevitable and Bevin was now

59

ready to play his last card. This aimed at taking advantage of the chaotic situation in Palestine in order to
gain for Britain's only reliable ally, Transjordan, access
to the Mediterranean. Such a move would make that country
suitable for the relocation of the bases from Iraq and
Egypt. Accordingly, Bevin encouraged King Abdullah to send
the Arab Legion, following the Jewish declaration of an independent state on 15 May 1948, to capture at least part
of the territory, which was allocated to the Arabs under
the partition plan.[88] This scheme backfired disastrously.
The intervention of Transjordan provoked other jealous
Arab countries to send in their armies to block her expansion as much as to fight the Jews. The Israelis offered
unexpectedly successful resistance to all the Arab armies
and barred Transjordan's path to the sea. Bevin tried to
turn these reverses to his own advantage by gaining Arab
gratitude for British arms, diplomatic support and delaying tactics at the UN. It was all to no avail and Britain
eventually had to submit to the UN resolution calling for
a cease-fire and an arms embargo.

The Arabs, far from being grateful, denounced this as
another example of British treachery and blamed their
defeat on their benefactor. The collapse of Bevin's
policy left Britain in an exposed and vulnerable position.
In the aftermath of the 1948 war, the Arab world was shaken
by a wave of nationalist agitation, violence and coups.
The revised Anglo-Iraqi Treaty signed early in 1948, which
Bevin hoped would mark the beginning of a series of treaties regularising Britain's relations with the Arab world,
was torn up by a Baghdad mob. In Egypt, 80,000 British
troops were beleaguered in the Suez Canal base, deprived
of supplies and harassed by guerrilla attacks. The
Egyptian Parliament twice rejected drafts for a revised
Anglo-Egyptian treaty before a new government came to
power and unilaterally abrogated the 1936 treaty. King
Abdullah of Transjordan, whose friendship with Britain
remained unshaken, was assassinated by a Palestinian to
ward off a possible Israeli-Jordanian settlement. Bevin's
efforts to replace Britain's bilateral treaties with the
Arab countries by a collective defence arrangement was
frustrated by nationalist opposition and inter-Arab
rivalties. Mounting political instability underscored
Britain's loss of control over events in the Middle East,
and in May 1950 America intervened alongside Britain and

France by means of the Tripartite Declaration which aimed
to stabilise the situation and bring all the Arab countries
into a regional defence organisation.

   In one of the rashest statements of his political career,
Bevin staked his reputation on solving the Palestine problem. He failed, and it was perhaps his greatest failure.
The brutality which characterised Bevin's handling of the
problem was attributed by his enemies to anti-Semitism.
Bevin was not, in fact, anti-Jewish, only anti-Zionist.
The idea of a Zionist state is reported to have given him
nightmares of thousands and thousands of Harold Laskis
pursuing him down the road. The real explanation of his
disastrous policy probably lies in the sense of frustration
he experienced in being caught up in the cross-fire from
all directions. In fairness to Bevin, it has to be said
that he inherited a position hopelessly enmeshed in incompatible claims, dating back to the First World War, which
British governments had made to the Jews and the Arabs.
It is difficult to see what other policy could have worked.
Nevertheless, his own handling of the situation, in Hugh
Dalton's apt phrase, was 'a crescendo of stupidity'.[89]

   In South-East Asia and the Far East, Bevin accepted the
necessity of relinquishing privileged positions and reducing commitments with more realism and grace than he did
in the Middle East. Here there was not the same clash
between the demands of Asian nationalism with which he
sympathised and the strategic requirements of Great Britain.
After the grant of independence to the Indian sub-continent,
which in itself was a major contribution to the transformation of empire into commonwealth in this area, the remaining
British interests were predominantly economic. Bevin,
therefore, aimed to create peaceful and stable conditions
in the interests of British trade and investments. In one
of his early surveys he outlined to the House of Commons
the main elements of this policy of utilising the colonial
heritage to the mutual advantage of Britain and Asia:

   There is Indonesia, Malaya, Ceylon and a new China
   emerging. There is all that new development and I
   think the policy we have to follow so far as the
   dependent territories are concerned which are emerging into independence, is to nurse them, guide them,
   help them to change over as a going concern, to keep

61

their administration intact, to provide them with experts. I am not too sure that from the point of view of our own interests in this country, we would not do far better by helping other countries and assisting them from a purely trade point in trade and commerce than we did under the old-fashioned Colonial system of the past. That is our policy in the Far East.[90]

Bevin found co-operation with America easier to attain in South-East Asia and the Far East because the interests of the two allies converged here to a far greater extent than they did in the Middle East. The common interest in preventing the spread of communist influence in the area found its expression in a joint strategy of 'containment'. But, whereas for America containment was more of a military policy which depended on American control of the island chain and bases around the Asian land-mass, Bevin preferred to practise containment by using friendship and economic links to build up a belt of pro-western states. He also assumed the role, whenever possible, of acting as an inter-mediary between America and the Commonwealth countries to remove mistrust and work out common policies. After agreeing with the Americans in September 1949 on the ne-gotiation of a peace treaty with Japan, for example, Bevin induced them to move at a slower pace than they intended in deference to the feelings of Australia and New Zealand and had a report drawn up on Commonwealth interests to be taken into account in the negotiations.

When the Chinese communists emerged in 1949 as the effec-tive government of China, Bevin tried hard to harmonise America's reaction to the communist victory with that of Britain and the Commonwealth. He reasoned that since the West did not have the power to reverse this victory, the best policy would be to recognise China and work for an accommodation between her and her neighbours. He regarded Dean Acheson's idea of Western intervention as dangerous and warned that American hostility would drive China into the arms of Russia. His policy of promoting diplomatic contacts and trade between China and the West was designed to have the opposite effect of preventing the integration of the two great communist powers. 'I believe we were right', he observed later, 'to recognise the People's Government and not to leave the Russians to assume that they were the only country to do anything at all for China'.[91] Consideration of British economic interests and the pressure exercised by the Far Eastern traders also inclined Bevin towards an early recognition of China.

But the decisive factor in granting de jure recognition on 6 January 1950 was to preserve a united front with the Asian members of the Commonwealth and retain the goodwill of India in particular. In a conversation with Acheson, Bevin had to recognise that the interests of their countries diverged in this issue. The US Government was withdrawing; the UK was trying to 'keep a foot in the door and see what happens'.[92] It was not long before America and China were involved on the opposite sides of a dangerous international crisis. The American policy-makers saw the North Korean invasion of South Korea in June 1950 as part of a communist plan co-ordinated by Moscow and Peking. They organised a concerted military intervention under the UN banner to repel this aggression, and Bevin supported them in this. But when they sent the Seventh Fleet to beutralise the Straits of Formosa, he privately remonstrated against this provocative act which he feared might plunge those countries who supported the American intervention in Korea into a war with China.[93]

Bevin's self-appointed task of mediating between American power and Asian sensitivity, his consciousness of the economic factors which underlay international questions, his inclination towards a functional Commonwealth serving as a bridge with non-Commonwealth countries and across different stages of economic development, all found their clearest expression in his promotion of the Colombo Plan. As the Commonwealth Conference of January 1950, decisions were reached to establish the machinery of co-operation as well as on specific technical measures for the development of South-East Asia. Bevin failed to draw American capital on the requisite scale and Britain's own contribution was necessarily limited. Nevertheless, his work at the Colombo Conference, which was one of the last international gatherings he attended, showed that to the end he retained the belief that a decent standard of living was the way to economic stability without which no political stability was possible, and that co-operation between the western powers in developing their colinial territories would contribute to the material welfare of

the latter, benefit the former and promote international
harmony. It was a fitting end for the career of a man who
wanted to be remembered, above all, as a bread-and-butter
statesman.

VII

In evaluating Bevin's overall record as foreign secretary,
one need not dwell on the domestic political setting in
which it was formulated, because this played a minimal role
in influencing the evolution of his policy. The organisational context, on account of Bevin's close collaboration
with his officials, enhanced Bevin's performance as foreign
secretary, but it cannot be said to have imposed on him the
main lines of the policies he pursued. The Foreign Office
was the instrument through which he carried out his policy,
not the policy-making machine of which he was content to
remain the mouthpiece. So much cannot be said for every
British foriegn secretary. Bevin's political status was
such that once his policies were formulated, he almost
invariably managed to secure their acceptance by the
Cabinet, the Labour Party and Parliament. This leaves as
the two crucial factors: Bevin, the individual, his views,
beliefs, attitudes and personal qualities; and the international environment.

   Bevin's personality was a mass of contradictions: so
rugged, simple and monumental if looked at from afar, so
gnarled, complicated and even mysterious on close viewing.
It is best seen as a series of contradictory impulses:
the nonconformism that was intolerant of minorities, the
anti-totalitarianism that required monolithic loyalty,
the humanitarianism that went hand in hand with obstinate
brutality, and the breadth of wisdom which co-existed
uneasily with prejudice and occasional vanity. But above
all others towered the qualities of pragmatism, toughness
and unshakable self-confidence.

   The international environment which confronted Bevin on
his accession to office was fraught with uncertainty.
Even before the final defeat of Germany, deep cracks had
developed in the wartime alliance between the Big Three
which was intended to provide the mainstay of the post-
war international order. The direction which Russian
policy would take in the aftermath of victory remained an

enigma. America's new leader was an unknown quantity and
it was by no means certain that America was ready to
assume global responsibilities commensurate with her vastly
expanded power. Britain emerged out of the war as one of
the principal architects of victory and with a richly deserved membership of the triumvirate of world power. In
terms of her responsibilities, she remained a world power,
but she was economically prostrate and militarily exhausted,
and her political influence owed more to her past reputation than to any solid, continuing source of international
power.

Fortunately, Bevin's qualities as an individual were the
ones most needed by Britain in the harsh and hazardous
international environment of the post-war period. He was
called on to preside over a phase of history which few
nations have conducted with ease and dignity, and he
carried out the task, except in the Middle East, not
gracefully, nor easily, but with great realism and foresight. To some extent, Bevin compensated for Britain's
reduced power and status with his own commanding personality and strength of character. Her economic weakness
could have had disastrous consequences, had it not been
for the shrewdness and skill with which he pleyed his
meagre hand. He took a whole range of difficult and grave
decisions without flinching and bore with fortitude the
ever-increasing burdens of his office which included the
most extensive and strenuous round of international conferences in the history of British foreign policy. It may
well be, as The Observer suggested in May 1948, that
'history will very possibly rate him as one of the greatest
Foreign Secretaries this country ever had and the best she
could possibly have had at this particular juncture'.

Meanwhile, in considering the verdict of his contemporaries, one is confronted with a curious paradox: Bevin's
most vociferous and persistent critics are to be found
within the ranks of his own party, whilst his political
opponents sustained him in Parliament and heaped praise
on him. This paradox can only be explained by the fact
that within weeks of coming into office Bevin began to
pursue a policy which the left wing of the Labour Party
regarded as the antithesis of a 'Socialist foreign policy'.
Bevin's very first speech in the House of Commons as
foreign secretary dashed their hopes that Labour's accession to power would mark a clean break with the past and

the promulgation of a new foreign policy. The nature of
this 'Socialist foreign policy' was never defined precisely
or authoritatively, but its main elements were a belief in
international co-operation, a commitment to international
proletarian solidarity, anti-capitalism and opposition to
the whole syndrome of power politics.[94] Bevin's critics
on the Left claimed that he reversed all these tenets by
initiating a policy which was nationalistic, anti-Russian,
pro-American, and which he conducted with the traditional
instruments of statecraft.

It was said, not altogether without reason, that the
Labour foreign secretary dropped nothing of the programme
of his Tory predecessors, except the aitches. He certainly
worked for a bi-partisan foreign policy and employed his
principal private secretary, Sir Pierson Dixon, as an
intermediary between himself and Anthony Eden.[95] It is
not surprising, therefore, that the guardians of doctrinal
purity remained highly critical of Bevin's handling of
foreign affairs.

The repudiation of a 'Socialist foreign policy' in
favour of 'continuity' also accounts for the support which
Bevin received from the Conservatives and the proponents
of the traditional or 'realist' approach to international
relations. Typical of this second group is Lord Strang,
who wrote: 'It is to the enduring credit of the Labour
Government, and of the Foreign Secretary, Ernest Bevin,
in particular, that, bypassing party doctrines, they
framed policies which were suited to strategic realities
and to the national interest as traditionally understood,
and which were well devised to take account of the change
in our place in the world and to enable us, even in the
altered circumstances, to continue to play a continuing
worthy part on the international stage.'[96]

Neither the criticisms nor the eulogies of Bevin can be
accepted without qualification. His refusal to be ideologically blinkered and to adopt a set of abstract and
dogmatic principles as the basis for his policy in a field
where flexibility and pragmatism are of the essence is
largely to his creidt. Moreover, the proponents of a
'Socialist foreign policy' were for the most part isolated
intellectuals and mavericks who spoke for no one but themselves. It was not they, but Bevin who represented the

true sentiments of the rank-and-file Labour supporters, their attachment to British sovereignty and their concern with the welfare of the working classes of this country.

At the same time, Strang's eulogy must be qualified by pointing out that Bevin's defence of 'the national interest as traditionally understood' is by no means synonymous with either wisdom or success in the conduct of foreign policy. Indeed, attachment to the traditional concepts of British statecraft could produce policies which were singularly unsuited to the new 'strategic realities'. Thus, Bevin's adoption of a traditional Tory foreign policy in the Middle East, bypassing Labour Party doctrines, precluded Britain from playing 'a continuing worthy part' on this section of the international stage precisely because it failed to take account of altered circumstances.

In Western Europe, too, Bevin's traditional outlook and methods made him a roadblock on the path to European unity. Altered conditions called for a reversal of Britain's negative balance-of-power precepts and offered new opportunities for constructive and imaginative statesmanship. It is true that no influential leaders of either party were prepared for a merger of British sovereignty in an organic European union and that there was not a great deal Britain could do on her own to reconstruct Europe's war-ravaged economies. But in the critical years of 1945 and 1946 Britain's prestige was higher than that of any other nation and the Social Democrats on the Continent looked desperately to Britain for a lead. But they looked in vain. There was not a word of encouragement from the Labour foreign secretary who was simply not interested because they were weak in power terms.

Bevin's sights were firmly fixed on the super-power relationship. His whole outlook was dominated by an acute perception of a Soviet threat and his policy was centrally directed at checking it. An assessment of his record must, therefore, largely turn on whether one shares his assumption that Russia was out to subvert the precarious post-war international order. Most Western politicians and commentators have shared it and were consequently inclined to praise Bevin for the realism and decisiveness with which he acted in defence of Western interests. Recent revisionist historiography, for all its limitations, does

serve to take us beyond the simplistic view of the cold
war as a defensive Western reaction to offensive Russian
actions. It suggests a more complicated pattern of defensive reactions on both sides to dimly-perceived threats
which eventually led to the formation of two hostile
military camps. To take this view is not to suggest that
the cold war was simply the result of a psychological process of misperception, only to point out that the fundamental divergence of interests was confounded by mutual
suspicion and mistrust. In defence of Bevin it should be
stated that the evidence regarding Soviet intentions was
not unambiguous, and to act on the assumption that it was
a status-quo power would have involved risks that he did
not feel justified in taking. What cannot be sustained
is the claim by Bevin and his apologists that he strained
every nerve to gain Russian goodwill and co-operation and
reluctantly abandoned this course only in mid-1947.[97]
Bevin's attitude to Russia was not only aggressive from
the start; he also endeavoured to persuade the sceptical
American leaders to adopt a tough line with their common
war-time ally. In this process of institutionalising
the cold war, Bevin played a larger part than is commonly
realised, but a final judgement as to whether this
constituted an act of statesmanship or an unfortunate
contribution to the deepening of the East-West rift must
be deferred until more evidence on Soviet aims and Anglo-
Soviet relations in the aftermath of the war comes to
light.

   Notwithstanding errors of Bevin's policy towards Western
Europe and the Middle East, and the possibility — by no
means a certainty — of errors in his policy towards Russia,
Bevin's overall record remains impressive. Almost single-
handed and with Olympian self-confidence, he kept the
British ship of state on an even keel, even in the stor-
miest seas of the post-war world. For six gruelling years,
he not only reacted to a succession of crises with a
steadiness of purpose and unflinching courage, but also
took the initiative in launching a number of novel and
constructive ideas. Foremost amongst his achievements
were the organisation of the European Recovery Programme
in response to the Marshall offer, and the key role he
played in laying the foundations of a broad Atlantic
alliance, and in effecting the transition from empire to
commonwealth. Considering the narrow margin at Bevin's
disposal and the unremitting pressure of the cold war,

his new departures and creative ventures appear all the
more remarkable.

   Part of the explanation for Bevin's uneven record and the
secular decline of his performance lies in the serious de-
terioration in his health. Growing illness, particularly
in his last three years in office, sapped his energy and
drive, relaxed his grip on policy, and made his interven-
tions unpredictable. The courage and direct approach with
which he had tackled great issues is a sad contrast to the
lack of purpose and fumblings which characterised his later
period in office. When physical exhaustion compelled him
to leave the conduct of affairs in the hands of the
Foreign Office, British policy became noticeably more
cautious, defensive and unimaginative, as witnessed by the
negotiations on the Schuman Plan. Perhaps Bevin's greatest
tradegy was that his opportunity to make his mark as a
statesman came to him so late in life.

   In assessing the ability and success of British foreign
secretaries, history, whatever it may decide about Ernest
Bevin, will not ignore him. He was not a man you could
ignore. By any standard of measurement, Bevin stands
forth as a man of great stature. He was cast in a large
mould, both politically and intellectually, and he played
a pivotal role in directing the course of events. His
unique and formidable personality left its mark on history
as it left a lasting impression on all who met him. He
had his weaknesses, he made his mistakes, some serious.
But there was no questioning his greatness. By his qualities, both as a man and as a statesman, he stands head and
shoulders above all Britain's other foreign secretaries in
the post-war era.

CHAPTER 3

HERBERT MORRISON

Controversy and criticism surrounded Herbert Morrison's last ministerial post. It was unfortunate that he was foreign secretary for only a few months, from March to October 1951; it was perhaps unfortunate that he was foreign secretary at all although, in fairness, it was difficult for him to develop his role at the Foreign Office in such a short time. Inevitably comparisons were made with his much respected predecessor, Ernest Bevin. Morrison claims that he was 'the inevitable choice',[1] and a strong case can be made in terms of his seniority for this view; his ministerial experience went back to 1929, when he became Minister of Transport. In the wartime coalition Morrison had served briefly as minister of supply and then in the difficult dual post of home secretary and minister of home security. In the post-war Labour Government, Morrison became deputy prime minister, lord president of the council and leader of the House of Commons. There is little doubt that Morrison was an ambitious man who hoped one day to lead his party and be prime minister. Although he denies complicity,[2] Morrison was the subject of a number of plots to replace Attlee during the 1945 Parliament, and this clearly affected relations between the two men. For a man hoping to succeed to the party leadership it was clear that a successful period as foreign secretary would greatly enhance his chances, especially as all Morrison's previous experience lay in the domestic area. Hence the eagerness to succeed Bevin: 'He worked to get the job. He brought every influence to bear. He turned down every other suggestion.'[3] Whilst the appointment pleased Morrison, it could be criticised on the basis that at such a critical time the appointment of someone who had no real expertise in foreign-policy-making either as a result of his career in Parliament or indeed outside it was a risk which should not have been taken, especially as he was already worn out by more than a decade of government. The same could be said, however, of most of his rivals.

Morrison had his introduction to international affairs in 1949 when he was appointed the leader of the Labour delegation to the Council of Europe in Strasbourg.[4] It was a far from happy experience. The Labour Party had not been well-disposed to 'Europeanism'; in the previous year the NEC (of which Morrison was a member) decided against participation in the Hague Congress. The 'Europeans' were somewhat disappointed to note that none of the members of the Government in the delegation to the Council of Europe were connected with the Foreign Office. Furthermore, neither Morrison nor Dalton, the delegation's deputy leader, was particularly noted for his enthusiasm for the European cause. The behaviour of the majority of the Labour delegation at the Council did little to enhance the already low reputation of the British Labour Party among its West European counterparts. For his part, Morrison saw the Council of Europe as a smaller version of Westminster in which he would try to reproduce his successful role as 'leader' of the House and thus be able to reorganise the proceedings in a manner which would be worthy of Westminster.[5] In this he was notably unsuccessful. Perhaps the best example of this came when the Labour delegation proposed William Whiteley, the Government Chief Whip, for the post of Vice-President of the Assembly. The European Movement controlled by Duncan Sandys, Churchill's son-in-law, proposed Lord Layton. After intense lobbying by both sides, Layton was elected by a small majority. The result was seen in a different light by both sides. Macmillan, who rather uncharitably compared Whiteley's nomination with Caligula's proposal that his horse should become Consul, regarded it as Morrison's 'first Parliamentary defeat since 1945';[6] the Labour delegation, on the other hand, thought it was 'a moral victory',[7] considering the overwhelming number of European Movement members present in the Assembly. Notwithstanding this rebuff, Morrison was elected chairman of the committee on detailed procedure, but Macmillan recorded that 'without a tame majority to carry all his points, he is lost'.[8]

It is particularly interesting to note here the insistence of the Labour members of the Council on calling themselves a 'delegation' whereas the Assembly treated all those

71

attending as individuals, seating them alphabetically
rather than by country. This led to some amusing juxta-
positions as well as a much less formal atmosphere. In
spite of this, Morrison attempted to treat the British
members as a delegation and to rule them all, regardless
of party, with the same iron hand with which he ruled in
London. In this venture also he was lacking in success.[9]
However, he quickly saw that the Conservative Opposition
was trying to use the European Movement as a vehicle to
further its own domestic interests, and his reaction to
this in part explains his lack of enthusiasm for the
Council of Europe and his behaviour at the Strasbourg
meeting.

Any of the Europeans who attended the Council of Europe
and who anticipated a softening of the Labour Government's
line on West European unity were bitterly disappointed.
This was not only due to the Labour delegation's composi-
tion but also its attitude, which was typified by
Morrison's speech to the Assembly. He failed to capture
the Assembly's mood and his speech merely reiterated
government policy, making no concessions either to the
moderate 'Europeans' or to the more extreme federalist
viewpoint. In making the most important speech by a
British politician on European Union since Bevin's
'Western Union' speech of January 1948, Morrison placed
the British Government firmly behind the principle of
inter-governmental co-operation rather than the supra-
nationalist solutions supported by many of those attending
the Assembly. Clearly he believed that the Assembly
should not get ideas above its station and should remain
a purely deliberative and consultative body. The main
emphasis of the speech was on co-operation rather than
union in the belief that changes should be based on consent. Instead of functionalism, which was usually contrasted with federalism and which sought to develop unity
by slow and steady steps in areas where agreement could
be reached, Morrison proposed 'positive and constructive
evolution'.[10] There was in practice little to distinguish
these views from those of the more cautious functionalists
except for the fact that in Morrison's mind, as indeed in
the minds of many other Labour leaders, the words 'co-operation' and 'unity' could be used interchangeably:
'Progress towards greater unity in Europe, which we all
desire, must be based on consent ... There can be no

question of coercing free people and democratic Parliaments into schemes to which they are opposed ... The progress towards greater European co-operation which has already taken place has been based on the willing action of responsible Governments sustained by responsible Parliaments.'[11] This speech along with his general performance in the Assembly led one opponent to comment on the relaxation of the atmosphere among the British representatives after Morrison had returned home.[12] Morrison's first venture on the international stage could hardly be described as a great success or a happy baptism.

The lessons of his visit to Strasbourg seemed to be lost on Morrison, who found it difficult to cope with matters when there was no certainty of victory and no assurance that his policies would be generally acceptable. This was again a reflection of his exclusive training in domestic politics where the Government was in practice the sole sovereign body; in addition it meant that he was ill-equipped to face the large number of unresponsive sovereign governments who were active in the international system.

Morrison returned home to join in the preparation for the general election due in the early part of 1950. As in 1945 he played an active part in the national campaign and in the drafting of the manifesto. The manifesto, <u>Let us win through together</u>, was one which did not find favour with the British electorate who dealt a bitter blow to the Labour Party by reducing its overall majority to a mere handful. Worse was to follow. First Cripps, then Bevin was overtaken by the effects of a decade of strenuous public service and forced to resign office. During much of the latter period before his resignation and death, Bevin had been unable to devote his full attention to the problems facing Britain, and Attlee had acted as his own foreign secretary. The strain of occupying both positions and trying to cope with a delicate political situation was also clearly too much for the prime minister who reshuffled his Cabinet in March 1951. Bevin, on his seventieth birthday, left his beloved Foreign Office and Herbert Morrison was appointed to replace him.

Morrison's appointment was not entirely a surprise. He was, after all, the deputy leader of the Parliamentary Labour Party and had since 1945 been in overall command of

the home policy of the government. It was natural that he
should consider himself to be a suitable candidate to play
the same role in foreign affairs now that Bevin was no
longer at the Foreign Office. Furthermore, he held a commanding position in the hierarchy of the Labour Party outside Parliament. He had been a member of the National
Executive Committee for many years and was a past chairman
of the party. He had been the architect and tactician of
the victories of 1945 and 1950. Morrison was thus highly
qualified in terms of his position within the Labour Party
as a whole to take on any appointment. However, in addition to his lack of foreign policy expertise, he was at a
distinct disadvantage in his relations with Attlee. He
had, as we have seen, been involved in plots to overthrow
Attlee and the latter had considerable reservations about
him. There was first of all a clash of personalities
which meant that Attlee was not prepared to give Morrison
as free a hand in foreign policy as he had given Bevin.
Whereas Bevin had always been a loyal lieutenant and was
content to control foreign policy under the general but
not detailed supervision of the Prime Minister, Morrison
was known to be ambitious and Attlee kept a tightish rein
on him. Furthermore, Bevin had a clear grasp of foreign
policy matters, and Morrison did not. Although it would
be too Machiavellian to suggest that Attlee appointed him
knowing that he would be a failure, it is quite possible
that, seeing the end of his administration as being imminent and a new rising star in Hugh Gaitskell, he did not
resist too strongly the pressures brought to bear on him
to appoint Morrison as the new foreign secretary.

Initially Morrison's appointment was welcomed outside
Parliament, especially by the press[13] who foresaw an end
to the delays and inaction which had characterised the
latter days of Bevin's tenure at the Foreign Office. Almost immediately after his appointment and before he had
time to familiarise himself with his new job, Morrison
found himself as Attlee's deputy in temporary charge of
the government as a consequence of the premier's illness.
He was thus not only faced by problems abroad in the shape
of German rearmament, European union, Iranian oil, the
Egyptian crisis and the war in Korea but also had to nurse
a tired and demoralised government divided amongst itself
over the question of domestic rearmament and Budget proposals to raise charges on false teeth and spectacles.

Whilst Attlee was in hospital Morrison unsuccessfully tried to avoid a Cabinet split. His failure further aggravated his relations with the Prime Minister.[14] In addition, Morrison was faced with his own personal problems in the form of his wife's serious illness from cancer, from which she was dying during the whole of his period at the Foreign Office.

It was against this rather stormy background that he took up his appointment. Despite the hopes that the change would be for the better, it soon became clear that Morrison was not really in tune with the Foreign Office. He demonstrated in a number of ways that he did not believe, as did most people in the Foreign Office at this time, that the Foreign Office was something special. His first appearance in Parliament as foreign secretary was marked by the fact that a junior minister, Kenneth Younger, answered the questions on foreign policy, whilst he dealt with questions on domestic policy.[15] He continued to show an interest in the Festival of Britain almost to the exclusion of everything else; for instance, instead of attending a meeting of the Council of Europe Committee of Ministers, he went to an 'eve of Festival' dinner. Furthermore, in May 1951 he told his Conservative opposite number, Eden, that he did not share the latter's 'superior' view of the Foreign Office.[16] This would have been bad enough, but it soon also became clear that Morrison's political style contrasted sharply with the standards expected at the Foreign Office. Whilst he liked whirlwind tours, political hurly-burly and informality, the formality and strict etiquette required by the Foreign Office irritated him. The view of the Foreign Office was that, apart from being unsuitable in terms of style, he also understood little about foreign policy and cared less about developing a long term strategy: 'It was evident that he knew practically nothing about foreign affairs and his whole outlook was parochial.'[17] Such views as this led inevitably to unfavourable comparisons with Bevin, who had not concealed his dislike of Morrison during his term at the Foreign Office. In a brief checklist of qualities and abilities it was difficult to find anything in Morrison that they could appreciate. Except in their staunch anti-communism,[18] Morrison and Bevin were almost a complete contrast. Whereas Bevin was quick and decisive and disliked attending the House of Commons, Morrison was slow and muddled and a real

'House of Commons' man; Bevin had vision and a mastery of
his subject, but Morrison never really got to grips with
foreign policy at all. In addition he kept providing evidence of his inability. He said:

> I am worried about Morrison. Dick Law told me that
> his speech on Foreign Affairs on Monday was absolute-
> ly deplorable. Everybody squirmed in agony. He
> pronounced the first syllable of 'Tigris' to rhyme
> with 'pig', and called the Euphrates the 'You Frates',
> in two separate words. Now, I do not mind people
> pronouncing foreign names incorrectly, but to pro-
> nounce the Tigris and Euphrates in that way indicates
> not only lack of education, but also the fact that
> one has never heard the Middle East discussed by men
> of experience. It is that which is so terrifying.[19]

Even if one accepts that, as a Conservative MP, Law was an
unfriendly informant it is hard to overlook this insight
into the views of the Establishment and its friends on
Herbert Morrison. It is evident that he failed to win the
respect of his officials and he was too easily distracted
by other things, particularly on the home front. Finally,
he was not able to establish the kind of relationship that
Bevin had with his officials and hence did not get from
them the support necessary to enable a man so lacking in
foreign policy experience to make a success of his period
in office.

Although there were several important issues in foreign
policy at this time, not least the Korean War, the most
pressing of them flared up in Iran and Egypt late in April
1951. Morrison got off on the wrong foot by cancelling a
meeting with the Egyptian Ambassador at short notice on
25 April. A few days later, a much more serious challenge
to the British position in the Persian Gulf than had been
made hitherto came about with the announcement of a take-
over by the Iranian Government of all foreign holdings in
Iranian Oil. From this point the situation deteriorated
rapidly. Although he was able to announce the ending of
the state of war with Germany, Morrison was hurt by the
double blow of the mysterious disappearance of two British
diplomats, Burgess and Maclean, who later reappeared in
Moscow, an affair for which he had ministerial responsibility, and by his failure to deal effectively with either

the Egyptian or Iranian crises. His performances at the
Despatch Box lacked the old authority, and he was frequently
unable to satisfy any section of the House. The reasons
for this lay in his general lack of understanding of the
situation on the one hand, and on the other the failure of
his Cabinet colleagues to give him support. Although privately he was 'more hawkish than expected',[20] publicly
Morrison had to oppose military action in the Middle East.
He was therefore never wholeheartedly behind the policy
which he had to defend in the House of Commons.[21] In
addition, the growing belief that his heart was not in his
job was confirmed in many ways by his two months' absence
from London during August and September. The first of
these months was spent on holiday in Scandinavia, having
left Attlee and the junior Foreign Office ministers to
deal with the rapidly deteriorating situation in the
Middle East. A story, possibly apocryphal, has it that
Morrison confided to a local official he met on holiday
that his interests had always lain in 'municipal' politics.
This official later became the foreign minister of his own
country and could hardly have believed this statement
coming from the British foreign minister. On his return
from this holiday, Morrison left almost immediately to
attend to Foreign Office business abroad. A more sensitive
foreign minister might well have gauged the public mood and
stayed at home dealing with the Iranian crisis rather than
attending to the important but less 'urgent' matters of the
Japanese Peace Conference, the Washington Foreign Ministers'
Meeting and the NATO meeting in Ottawa. As a result of
these meetings in the United States, it became clear that
there was to be no American help for Britain in Iran.
Furthermore, Morrison did little to enhance his reputation
abroad.[22] On his return home on the Queen Mary, Morrison
suffered eye trouble but soon recovered and was forced,
against his better judgement, to give a party for his
officials and other distinguished passengers on board.
The press were delighted to report that the foreign minister
danced publicly with an actress at this party, an action
which they regarded, along with many ordinary men and women,
as being most unbecoming in a British foreign secretary.

During the course of Morrison's journeys abroad, Attlee
had taken charge at the Foreign Office but it was left to
Morrison to pick up the pieces of the Iranian policy which,
as a result of the American refusal of help and the failure

of the Stokes Mission which attempted to reach a negotiated settlement, had crumbled almost to nothing. Although
personally disagreeing with the decision and the 'brief'
from the Foreign Office,[23] Morrison found that Attlee and
the Cabinet had decided to refer the Iranian dispute to
the United Nations. The dispute remained unresolved when
Labour left office the following month. During the election campaign, the press and the Opposition strenuously
attacked Morrison for his handling of foreign policy in
general and his Iranian policy in particular. Almost on
the eve of the election, the decision to withdraw staff
from Abadan under threat of their expulsion added fuel to
the fire and led to charges of 'capitulation'. Although
Morrison responded quite firmly to these attacks, the
damage was already done. In addition, the crisis in Egypt
deepened at this time, when Egypt turned down the British
proposals designed to forestall the abrogation of the 1936
treaty and the annexation of the Sudan.

It was, however, not just in the handling of the Egyptian
and Iranian crises that Morrison found himself at odds with
his colleagues in the Labour Party. On other issues also
there was division, most notably on the question of West
German rearmament. This had been agreed in principle by
Bevin under duress in September 1950. Subsequently it
had been hedged round by the so-called 'Attlee conditions',
that the rearmament of West Germany should be preceded by
the rearmament of the rest of Western Europe, that there
should be a clear indication that the German people wanted
rearmament and that, in order to prevent the re-emergence
of an independent German army, the West German contribution
should be part of an integrated force.[24] Morrison, on the
other hand, was much less cautious and appeared to be more
favourably disposed to West German rearmament than his
colleagues, although he too was strongly opposed to the
Pleven plan for a European army. As a result of his experience at Strasbourg before he became Foreign Secretary,
Morrison was very opposed to the Council of Europe and at
the time of his appointment was even considering recommending British withdrawal, particularly over the suggestion
that the Council should be allowed to discuss defence
matters. Later, however, he climbed down[25] and accepted
that the Council should be allowed to discuss the political
aspects of defence but not to make any defence decisions.
By the middle of September 1951, Morrison seems to have

completely reversed his position and associated himself
with a statement welcoming both the Pleven plan and the
Schuman plan for a coal and steel pool. 'Britain', said
the declaration, 'desired to establish the closest possible
association with the European continental community at all
stages of its development'.[26] Finally, he seems to have
been at odds with at least some members of his party over
policy towards Korea. When it was revealed in February
1952 that the Labour Government had agreed to the extension of the war outside Korea to involve the bombing of
airbases north of the Yalu in the People's Republic of
China, there was a considerable outcry from many members
of the Labour Party. Morrison's claim that he and his
colleagues 'had done nothing to be ashamed of' may be
true, but many of his fellow MPs were hurt and embarrassed
by Churchill's revelation.[27]

By any standards, Morrison's short stay at the Foreign
Office was far from happy. Although he stayed on as
'shadow' foreign secretary after the 1951 election, there
is evidence to suggest that Attlee was thinking of replac-
ing him had Labour won the election. 'P.M. ... said he
was disappointed with H.M(orrison) as foreign secretary
and, if he won the election he wouldn't put him back at
the F.O.'[28] His style and his lack of understanding of
foreign policy clearly made him unsuitable as a foreign
minister. The real problem lay in the lack of a clear
alternative once Bevin resigned. According to Hugh
Dalton, the alternatives lay between Morrison, Bevan, who
was regarded as an unacceptable choice because he was too
left-wing, and James Griffiths, whom some people thought
might be a compromise candidate. In his memoirs, Dalton
recorded that with the benefit of hindsight much of the
troubles of the Labour Party in opposition might have
been avoided had Bevan been given promotion at this
time.[29] To Dalton's list, Lord Gladwyn added the names
of Hartley Shawcross, the Solicitor-General, and Hector
McNeal, the Minister of State at the Foreign Office.[30]

The longer Morrison remained in his post the more disillusioned his colleagues became. Attlee particularly
regretted the appointment: 'I think it was a bad mistake
allowing Herbert to be Foreign Secretary. I didn't know
he knew so little. I had no idea he was so ignorant.'[31]

A further reason for Morrison's lack of knowledge may be
found in the confession made in an interview 'that he
rarely read Foreign Office papers: he made do with briefs
prepared by his own staff on whatever topics were up for
discussion' in Cabinet.[32] He was clearly not in a position to give the Cabinet the kind of lead necessary in
foreign affairs. 'His very training as Party strategist
encouraged him to take short-range views and to be ingenious without reference to overall ends... (He) had
neither the time nor the inclination for careful study of
foreign policy.'[33]

It is quite clear that Morrison's disastrous period at
the Foreign Office did much to destroy what little chance
he might have had of succeeding Attlee as leader. That a
man who could reportedly say 'foreign policy would be okay
except for the bloody foreigners'[34] should ever have been
appointed foreign secretary throws little credit either on
himself or on the man who appointed him. It may be that
the key to Morrison's behaviour as foreign secretary could
lie in a conscious - or unconscious - attempt to compensate
for his pacifism in the First World War - a view borne out
by the fact that one of his first acts as foreign secretary
was to ask for a biography of Palmerston.[35] It is hard to
escape from the conclusion that 'Morrison lacked the supreme
qualities of vision and style, as well as luck, necessary
to succeed as British Foreign Secretary in 1951'.[36] It
would have been far better for all concerned if Herbert
Morrison had ended his ministerial career in al office
which would have been more in keeping with his interests
and his expertise.

CHAPTER 4

ANTHONY EDEN

From the mid-twenties until the mid-fifties Anthony Eden
was more closely and intimately involved in the conduct of
British foreign policy than any other single figure. His
influence was not always decisive, his status ranged from
parliamentary private secretary to prime minister, and
there were some intervals when he was out of office altogether. But in sheer experience of foreign affairs and
longevity of tenure few could approach him. In one way
or another he dominated the British diplomatic scene for
the best part of three decades, and during this crucial
period in British history he personified the spirit of
British diplomacy at home as well as abroad. Few politicians have been more exposed to the public eye. No other
twentieth-century British foreign secretary has written
about his stewardship and been written on at greater
length than Eden.[1] Yet in a very real sense he remains
an elusive and enigmatic personality.

Eden came from an aristocratic and well-connected family.
After an undistinguished career at Eton and an impressive
record of service during the First World War, Captain
Eden went up to Oxford where he read oriental languanges
with a view to joining the diplomatic service. Although
he had not previously displayed any deep interest in
politics, Parliament appealed to him as an alternative
approach to foreign affairs, and in 1923, at the age of
twenty-six, he entered the House of Commons as the representative of Warwick and Leamington. From then on Eden
proceeded swiftly up the rungs of the political ladder.
In 1926 he became parliamentary private secretary to Sir
Austen Chamberlain, the foreign secretary, and served in
that capacity until 1929. From 1931 until 1933 he was
under-secretary of state at the Foreign Office. For the
next three years he was in double harness with two
successive foreign secretaries, Sir John Simon and Sir

Samuel Hoare, first as lord privy seal and then as minister for League of Nations affairs. In 1935 Eden became, at thirty-eight, the youngest foreign secretary since Lord Grenville in the eighteenth century, and he held the post until he broke with Neville Chamberlain in 1938.

In the thirties Eden's popularity was at its peak. The public saw in him the embodiment of the highest principles in a world of depraved and cynical power politics. His colleagues inside the Cabinet, however, did not share his faith in collective security and the League of Nations. His whole conduct of foreign policy was subjected to frequent and humiliating interference from Neville Chamberlain and the Inner Cabinet. And he acquiesced far too meekly and for far too long in the anomalous position of having the responsibility of defending government policy while being excluded from having a say in shaping its direction.

It is surprising that Eden did not make a firm stand earlier. When he belatedly resigned in 1938 it was over a secondary issue, Chamberlain's plan to open negotiations with Mussolini, and he went out of his way to play down the differences which divided him from the prime minister and his clique. Ironically, Eden's resignation probably saved his career, for he emerged untarnished by the brush of appeasement and stood out in the public eye in glittering contrast to the men of Munich. The impact of Eden's resignation can to some extent be gauged from Winston Churchill's description of his personal reaction: 'Late on 20th February 1938 the news reached me. I must confess that my heart sank and for a while the dark waters of despair overwhelmed me... There seemed one strong young figure standing up against the long, dismal, drawling tides of drift and surrender... he seemed to me to embody the life hope of the British nation, the grand old British race'.[2] This was the popular mythology which surrounded the role played by Eden in the thirties, but in reality his stand against the drift was neither strong nor effective.

With the outbreak of the Second World War Eden was swept back into office as secretary of state for the dominions in Neville Chamberlain's reconstructed government. He proved to be a good choice for organising and co-ordinating the Empire war effort. When Churchill became prime

minister in May 1940, he moved Eden from the Dominions
Office to the War Office. Here Eden's flair for administration, his love of action, his tremendous appetite for
hard work and his understanding of the army and the men in
it were put to good effect. He stayed at the War Office
for only seven months but during that period he presided
vigorously over the reconstruction of the British Army and
the launching of the victorious offensive in North Africa.
Quite possibly Eden's achievements during those crucial
months will be remembered as the most notable of his long
career. He was understandably sorry to leave the War
Office, but he returned to the Foreign Office, in
Churchill's words, 'like a man going home'.

   Throughout the war Eden worked exceptionally hard and
showed his real worth as an administrator and organiser.
The endless chain of international conferences he had to
attend provided wide scope for the exercise of his skill
in negotiation. But his passionate interest in the day-
to-day conduct of foreign policy was not matched by an
interest in long-term planning for the post-war international order. He was noticeably lacking in any broad
ideas of his own and to a large extent acted as a passive
intermediary between the Foreign Office and the prime
minister who held widely divergent views on the structure
of post-war international security. During the six years
which followed the Conservative defeat at the 1945 election, Eden had ample time to reflect and develop his
ideas. But his speeches contained few original or distinc-
tive thoughts. They were carefully considered, packed with
factual information and dispassionate. He instinctively
shunned controversy and uttered endless platitudes. The
bulk and variety of his speeches, which have been published in three volumes, are a tribute to his industry if
not to his imagination, wit or vision.[3] But though his
speeches lacked fire, their manner was always impeccable.
The House of Commons listened to him attentively, and
political opponents as well as colleagues have given him
credit for the effectiveness with which he handled parliamentary debate and procedure.[4]

II

That Eden should have had the Foreign Office when the
Conservatives were returned to power in October 1951 was
a foregone conclusion. The chancellorship of the

Exchequer or the Foreign Office usually go to the second most influential politician of the ruling party, and by experience and personal preference Eden was clearly marked for the top foreign affairs post. As foreign secretary during the 1951-5 administration, Eden's personal position was immensely powerful. He enjoyed a high standing in the country at large. Within the Conservative Party he was not only regarded as a formidable authority on foreign affairs but also recognised as Churchill's No 2 and eventual successor. In this latter position Eden was so firmly entrenched that it was never openly questioned by any of his colleagues. In the House of Commons Eden could rely on a dependable Conservative majority and to some extent on the support of the Opposition for the substance, if not always for the details, of his policy. There were thus no major domestic political constraints to limit Eden's freedom of action.

The key to Eden's role and performance as foreign secretary was his relationship with the prime minister. Working with Churchill in double-harness in the 1951-5 government was, of course, not a new experience but a continuation of the close personal and political partnership which developed during the war. It was only natural that Sir Winston with his commanding personality, prodigious experience and unrivalled fame as a world statesman should want to play a leading and active role in the making of foreign policy by his government. His main interest continued to be in international affairs and he concerned himself closely with the broad lines of foreign policy, leaving the detailed execution to his Foreign Secretary. Co-operation was enhanced by a remarkable concensus on most foreign policy issues. Winston Churchill once said that you could put him and his foreign secretary in separate rooms, 'put any questions on foreign policy to us and nine times out of ten we would give the same answer'.[5] For his part, Eden recorded that 'in all the years that Sir Winston Churchill and I worked together, it was this comprehension... that was most remarkable... the result of our lifetimes' experience of world affairs'.[6] Eye-witnesses have also written a great deal about the complementary qualities of character, age and mind and on 'the pride and indulgence of the old prophet and the devotion and patience of the chosen successor'.[7]

What is less well known is that during Churchill's last years in office this carefully cultivated impression of harmony concealed serious cracks. The relationship was no longer always easy and the two men could not but frustrate one another on occasion. Churchill, who was much the more forceful and decisive of the two, criticised Eden for being too much like a traditional diplomat. When he produced a neatly balanced but inconclusive paper with 'on the one hand' duly succeeded by 'on the other', Churchill commented that it contained every cliche except 'please adjust your dress before leaving'. The diaries of Lord Moran, Churchill's doctor, give a highly revealing account of the tensions rankling below the surface. 'It makes things difficult', Churchill complained, 'when Anthony cannot distinguish between a big issue and a small issue'.[8] When Eden was ill Churchill felt that 'It is a great relief to have charge of the F.O. instead of having to argue with Anthony. I can get something done'.[9] He thought Eden was tired and detected a strain in his telegrams: 'Sometimes he sends three thousand words in one day and there is nothing in them'.[10]

In part this was Churchill's fault. For fifteen years he had harried Eden unmercifully, lectured him and interfered with his work until Eden was afraid to make a decision on his own. It is true that Churchill groomed Eden for the leadership, but he still regarded him as a young man and was not very influenced by his views.[11] He also rendered Eden a great disservice by making him wait too long. Eden's patience was strained to breaking point by the eighty-year-old leader who kept postponing the date of his retirement. In a sudden display of nerves and temper Eden revealed to Sir Henry Channon that he was on bad terms with Winston: 'I get all the knocks; I don't think I can stand it much longer.'[12]

Lord Moran, who had the opportunity to observe both men at close range, concluded 'Everything Anthony said was sensible, and his judgment of men was discerning. He is not like Winston; he looks behind the facade... Both as a judge of men and as a cool appraiser of events, Anthony is much sounder and more discriminating than Winston, but the personality of the P.M. and his power over words raise him into another world, which will always be closed to Anthony, who was born, and will remain, a secondary

figure.'[13] The disparity in the weight of the two personalities precluded a partnership of equals and in the
last years of his administration Churchill increasingly
began to wonder whether Eden had the qualities which make
for success at the top. After his retirement, when Lord
Cherwell spoke to him of Eden's weakness, Churchill
replied: 'I have gone too far in building him up to go
back on it now'.[14] 'I wonder if he can do it', he
muttered on another occasion. 'Courage, Anthony has
courage. He would charge a square, but would he charge
at the right time and in the right place?'[15] These
doubts were amply justified by subsequent events.

   The point to note in relation to the period 1951-5 is
that Churchill did not confide his doubts to any of his
political colleagues, and carefully refrained from doing
anything which would damage Eden's public image. In fact
he went to great lengths to emphasise that he had the
utmost confidence in his deputy. In Cabinet, far from
being treated as an underling, Eden was treated as an
eminent statesman in his own right. On this point we have
the testimony of Lord Kilmuir (home secretary and later
lord chancellor) who refers to Eden's 'silencing authority'
when he spoke — in private or public — on his subject of
foreign affairs. 'Looking back', writes Kilmuir,

   I am not sure that his great authority and knowledge
   of foreign affairs was not a defect in the Government.
   Winston was determined not to oppose his successor,
   and none of the other members had the knowledge or
   experience to contradict Eden's policies. I doubt if
   a Foreign Secretary has enjoyed so much freedom since
   Lord Rosebery — in very different circumstances —
   reigned at the Foreign Office in 1892-1894. This en-
   trusting of a vital aspect of government to one man,
   however, competent, was in a sense an abrogation of
   the role of the Cabinet.[16]

As the minister in charge of the Foreign Office Eden was
not a new face. This was his third term as the political
chief of the Office. He had risen within the Office to a
degree rare in a party politician, and shared in its outlook, beliefs and collective temperament. In his style
of work Eden was very much like a Foreign Office mandarin:
cautious, methodical and bureaucratic. His specialised

training in foreign affairs was such that one colleague
was led to comment that 'he could have stepped down to be
a Permanent Under-Secretary as a civil servant without
shaking the organisation'.[17] Eden's natural inclinations
and the length of his association with the department
combined to blur the distinction between his amateur status and the professional status of his advisers.

But Eden's recognised expertise and exceptional familia-
rity with the work of his department did not necessarily
make him an effective political master. He relied excess-
ively on his own intuition and judgment, to the chagrin of
his advisers, and he was much less open to argument and
persuasion than a minister who recognised his own limitations. This fact goes a long way to explain the apparent
paradox that this old Etonian was much less popular with
the Foreign Office staff than his working-class predecessor
who was a good, if critical, listener.

In general Eden was courteous and considerate towards his
officials, but under stress he became snappy and irascible.
Outwardly he gave the impression of a cool, self-assured
and even languid figure, but in his dealings with his staff
he was anything but imperturbable. Particularly when his
health was adding to the anxieties of his office he was
liable to become fussy, petulant and irritable. No one in
public life, commented one colleague, lives more on his
nerves than Eden.[18] Behind the decorous facade of urbanity
there was a relentlessly gnawing tension. In a field where
strong nerves are of the essence, this made Eden an awkward
master to work for. His permanent under-secretary during
the war, Sir Alexander Cadogan, described him as 'a cat on
hot bricks' and recorded in his diary that 'He is always
jumping about the room, itching to "do something"'.[19]

Part of the trouble was that Eden, unlike R.A.Butler and
Sir Alex Douglas Home, was very bad at delegating. The
flow of papers and telegrams at the Foreign Office is
remorseless and it is not easy to escape from the ubiqui-
tous despatch boxes. Some ministers ease their burden by
exercising only remote control over the most important
business. Eden's reluctance to delegate led him to tax
himself considerably; he was often exhausted, sometimes
dangerously so. When Eden was absent from the Foreign
Office through illness either Churchill or Lord Salisbury

was nominally in charge, but the day-to-day running of the Office was entrusted to the minister of state, Selwyn Lloyd, whom Eden liked and with whom he worked smoothly and harmoniously.

The charge of neglecting the work of his department could never be levelled against Anthony Eden. He was assiduous, hardworking and meticulous in his attention to detail. His subordinates were impressed by his prodigious energy and the sustained application with which he read his papers and mastered his briefs. The real charge is that he lacked imagination and vision and consequently failed to provide inspiration and leadership. As Churchill once observed: 'Anthony works very hard and is most conscientious, plugging away at routine. But that is not what is wanted at the Foreign Office, where you must take up the big issues and deal with them'.[20]

Eden's preference for day-to-day business over the much more challenging tasks of policy evaluation and innovation is clearly reflected in his attitude to planning. He was fond of quoting Lord Kitchener's aphorism: 'One cannot conduct foreign policy as one would but only as one can'. His attitude to the committee set up by Bevin to examine long-term policy and which had in the meantime proved its worth as an embryonic planning machinery was decidedly cool. Like many traditional diplomats Eden felt that in foreign affairs there is no possibility of planning, the right approach being to deal with problems as they arise. This view errs in construing difficulty as impossibility, and it may be that Eden was unenthusiastic about the work of the long-term committee because he felt out of his depth in this unfamiliar and intellectually strenuous activity. At any rate, he discouraged its work and the committee gradually faded out.[21]

From the beginning until the end of his career, Eden showed a diplomatic, not a political interest in foreign affairs and he took on the position of ambassador-at-large with obvious enjoyment. He had a flair for diplomacy and was highly skilled in the art of personal negotiations. Harold Macmillan gave the following example of Eden's prowess and virtuosity:

The other day Dulles brought forward a plan that was totally unacceptable to us. I wondered for a moment how Anthony would handle the situation. But he was quite wonderful. I thought his patience would never give out. An hour went by, and gradually I discovered Dulles changing his position. At last he brought forward another scheme, which was about the exact opposite of the first, and incidentally just what we wanted. Anthony did not rush at him and say: that's just what we wanted all along. He murmered that there were parts of the plan he did not like, and then he appeared to give way to Dulles a little reluctantly.[22]

Curiously, for a man who spent a lifetime in diplomacy and was so adept at it, Eden neither liked nor understood foreigners. Representatives of other countries who came into contact with him were struck by his courtesy and gracious manners but were rarely able to establish human relations with him. Harold Nicolson, after quoting the observation of the French ambassador to London, 'Il s'esquive derriere son charme', exclaims 'How true that is! Anthony has managed to create out of affability a smoke-screen more impenetrable than any cloud of sullenness'.[23] Eden was also elusive and fifficult to pin down: 'One goes away thinking how reasonable, how agreeable and how helpful he has been, and then discovers that in fact he had promised nothing at all'.[24]

Eden was the personification of what Harold Nicolson called the 'mercantile or shopkeeper' conception of diplomacy to distinguish it from the 'heroic' conception. The former conception is based on the assumption that a compromise between rivals is generally more profitable than a complete destruction of the rival. Negotiation is not a mere phase in a death-struggle but an attempt by mutual concession to reach some durable understanding. A middle point can reconcile opponents; national prestige must not intrude. To find this middle point all that is required is a frank discussion, the placing of the cards on the table and the usual processes of human reason, confidence and fair dealing.[25]

This mercantile conception of diplomacy is not an inaccurate summary of the british diplomatic tradition which

is so deeply pragmatic and empirical. The distinction
with which Eden represented this particular style and
approach won a number of admirers inside the Foreign
Office. It also brought a number of concrete achievements.
The problem of Trieste which had poisoned relations between
Italy and Yugoslavia for nearly a decade was settled in
1953 largely thanks to Eden's initiative. He himself
proudly presented it as 'a classic example of the true
function of diplomacy, an open agreement secretly arrived
at'.[26] More substantial were Eden's contributions in 1954
to the solutions of the Indo-China conflict and the problem
of European defence. Unfortunately Eden also acquired the
language of diplomacy as second nature: the blurred edge,
the softened meaning, the studied understatement. He
became addicted to cliches, ambiguities and homilies which
deprived his speech and thought of any vigour and force.

Eden's views on international relations are depressingly
bland and superficial. The need for restraint and moderation, give and take and civilised behaviour are recurrent
themes. The sanctity of international law is the subject
of high-sounding but singularly vague orations. To give
just one example, in his address to the General Assembly
of the United Nations in November 1951 he said:

 I am more than ever convinced that, if we are to
 succeed in this task, the nations of the world must
 submit to the rule of law and abide by it. Confidence can only be created and maintained on the
 basis of respect for international engagements. It
 is therefore the duty of all nations, as indeed it
 is their interest, to respect international authority
 and to uphold it...
 I do not believe, or ask you to believe, that in any
 dispute one party is one hundred per cent a black
 villian, and the other party one hundred per cent
 snow-white. That is against the law of averages.
 All men are fallible, and peace can only rest on
 mutual forbearance and restraint.[27]

The conception Eden had of Britain's own role in international affairs was out of touch with reality. He had
never adjusted his thoughts to the altered status of
Britain. When the Conservatives were returned to office
in October 1951 and Eden became foreign secretary again

90

after a lapse of six years, he apparently expected to play the diplomatic starring role which he had performed for so long between the wars and during the Second World War. A fundamental reappraisal of British strategy and foreign policy was called for by the advances in the technology of war and nuclear weapons; the changing configuration of international power and the decline in Britain's economic resources relative to the United States and the Soviet Union. Framing realistic objectives which adequately register changes in the international environment and Britain's own shrinking material base constituted the ultimate test of British statesmanship in the 1950s. Eden failed the test and the result of this failure was that the gulf between national resources and the multitude of political problems whose outcome the United Kingdom desired to influence steadily widened.

Eden's utterances on Britain's role reflect a profound debt to Churchill and particularly to the idea of Britain standing at the centre of three interlocking circles which the Conservative leader began to popularise in the late 1940s. 'Our foreign policy', said Eden to the 1948 Conservative Conference, 'should pursue three immediate objectives, which we can call the three unities. First, unity within the British Commonwealth and Empire. Second, unity within Western Europe. Third, unity across the Atlantic. The three unities I maintain... are not antagonistic, but complementary'.[28] This was very much watered-down Winston but it should be noticed that the order of priorities had been reversed. Whereas for Churchill what he called the 'alliance of the English-speaking peoples' always came first, followed by the Commonwealth and Western Europe, Eden, in this and other speeches, put the Commonwealth first and the Atlantic alliance last. He attached an exaggerated importance to Britain's position as 'the heart and centre of a great Commonwealth and Empire'. 'If we really work together', he claimed on another occasion, 'there are no limits to our joint endeavour. There are no difficulties that we cannot overcome'.[29]

The idea of three interlocking circles with Britain at the centre has obvious affinities with the nineteenth century idea of Britain controlling the destiny of the world by manipulating the European balance of Power.

Sometimes Eden would use the illustration of a stool standing on three legs, each of which must be given equal care and attention. The only trouble was that all through the fifties two of these legs were being whittled away. The Commonwealth was becoming not so much an instrument of British power as a vehicle for the peaceful liquidation of British colonies. Meanwhile in Europe the success of the Six after the formation of the Coal and Steel Community in forging an organic unity between themselves gradually led to the freezing of Britain out of her old role of independent influence in continental affairs.

If Eden had any understanding of the implications of these transformations, he effectively concealed that understanding. A broadcast he made in 1952 brings out clearly his outdated view of Britain as a global and oceanic power and the hub of the international system. In a tone reminiscent of Sir Eyre Crowe's famous memorandum of 1907 he said:

We are on the one hand, of course, a part of Europe, both by tradition and by geography. On the other hand our significance as a Great Power depends largely on our position within the British Commonwealth and on our connections with many other parts of the world, including the United States of America. That is why we warmly welcome the growth of the North Atlantic Community. Here is an association in harmony with so many of our thoughts and feelings. In this wide forum we feel ourselves at home...
The Atlantic Community is developing quietly without fuss but quite inevitably, around... common purposes. Bounded by the United States and Canada in the West and by Europe in the East, it transcends the national interest of us all. In this century the Atlantic has become a Mare Nostrum, a sea of links rather than a barrier which divides. I believe that Great Britain can render a particular service to this Atlantic Community. We are the nearest of the European nations, by our language and background, to the Commonwealth and to the United States, and we can act to some extent as the interpreters of each world to the other. I claim no special merit for Britain in all this. But I believe that by accident of geography, through our position on the fringe of these three interlocking

worlds, we have a special part to play, to which we must be true.[30]

III

Eden's actual conduct of British foreign policy in the 1950s was influenced to an exceptionally high degree by his experience of dealing with Hitler and Mussolini in the 1930s. As a result of that experience Eden developed very fixed images of 'dictators' and 'democracies' and highly dogmatic rules for ordering the relations between them. His memoirs are strewn with remarks to this effect. On his dealings with Hitler he writes: 'Here was a lesson I learnt, and was determined to apply if I could, twenty years later. A militant dictator's capacity for aggrandisement is only limited by the physical checks imposed upon him.'[31] And again on the need to be firm with dictators he writes that 'a leading democracy, in negotiating with a militant dictatorship, must not go cap in hand in search of fresh negotiations to cover longstanding differences, until there is evidence that the dictator is going to carry out the engagements he had already undertaken to the democracy. If, either from weakness or impatience, the democracy ignores this rule, other countries will take their cue from this action. As a consequence, potential friends will be in disarray, the public in the democracy will be bewildered and the dictators will underestimate the toughness of the democracy at the hour of decision.'[32] After dwelling at length on the tendency to find excuses for not upholding international order in the 1930s, Eden writes: 'All of which has its lesson for today. Once the obligation not to uphold international engagements is evaded, pretext will follow pretext, until the structure of confidence is destroyed and respect for treaties hangs 'like a rusty nail in monumental mockery'... The West must be on its guard, therefore, and be punctilious in fulfilling its word, to the newfound ally and to the old one, to West Germany as to France. For the issues that concern any of the free nations concern us all. The Soviets will not then be deceived into thinking that they can divide us, and there will be peace.'[33]

The Soviets, in Eden's belief system, were equated with the dictators of the inter-war period, and he was convinced that the new challenge could be effectively countered if only the lessons he distilled from his dealings with the earlier dictators were applied. 'Let us make no mistake,' he told an American audience, 'the Communist assault on free and democratic thought is more formidable than its Fascist counterpart of yesterday. Taking advantage of every contradiction and weakness in Western society, communism nearly absorbed a Western Europe confused by the aftermath of war... Side by side with this policy of penetration, the Communists have not hesitated to use the threat of rorce... To all this there is only one answer. We had to look to our physical defences.'[34]

This simplistic diagnosis and prescription, embedded in the arbitrary parallel posited between Communism and Fascism, blindered Eden's outlook and made his posture towards Russia more inflexible than it need have been. Even after Stalin's death, in March 1953, he writes, 'I did not share the optimism of those who say in this event an easement of the world's problems. The permanent challenge of communism transcends personalities, however powerful.'[35] Churchill took a much broader and more subtle view of relations with the Russians. He believed that the time was ripe for an attempt to achieve an understanding with the new rulers of Russia at a summit meeting between himself, Malenkov and, if possible, the President of the United States. Despite Eden's serious reservations about a personal approach to the new Soviet leaders, in a major speech on 11 May 1953 Churchill proposed big-power talks. Eden was afraid that Churchill (of all people) would give away too much to the Russians. Just before he was taken to a Boston clinic for an operation he phoned his under-secretary at the Foreign Office, Anthony Nutting, and told him, 'Don't let that old man appease the Bear too much in my absence.'[36] In July 1954 after Churchill had obtained Eisenhower's agreement to 'a reconnoitring patrol' Eden was still opposed to a direct approach to the Kremlin. Thus when even the author of the 'Iron Curtain' speech wanted to cash in on the post-Stalinist thaw to explore the possibilities of detente, the foreign secretary, tied to frozen images and ideas derived from his experience of dealing with Hitler and Mussolini twenty years earlier, was obdurately opposed to any movement.

Eden's rigid perception of the communist adversary was

matched by an unequivocal belief in the importance of close relations with allies. In an article in the American journal Foreign Affairs, he wrote: 'The West can survive only to the extent that individuals accept their obligations as members of a free community. As such our duty is clear. First, last and all the time we must stand together.'[37] Solidarity with Britain's principal Western ally, the United States, was, however, extremely difficult to maintain with Anthony Eden and John Foster Dulles as foreign secretaries. The two men were dissimilar in character, temperament and sense of values; incompatible in personality and divided by mutual personal antipathy. In 1952 Eden expressed to Eisenhower the hope that he would appoint someone other than Dulles as secretary of state if he became president.[38] After Eisenhower appointed Dulles and gave him a free hand over American foreign policy, relations between the two countries were dogged by endemic friction. Their foreign secretaries were simply not on the same wavelength. Dulles was essentially intellectual in his approach, calculating, legalistic and intricate. Eden as a politician was intuitive and not very open to argument. He was baffled and frustrated by Dulles's tortuousness; time and again he was put out of his straightforward stride by the American's roundabout and shifting tactics.

Incompatibility of leaders was not the only source of strain in Anglo-American relations, but it certainly exacerbated policy differences. Although he never underestimated the importance of Western Europe, Dulles supported an 'Asia first' strategy which was very unwelcome to the European allies. In relation to Afro-Asia Dulles's condemnation of non-alignment as a shortsighted and immoral policy and his attempts to bludgeon new states into an anti-communist crusade contrasted with Eden's more tolerant attitude. In the Middle East Eden was peeved by America's prolonged coolness towards the Baghdad Pact when the inspiration for the unity of the 'northern tier' seemed to him to have been shared by Washington. Underlying everything else was the fact that Eden did not grasp the implications of the changes in the distribution of global power and consequently did not appreciate as well as Churchill did the need to be less assertive and more persuasive with Britain's senior partner. Eden saw Britain and the Commonwealth as an independent world force and a link between the two sides of the Atlantic. Dulles wanted Britain to be part of the European pillar of a two-pillar Atlantic alliance and thought that British foreign policy suffered from delusions of grandeur.

Both secretaries would have been more successful in achieving their ends had they been prepared to concede that a close alliance required each country to support its partner's basic interests. Dulles wanted to win over the Middle Eastern countries so that he might have a reliable southern bulwark against Soviet expansion. Eden wanted to win over the Asian neutralists in order to strengthen the Commonwealth as a political entity. In the end each failed in his objective. America did not gain political support in the Middle East; Britain lost it in the Far East. The divergence in the Anglo-American alliance was essentially responsible for the respective national failures of each.[39]

IV

On the German problem, the main bone of contention in the struggle between East and West, the convergence of official British and American views on the Russian threat and the importance of maintaining Western cohesion and strength produced a united diplomatic front. In his first general survey after his return to office in 1951 Eden told the House of Commons that finding a solution to the chasm which divided East and West was the cardinal issue of international affairs.[40] The German problem was the principal obstacle to any move forward, and Eden's approach to this problem clearly reflected the main lines of his thinking on relations with allies and adversaries in a bipolar world.

The Soviet Union launched a major initiative on 10 March 1952 with a note calling for immediate four-power talks to discuss the question of a peace treaty with Germany and proposing the neutralisation of Germany and the withdrawal of all occupation forces. Eden made the largest contribution to analysis and policy on the Western side.[41] He viewed the Soviet note as part of a propaganda campaign designed to disrupt the Atlantic alliance and distract German attention from the European Defence Community project by raising hopes of German reunification and a peace treaty. America, France and Britain accordingly sent identical notes rejecting detailed discussions on a peace treaty until conditions had been created for free elections, and until a freely elected all-German government had been established. They also insisted on the freedom of such a government to enter any associations after the conclusion of the peace treaty.

The Western proposals can only be regarded as unrealistic. By insisting on free elections and subsequent freedom to join alliances the West presented the Soviet Union with the prospect that not only Western Germany but a united Germany would become a member of the Atlantic alliance. On the other hand the Soviet proposals were fraught with risks and uncertainties and could have ushered in an important shift in the power balance of the cold war. Eden was therefore strongly in favour of pressing ahead with the parallel policies of removing the contractual limitations on West German sovereignty and integrating it as an equal partner in Western defence. When moving the ratification of the Bonn and Paris agreements which gave effect to these policies Eden told the House of Commons that if a new Germany was created along the lines proposed by Russia, 'It would be a Germany left in dangerous and irresponsible isolation in the heart of Europe and it would be a Germany allowed to raise national armed forces.'[42]

When Dulles took over from Dean Acheson as American Secretary of State in 1953, Western policy became increasingly doctrinaire and uncompromising. Eden, Dulles and Chancellor Adenauer kept insisting on free elections at a time when the East German uprising left no room for doubting the outcome of such elections. When the four foreign ministers met in Berlin in February 1954, Anthony Eden presented what came to be known as the Eden Plan for German reunification. This was to be achieved by five stages: free elections throughout Germany; the convocation of a national assembly resulting from those elections; the drafting of a constitution and the preparation of peace treaty negotiations; the adoption of the constitution and the formation of an all-German government responsible for the negotiation of a peace treaty; the signature and entry into force of the peacy treaty.[43]

Eden's claim that if only his plan were accepted in broad outline it could have led to the solution of the German problem[44] was astonishingly naive in its disregard of the existence of any Russian interests in the matter. It exemplified the disposition to equate British national interests with universal justice and morality. Moreover, Eden's posture at the Berlin conference was not only un-realistic but extremely uncompromising. When the dead-lock over free elections versus a peace treaty made it apparent that a permanent settlement for an all-German state was no nearer, the Soviets tried a different approach by proposing the evacuation of foreign troops from the two Germanies and the signing of a general Euro-pean treaty on collective security in Europe. This pro-posal never received the attention it deserved because Eden and his colleagues brushed it aside as a propaganda gambit designed to dissolve NATO, although Molotov assured Eden that the dissolution of NATO was not a precondition of his plan.

Throughout the early 1950s Eden's obdurate clinging to fixed positions stood in marked contrast to Russia's tac-tical flexibility. Whether a more supple position would have ushered in a solution to the German problem is a matter for speculation. But Eden's whole approach to the problem does reveal the stultifying effect which his rigid image of 'dictatorships' had on his policy towards the Soviet Union; his failure to take into account the inter-ests of the adversary in working for a settlement and his reluctance to get involved in serious discussions with the adversary for fear this would open up fissures in the united Western diplomatic front. He must therefore bear his share of responsibility for the fact that no progress was made during these years in attenuating the division between East and West and working towards a compromise on the problem of Germany.

Eden considered a German contribution as an indispensable means to the goal of a strong and prosperous Atlantic com-munity, and thought the integration of West Germany on a footing of equality within an evolving European Community was the most promising way of working towards this goal. But he did not support European unity as an end in itself. Some of his political colleagues have suggested that his exclusion from the European Movement, which he tended to

view as a 'party stunt' of Winston's, and his absense from
the British delegation to the Council of Europe were partly
responsible for his subsequent hostility.[45] It has to be
said for Eden, however, that, unlike other members of
Churchill's European Movement, he was a least consistent
in his attitude and had indeed warned against the danger
of raising false hopes on the Continent as to exactly how
far Britain would be prepared to go if the Conservatives
got into power.

In any case Eden's attitude to European unity was dictated to a far greater extent by his conception of Britain's
role in the world. He shared the Foreign Office's opposition to the European concept, to the Council of Europe and
all it stood for. 'Association, not participation', he
once said to Robert Boothby. 'Association is as far as I
am prepared to go in any European connection', adding that
he was basically 'an Atlantic animal'.[46] His conception
of Britain as a global and oceanic power as well as an
Atlantic one militated against an exclusive commitment to
Europe. Referring in 1952 in front of an American
audience to the suggestion that the United Kingdom should
join a federation on the Continent of Europe, Eden said:
'This is something we know in our bones we cannot do. We
know that if we were to attempt it, we should relax the
springs of our action in the Western Democratic cause and
in the Atlantic Association which is the expression of
that cause. For Britain's stody and her interests lie
far beyond the continent of Europe. Our thoughts move
across the seas to the many communities in which our
people play their part, in every corner of the world.
That is our life: without it we should be no more than
some millions of people living on an island off the
coast of Europe'.[47]

The degree of division between the Atlanticists' and the
'Europeans' was shown up quickly after the Conservatives
got back into office. In November 1951 Sir David Maxwell-
Fyfe (later the Earl of Kilmuir) told the Consultative
Assembly of the Council of Europe that 'there is no
refusal on the part of Britain' to join the projected
European army. A few hours later, at a press conference
in Rome, Eden stated that the United Kingdom would not
participate in a European army on any terms whatsoever.
In Kilmuir's opinion this 'single act, above all others,

destroyed our name on the Continent'.[48] The sense of be-
trayal felt by the Europeans at Strasbourg was acute and
their condemnation was bitter. M. Spaak resigned the
presidency of the Assembly to lead the campaign for a
'little federation of the Six' without Britain.

The split which began to develop in Western Europe,
between the Six who successfully launched the European
Coal and Steel Community and agreed to proceed towards
the establishment of a European Defence Community and the
rest was a cause of concern to Eden. In March 1952 he
submitted proposals to the Committee of Ministers of the
Council of Europe which were dubbed by the press the 'Eden
Plan', the first of manu such. The plan was to create
organic links between the Council of Europe and the institutions foreshadowed in the treaties setting up the
European Coal and Steel Community and the European Defence
Community.[49] Eden's aim was to ensure - while maintaining
Britain's sovereignty intact - that his country was not
cut off from the Europe which was beginning to take shape,
and to help it retain a measure of influence over this
process. He thus remained faithful to the concept of a
European balance of power guaranteed by Britain. The plan
was accepted politely but it was seen for what it was and
no action followed. Spaak told Nutting, who was the real
originator of the plan, that the federalists 'had waited
long enough for Britain to get aboard the European bus...
the Eden plan was a neat halfway-house arrangement which
might suit Great Britain, but halfway-houses were not
enough for Europe'.[50]

The failure of this initiative left Eden's policy towards
the EDC unchanged: he supported the project and promised
close British association but was firmly opposed to full
British membership. He was acutely aware of the faults
and failings of the plan but it was the only plan available
for German rearmament with adequate safeguards.[51] To
reassure France against the danger of resurgent German
militarism, when the EDC treaty was signed in May 1952,
the British Government entered simultaneously into a treaty
with the Six pledging support in the case of attack.[52]
But when the French National Assembly rejected the EDC
Treaty in August 1954, after a prolonged and agonising
debate, the whole house of cards came tumbling down.

100

The defeat of the EDC was not altogether unanticipated, and in line with a contingency plan Eden had outlined to Churchill as early as December 1951[53] he moved swiftly to work out with Britain's allies a more modest scheme based on technical military arrangements but without an elaborate political superstructure. This actual scheme had not been worked out in advance, and in his memoirs Eden says that while he was in his bath the idea occurred to him of converting the Brussels Treaty of 1948 - which had Britain, France, Italy and the Benelux countries - into a wider pact to include West Germany and provide the treaty framework for controlled German rearmament and German entry into NATO. The idea in fact came from Sir Christopher Steel, then British ambassador to NATO, but Eden deserves all the credit for its masterly translation into action.

He set off on a tour of the European capitals, and, with a perfect sense of timing and using all his skills as a negotiator, he built up support for his idea, isolated the French and bypassed the opposition of Dulles who had been sold on the EDC and regarded any solution which did not provide for the creation of supranational institutions as makeshift.

The French had still to be won over and American opposition had not been effectively neutralised, but Eden was content that his European tour had at least opened the way to the nine-power conference which he convened in London for 28 September 1954. A day before the conference opened Eden explained in a note to Churchill that the key to the success of the conference would be a new commitment by the United Kingdom to maintain her existing forces on the Continent and not to withdraw them against the wishes of the majority of the enlarged Brussels Treaty powers. He realised, the note continued, that this would be an unprecedented commitment for Britain, but if it were not made 'the conference may fail and the Atlantic alliance fall to pieces'.[54] Thus, ironically, Eden was now urging a course which he had persistently and scornfully rejected and which might have saved the EDC had it been made earlier. The British ambassador to France, Sir Gladwyn Jebb, had called for such a pledge long before the defeat of the EDC, but Eden dismissed it as 'a high blown idea'.[55] Eden at least saw the light before it was too late.

Since Dulles did not have an alternative plan, the argument went to Eden by default. The two secretaries agreed
a scenario which they duly followed at the London conference. Dulles offered to renew to the enlarged Brussels
Treaty powers the pledge which had been made by the US
Government to the EDC. Eden then gave the assurance that
Britain would maintain on the mainland of Europe four
divisions and the Tactical Air Force for as long as the
majority of the Brussels Powers desired it. The European
representatives immediately hailed this as an historic
decision and from this point the conference moved rapidly
forward.

The series of negotiations following the defeat of the
EDC rank among the most successful in Eden's entire career.
In less than a month he succeeded in ending the prevailing
disarray. The Brussels Treaty Organisation was renamed
Western European Union and extended to include Germany and
Italy. Within this new framework, set up in October 1954,
German rearmament could take place under safeguards and
Germany became a member of the NATO alliance. Eden himself hoped that Western European Union would take its place
as the leading authority in the new Europe. But the proponents of a united Europe did not view this technical
intergovernmental organisation as the fulfilment of their
federalist ambitions. In April 1955 the Benelux governments proposed a conference on West European integration
at Messina which was duly held in June and set the ball
rolling for the creation of the EEC and EURATOM. Eden,
who persistently underestimated the seriousness and force
behind the drive for European unity, remained aloof. His
contribution to solving the problem of European defence
must therefore be set off against his failure to appreciate
the political currents on the Continent — a failure which
was to prove as costly as it was difficult to rectify.

V

In the Middle East, similarly, Eden's insensitive disregard
of the new political currents, in this case the nationalism
and the desire for independence from foreign influence,
redounded to Britain's disadvantage. Eden prided himself
on being an expert on the affairs of the Middle East, but
his knowledge and whole approach were out of date. Soon
after he returned to office he sent a stiff note to the

Egyptian Government castigating its unilateral abrogation
of the treaty which he himself had negotiated in 1936.
Implicitly he expected the old type of colonial relations
to continue in the new world of the 1950s, and was infuriated when King Farouk's Government rejected outright the
plan for a Middle East defence organisation on the grounds
that it would not only not end the universally unpopular
British presence but bring in American, French and Turkish
troops as well. The bloodless coup which brought General
Neguib to power in February 1952 provided an opportunity
for opening a new chapter in Anglo-Egyptian relations, but
Eden's barely concealed disdain for Egypt's new rulers, to
whom he referred privately as 'these young and transitory
majors in Cairo',[56] could only lead to the intensification
of anti-British sentiment.

Early in 1953 Eden began to grope for an agreement which
would allow the phased withdrawal of British troops, the
maintenance of a British base which could be used in time
of war, and Egyptian participation in a Middle East defence
organisation. He won President Eisenhower's support for
this approach, but America did not take part in the tor-
tuous negotiations which followed because the Egyptians
insisted that an agreement on British withdrawal must be
reached before Middle East defence as a whole could be
considered. Eden was anxious to secure American participation so that she might use her economic and military aid
as a lever for getting concessions from the Egyptian
rulers, but in this aim he was frustrated: the Americans
were intent on gaining Egyptian friendship and declined to
be embroiled in Britain's colonial-type policy.

An agreement was eventually reached in October 1954,
largely thanks to the efforts of Eden's pro-Arab under-
secretary, Anthony Nutting, on a phased withdrawal of
British troops coupled with a British right to reactivate
the Canal base in the event of an armed attack on either
Egypt or any other member of the Arab League. In defence
of such an arrangement Eden had argued that it would bring
a gain in strategic mobility: 'There is no vacuum because
as a result of these arrangements we shall be able to re-
deploy our forces and make them mobile to an extent that
they had not been hitherto.'[57] Churchill, however, did
not share this view: to leave Egypt, he argued, would be
a 'scuttle' comparable only to Britain's 'senseless'

departure from India. Eden also had to contend with a
section of the press and the Suez Group who, ignoring the
need for strategic redeployment and the fact that Britain's
treaty rights would have expired in 1956 anyway, bitterly
opposed the withdrawal of British troops from the Canal
Zone as a humiliating lowering of the imperial flag. It
was a mark of Eden's political courage that he pressed the
1954 agreement in the face of fierce opposition within his
own party.

   The prospects of healthier Anglo-Egyptian relations opened up by the agreement were unfortunately wrecked by Eden's
efforts to organise the 'northern Tier' of the Middle East
in a collective defence organisation linked to the West and
capable of resisting Soviet encroachment. Unless Britain's
special military rights in Iraq could be replaced by a new
collective defence treaty, there was the risk that they
might have to be abandoned altogether. Nuri es-Said, the
Iraqi premier and Britain's oldest friend in the Middle
East, therefore had Eden's full backing, if not direct inspiration, for establishing the Baghdad Pact. This pact
was originally signed by Iraq and Turkey in February 1955
and was soon joined by Pakistan and Iran. In April 1955
Eden announced Britain's decision to join the pact, but
Dulles, who had provided the original inspiration for the
strategy of the 'northern tier' for the containment of
Russia, did not follow suit. He probably wanted the benefits without the liabilities of membership. It was
Nasser's opposition, however, which crippled the Baghdad
Pact. At their only meeting, in February 1955, Eden tried
to persuade the new Egyptian ruler to become a member, but
Nasser took the view that by its bad timing and unfortunate
membership the pact set back the prospects of collaboration
with the West. There can be little doubt that by making
Nasser's rival, Nuri es-Said, the chief recruiting agent of
the West, Eden displayed indifference to the relative political importance of Egypt in the Arab world, not to speak
of the position of Nasser himself on whose co-operation
Britain now depended for the maintenance of the Suez Canal
Zone. It was a costly mistake, because within a few months
an antagonised Nasser signed a major arms deal with Russia
which permitted the latter to bypass completely the 'northern tier' and gain a foothold in the heartland of the
Middle East.

The Iranian oil dispute which erupted with the nation-
alisation of the Anglo-Iranian Company in 1951 continued
to bedevil relations with Itan for the first three years
of the Churchill administration. Eden's handling of the
dispute displayed the same mixture of self-righteousness
and inability to win the friendship of independent nationalist regimes which marred the rest of his Middle East
policy. Such friendship based on a relationship of equals
would have been the mainstay of Britain's strategic and
oil interests in this part of the world. But in the
manner of an imperial overlord Eden regarded the Iranian
nationalist leader, Dr.Mossadiqq, as a local troublemaker
who had to be put down firmly. His complaint that the US
Government was unco-operative and that its 'neutrality'
in the dispute aided Mossadiqq reveals the difficulty he
had in apprehending that the interests of other countries
may legitimately differ from those of Britain. Much more
justified were Acheson's criticisms that Eden followed the
advice of the bureaucracy of the Anglo-Iranian Oil Company
and the Treasury where Sir Leslie Rowan decreed that
Mossadiqq, leading the attack on British foreign investments, had to fail, to be crushed and punished.[58] Eden,
of course, rejoiced when Mossadiqq fell from power in
August 1954 (largely as a result of the efforts of the
Central Intelligence Agency rather than those of the
British Treasury). Soon after, a comprehensive settlement
was reached with the royalist regime and Anglo-Iranian
relations took a friendlier turn.

It is no coincidence that in South-East Asia, where
Eden's approach was more supple and more in tune with local
feelings and political currents, he achieved better results
than he was able to in the Middle East. In his memoirs he
states that the restoration of peace in Indo-China was the
most dangerous and acute of the problems with which he had
to deal during his last four years as foreign secretary.[59]
Matters came to a head in the spring of 1954 when, following a long series of reverses in imposing control over
Indo-China, the French forces were besieged by the Vietminh in the fortress of Dien Bien Phu. Dulles concluded
that if the French position in Indo-China was allowed to
collapse, the whole of South-East Asia would eventually be
overrun by the rising tide of communism. On 4 April
Eisenhower formally asked Britain for joint military intervention together with friendly Asian nations to defeat the

communist forces in Indo-China and simultaneously begin
organising the collective defence of South Asia. Eden
felt that the proposed military action would be ineffective, that it would prejudice the chances of a negotiated
settlement at the forthcoming Geneva Conference and that
it might internationalise the war by forcing a showdown in
which Russia would be obliged to support China on the
Vietminh side. Churchill summed up the position by saying
that 'what we were being asked to do was to assist in misleading Congress into approving a military operation,
which would in itself be ineffective, and might well bring
the world to the verge of a major war'.[60]

The Indo-Chinese sessions of the Geneva Conference opened
on 8 May in the shadow of the failure of the American
scheme for joint military intervention and the overwhelming
Vietminh victory at Dien Bien Phu the previous day. Believing the conference was doomed to failure, Dulles depar-
ted from Geneva before it started, leaving his under-
secretary, Bedell-Smith, in charge. Over the next ten
weeks, Eden, despite Dulles's elephantine obstinacy,
steered the conference towards a successful conclusion
almost single-handed. As co-chairman of the conference
his skills as a negotiator and a mediator were seen at
their very best. He kept in close touch with Commonwealth
leaders and elicited the co-operation of the Russian and
Chinese representatives, who feared the extension of the
conflict through full-scale American intervention if the
conference failed and put pressure on the Vietminh to
accept half a victory when a full victory was in sight in
order to secure a diplomatic solution.

Eden's untiring and versatile diplomatic efforts at
Geneva to achieve a settlement that, in the light of
France's desperate position, would necessarily involve
Western concessions, were regarded by many influential
Republicans as smacking of 'appeasement' and ushering in
an 'indo-Chinese Munich'. When the Geneva Accords which
settled the future of Vietnam, Laos and Cambodia were
finalised Dulles refused to associate his administration
with this settlement which handed over territory to the
communists. That the Geneva Accords had flaws and weaknesses is undeniable, but Eden was perfectly justified in
claiming that they were the best available under the circumstances. As Bedell-Smith perceptively observed: 'It

will be well to remember that diplomacy has rarely been able to gain at the conference table what cannot be gained or held on the battlefield'.

It will be equally well to remember that the continuation of the conflict in Indo-China for two more decades was not the direct cause of the Geneva Accords. The outcome sought by Eden in 1954 was a belt of independent and neutral states, Vietnam, Cambodia and Laos, which would 'bring prosperity to these states and confidence to their neigh- bours'. Though this 'did not come about, the purpose was right and as such in the interests of the great powers and of the three small states themselves'.[61] That the Accords collapsed was not the fault of those who framed them but largely of those Americans who subverted them through military intervention, through connivance in Diem's re- fusal to hold the general election in 1956 which was de- signed to lead to the reunification of Vietnam, and later through their violation of Laotian and Cambodian neutra- lity.

VI

The manner in which Sir Anthony Eden's career ended in 1957, following the Suez debacle, has helped to make him one of the most controversial figures in twentieth-century British foreign policy. His apologists have tended to view the Suez affair as a temporary aberration which brought a brilliant career crashing down in flames. His detractors see in it the final proof that he never possessed the qualities required of a leader and a statesman. Eden's record as foreign secretary from 1951 to 1955 should not, however, be evaluated in the light of subsequent events. It is possible, too, that ill-health impaired Eden's judgement as prime minister to a degree not paralleled during the period preceding his move to No 10 and that sickness rather than ingrained ineptitude was the decisive cause behind the disastrous Suez adventure.

There was a great deal in Eden's record of which he could justly feel proud. When he came into office in October 1951, he was faced with a baffling array of pro- blems and crises. Realising that these could not be solved by a sudden and spectacular move, he resolved to grasp definite but specific problems and work for their practical solution. Over the next three and a half years he stuck to this task with courage and tenacity. There were trials and tribulations, major reverses and temporary setbacks, but in the end he secured a settlement of the Iranian oil dispute, and a satisfactory agreement with Egypt on the withdrawal of British troops from the Canal Zone. His contribution to the settlement of wider international problems, notably that which followed the defeat of the EDC, the Indo-China conflict and the Yugoslav-Italian quarrel over Trieste, was second to none. The sheer number of international agreements which he helped to bring about in 1954 is impressive by any standards.

And yet Eden cannot be regarded as a great foreign secretary. He was an outstanding negotiator and a mediator par excellence, and most of his achievements can be directly traced to his skills in personal diplomacy and at the conference table. But he lacked the attributes of realism, breadth of vision and the capacity to think ahead which mark the true statesman. 'He was not a strategist', as Nutting rightly points out, 'who set a course for five, ten or twenty years and stuck to it with bulldog determination. He was essentially a tactician who planned his advance in limited moves, stopping and starting, veering and tacking according to the strength and direction of the prevailing pressures.'[62]

Eden's conduct of foreign affairs was not subjected to major domestic constraints. His standing and influence in the country, in the Conservative Party, in Parliament and in the Cabinet gave him considerable latitude. If his policy lacked an overall sense of direction, it was partly the result of the inescapable constraints imposed by the international environment, but the more decisive reason was his own failure to produce a long-term strategy based on a realistic assessment of Britain's capabilities, and the objectives they could reasonably be expected to support. A foreign policy which is not backed by adequate instruments and capabilities is mere posturing, and Eden's grandiose conception of Britain's world role, because it was so divorced from the underlying distribution of international power, strained relations with Britain's allies and made little impression on Britain's principal adversary. Moreover, this misleading conception of Britain as the centre of three great circles had the effect of

blinding Eden to the real opportunity which Britain had
in the early 1950s, that of assuming the leadership of a
united Europe. In short, Eden's conservative outlook,
his uncritical acceptance of orthodox assumptions, his
intuitive and pragmatic approach to events, his pre-
occupation with day to day problems as opposed to overall
strategy and his aversion to planning all predisposed him
towards continuing along the traditional lines of British
foreign policy and militated against any fundamental reappraisal of Britain's role in the world, let alone any
bold and imaginative departures.

CHAPTER 5

HAROLD MACMILLAN

The question which comes to mind when considering Harold Macmillan's term at the Foreign Office is quite simply, 'How was it that a politician of great ability and experience should have been judged relatively unsuccessful in that office?'. On the face of it, this seems to have been the contemporary view. Indeed one of his Cabinet colleagues, Lord Kilmuir describes the appointment as 'a major error of judgement'.[1]

This verdict is, of course, an over-simplification, as all such judgements must be. But, in so far as there is truth in it, the reasons appear to be twofold. Firstly, he was not there long enough to make an impression. Eight months is not quite enough time to take a full and firm grip on a department as powerful and talented as the Foreign Office, or on a field such as foreign policy, in which one inevitably inherits much that is in motion from one's predecessor. Macmillan himself clearly shared this view, and felt that when he agreed to move to the Exchequer in December 1955, it was in fact a mistake; he should have remained at the Foreign Office long enough to make a more significant contribution to foreign policy.[2]

The second reason for Macmillan's relative lack of impact is equally generally agreed, and has to do with the character of the prime minister of the day, Sir Anthony Eden, and Macmillan's relations with him. Eden had a unique knowledge of foreign affairs, and a unique prestige in that field,[3] having served three times as foreign secretary. During the war years he had attended all the major international conferences, and again between 1951 and 1954, when he had gained major successes in the field of foreign affairs. He was a world figure. It was natural that such a man should continue to take a close and continuous interest in foreign affairs; but it was equally inevitable that this should sometimes make things

difficult for his foreign secretary and be irksome,
especially to a man of the ability, force of character
and spirit of Macmillan.

It would not have mattered so much had there been a
greater degree of temperamental compatibility between the
two men, but this was not unfortunately the case. Eden
was temperamental, highly strung and inclined to fuss. He
was in the habit of ringing up frequently and asking a
minister or a department for information, sometimes early
in the morning. This irritated Macmillan, who was not the
most equable of men and had quite as much confidence in
his own judgement as in Eden's. That Eden himself was
defensively aware of the difficulty is shown by a revealing conversation with R.A.Butler in September 1955, when
he disclaimed 'undue interference' with the Foreign Office
but admitted that he found it difficult to work with as
strong a character as Macmillan.[4] Macmillan himself,
equally revealingly, cites an instance, clearly one of a
number, in which he felt obliged to insist that Eden
delay a message to the Soviet premier on the Soviet-
Egyptian arms deal of 1955 and the Arab-Israel dispute,
which Eden proposed to send in Macmillan's absence.
Macmillan records that he differed from Eden on the word-
ing and scope of the message and adds that he felt himself
drifting into a dangerous position vis-a-vis the prime
minister, that of accepting undue control, without proper
consultation, in his own field of responsibility.[5] He
recalled Eden's own unfortunate experience with Neville
Chamberlain which Macmillan clearly regarded as a warning
to future foreign secretaries. Later, reflecting on his
transfer to the Treasury at the end of 1955, Macmillan
concluded that while Eden certainly felt at that time
that a stronger hand was needed in economic affairs,
there was also the desire, 'consciously or unconsciously
to have more control over foreign affairs'.[6] Though
Macmillan's own comments on the relationship are both
restrained and balanced, it is clear that he himself felt
the difficulty, and the clash of temperament and occasionally judgement. Indeed his own account of his period at
the Foreign Office is curiously anonymous, almost as
though he is saying to the reader that he felt he was not
the main initiator in foreign policy, and in a sense was
not fully responsible.

Harold Macmillan was born in 1894, the son of a wealthy publisher and an American mother. After education at Eton and Oxford, he served in the First World War and entered politics as a Conservative M.P. His opposition to the orthodox policies of the Baldwin-Chamberlain governments of the thirties kept him out of office until the Second World War, when he made his reputation as a successful Minister of State in North Africa and Italy. When the Tories came back to power in 1951, he was offered the Ministry of Housing by Churchill, where he demonstrated considerable administrative ability. Churchill promoted him to the Ministry of Defence in 1954, and six months later, Eden made him foreign secretary – though, significantly, only as second choice. Eden would have preferred Lord Salisbury, but regarded the latter's peerage as a disqualification.[7]

The Macmillan who came to the Foreign Office in 1955 therefore was a politician of wide experience at home and abroad, and of proven independence of mind, intellectual and practical ability and strength of character. He was apparently an ideal choice for the post. It is this which makes it necessary to ask, and answer, the question posed at the beginning of this chapter. In so far as the answer does not lie in the shortness of his term of office and his relations with the premier, it relates to certain aspects of his character and judgment. On the first point, it must be said that he was not, as his contemporary image portrayed him, particularly 'unflappable', nor indeed did he himself claim to be. He was in fact like his predecessor in being somewhat sensitive and temperamental, even explosive at times.[8] He was, however, much more successful than his predecessor in giving an impression of calmness and conveying this to others. But he also had at times a certain tendency to ambiguity in his pronouncements so that it was not always clear what he was aiming at.[9] More than one of his colleagues has said that he tended to 'paint with a broad brush', which meant that people did not always understand him. As far as judgement was concerned, moreover, he was apt sometimes to be too self-confident on issues where he felt he had wide experience. Thus in spite of the unsatisfactory nature of British dealings with the Eisenhower administration over the Middle East before 1955,[10] he continued to press ahead with British plans for Middle East defence,

112

believing that US support would be forthcoming. Equally,
in spite of French attitudes to Britain, as demonstrated
over previous plans for European integration, he allowed
himself to be persuaded, admittedly with the encouragement
of some French leaders, that if the European Economic
Community succeeded, the French would then be prepared to
associate it with a wider free trade area.[11] The full
consequences of these miscalculations were not to come
until later.

On the other hand, Macmillan, at sixty, was capable of
learning and adapting. He had already, during the war,
absorbed the reality of Britain's declining power vis a
vis the United States, and he was aware too of the impossibility of halting the transformation of the British
Empire into the new Commonwealth. He was also quick to
grasp the extent to which the very threat of nuclear war
helped to preserve peace.[12] Given time, he must have
learnt more. He had powerful assets also in the support
of the mass of the parliamentary party, who liked his
combative and somewhat arrogant attitude to the Labour
Opposition, in the benevolent support from retirement of
Winston Churchill, who later recommended him as premier
in preference to R.A.Butler, and the goodwill of most of
his Cabinet colleagues, the vast majority of whom were to
concur with Churchill's judgement. He enjoyed, too, a
good relationship with most of his civil servants at the
Foreign Office, and ambassadors. They found him a strong-
minded minister who could not easily be 'managed'; and
liked him for it.

Macmillan, of course, operated in a field, as all foreign
ministers do, where events cannot always be mastered, nor
always foreseen, and one which was becoming less 'manageable' as Britain's power declined. In relations with the
two super-powers, the USA and Russia, Britain's capacity
to influence and occasionally mediate now rested more on
the respect for her experience and past role and on the
wartime friendship of Macmillan with Eisenhower than on
actual British power. The 'special relationship' with the
US still meant something, as did ties with the Commonwealth, but both were a declining asset.

Equally, as with all foreign ministers, Macmillan was
the inheritor of policies already well established in

relation to various problems and areas, policies largely shaped by Eden. There is little evidence, however, that he markedly differed from Eden on the main basis of policy. So far as East—West relations were concerned, and particularly in relation to the major problems of European security, disarmament and German reunification which bulked so large in this area, Macmillan inherited the Churchill—Eden belief in the effectiveness of the 'summit' meeting of heads of government as a means of reducing tension and making progress. He loyally pursued this aim against considerable scepticism within his own ministry[13] and persuaded the reluctant Americans to agree, having established a good relationship with the difficult John Foster Dulles. Macmillan found Dulles 'hesitant and uncertain' yet came to like him. Dulles, for his part, regretted Macmillan's departure from the Foreign Office after only a short period there. The four heads of government — British, Russian, American, French — duly met in Geneva from 18 to 25 July 1955, but little was achieved on the concrete problems mentioned above.[14] Macmillan, indeed, must have been well aware that decisions already taken by the West — the rearmament of Western Germany and her admission to the North Atlantic Treaty Organisation on 9 May of that year — virtually precluded agreement on German reunification; for the Soviet government would never agree to a united Germany which was rearmed and a member of the Western defence system. Yet free elections for the whole of Germany, which the West demanded, would in practice have meant just that. Not surprisingly, the foreign ministers' meetings which followed, from 27 October to 6 November, soon broke down in recrimination. The 'summit', then, had produced only a temporary amelioration of the atmosphere between East and West, and Macmillan conceded that the 'Geneva spirit' had soon burnt low; though he continued to believe that, with the emergence of Khrushchev and Bulganin, 'new forces were at work in the Soviet Union'.

Similarly, in the Middle East, Macmillan continued Eden's policy of building a defence system around the Defence Pact between Turkey and Iraq, signed on 4 February 1955 and adhered to by Britain on 4 April — the Baghdad Pact'. Macmillan worked hard to extend its membership, and above all to get the United States to join: but Dulles hung back, fearful of antagonising both Egypt and

Saudi Arabia which were hostile to and jealous of Iraq, and believing rightly that the pact might exacerbate inter-Arab rivalries: moreover, pro-Israeli sentiment in the United States made it a ticklish business for the US to join an Arab pact. Macmillan therefore was only able to secure the adhesion of Iran and Pakistan, and in fact no other Arab state joined the pact. As Macmillan might have foreseen, Arab nationalism saw any British sponsored pact as an attempt to buttress Britain's imperial interests in the Middle East - as indeed it was. A year later the mere suggestion that Jordan should join the pact nearly cost King Hussein his throne, and the Suez crisis largely destroyed it as an effective organisation.[15]

Macmillan himself seems to have had doubts in retrospect, wondering in his memoirs whether it was 'a prudent move' or in fact 'provocative' to Russia.[16] If he had doubts at the time, however, they did not inhibit his pursuit of the policy or his public defence of it as 'in the long run likely to unite the Arab world'.[17] Whether as a consequence or not, the pact was soon followed by the Soviet-Egyptian arms deal of 27 September 1955, which represented the first major Russian breakthrough into the area and led Macmillan himself to speculate whether 'this was the beginning of a new offensive in the Middle East'.[18] If Macmillan's policy was partly responsible for the beginnings of Soviet influence in the area, then his responsibility is a heavy one.

In the sphere of European unity Macmillan's role as foreign secretary was ambiguous. Although a committed 'European', who had contemplated resigning in 1952 on this issue, he responded to the first steps towards the European Economic Community in a negative fashion, apparently accepting until it was too late the general Foreign Office view that it would fail, and the participants come round to the British plan for a free trade area.[19] This proved a costly miscalculation, though it is easy to be wise after the event; and Macmillan could certainly claim that some of the European leaders were themselves pessimistic about the prospects for the EEC and that the Six later went back on a fairly clear commitment to enter into arrangements for a larger free trade area, whatever the outcome of the EEC negotiations.[20]

115

One major achievement certainly marked Macmillan's tenure of the Foreign Office, namely the signature of the
Austrian Peacy Treaty on 15 May 1955. But this was again
the product partly of his predecessor's painstaking negotiations, and perhaps even more of a change of tactics by
the Soviet leaders, rather than of Macmillan's efforts.
At that time the Soviet leaders wished to forward a
detente with the West, and perhaps also had it in mind to
create a precedent for a 'neutralised' Germany.

In short, it is difficult to dissent from the judgement
that Macmillan's term at the Foreign Office was not one
of his most successful phases. But it is possible, perhaps, to look at this in two different ways. The harsher
judgement might be that Macmillan was an undistinguished
foreign secretary who was lucky to leave the Foreign
Office before all his chickens came home to roost and particularly before the trauma of Suez fell upon his country.
A more generous judgement is tenable, namely, that this
was a politician who had already shown in his sixties a
remarkable capacity to absorb new concepts of Britain's
role in the world and of the changing world itself, and
that, given more time, he would have made a great foreign
secretary. Time, however, was not given him.

CHAPTER 6

SELWYN LLOYD

I

Selwyn Lloyd had the not altogether enviable distinction
of serving one of the longest post-war terms at the
Foreign Office yet at the same time incurring greater
criticism and denigration than any of his contemporaries
in that role. There is a paradox here which needs to be
resolved.

Lloyd came to the Foreign Office in December 1955 as the
first of a new generation to make its impact on British
foreign policy. Unlike his immediate predecessors, he had
entered politics after the war, was a comparatively junior
figure in the party's hierarchy, and was little known to
the general public. He had served only eight months in
the Cabinet and at fifty-one was a decade or more younger
than his predecessors. He was in fact the first of his
generation in the Conservative Party to reach one of the
highest offices, moving ahead of near-contemporaries such
as Peter Thorneycroft, Quintin Hogg and David Eccles. For
this advancement he was to pay a heavy price, for few
foreign secretaries have been confronted with a more
gruelling ordeal during their first year or two in office:
and this he had to meet without the advantages of party
and parliamentary stature and long Cabinet experience
enjoyed by his predecessors.

There is indeed a certain symbolism in the advent of
this new and relatively junior figure at the Foreign
Office, for it coincided with the moment, dramatically
epitomised by the Suez crisis, when the realities of
Britain's decline in world power became impossible to
ignore: and in a sense with the moment when, because of
her lessening influence in the world, and the economic
weakness which was a major cause of it, the Foreign

Office itself suffered a relative decline in importance vis-a-vis other government departments, particularly the Treasury. It is the view of many of those who served in the Foreign Office at the time that Eden was the last foreign secretary who could really dictate to the Treasury, for example in the case of the negotiations over Western defence in 1954, where there was some feeling that the Treasury was inadequately consulted.[1]

Developments of this kind take place slowly, over a period of time, and one cannot point to a specific date such as November 1956 and say 'After this date, Britain ceased to count in the world'. But Suez clearly marked a turning-point. Until then Britain had continued to live on her reputation as a world power, her imperial past, and her wartime achievement. There was still a gap between her real strength and her power and influence, the latter always depending to some extent on 'reputation'. The United States and the USSR, the two super-powers, had continued to treat Britain as a world power, and other states followed suit. In particular, the wartime 'special relationship' with the United States was still meaningful to the latter and paid dividends to Britain.

Suez really ended this phase in British history, by re-vealing the naked facts of power. It was made clear that Britain could not defend even national interests that were regarded as vital, without the goodwill and consent of one of the two super-powers, which, in the context of the time, could only be the United States. After Suez, in spite of the able and partially successful 'repair job' done by Macmillan and Lloyd, in restoring both the Anglo-American relationship and the British position in the Middle East, it was no longer easy for British politi-cal leaders to deceive either themselves or others as to the reality of British power. It is fair to add that during the decade which followed Suez the Macmillan govern-ment continued the process of voluntary liquidation of empire, which inevitably further diminished the effective power of Britain in the world.

Selwyn Lloyd's tenure of the Foreign Office must there-fore be seen in the light of this decisive change in British power: and the final judgement must rest ulti-mately not just on the Suez crisis, but on the extent to

which he was able, with Macmillan, to come to terms with
the fact, to adapt British policies to it, and to make the
right decisions consequent on this adaptation during his
five-year period in office.

Few foreign secretaries before or after Lloyd have been
the centre of such bitter controversy or subject to such
harsh criticism both within Parliament and outside it.
Not merely at the time of Suez but on a number of occasions
afterwards he had a bad press, and apart from the tributes
paid by both his prime ministers, little has been done
since to offset this unfavourable contemporary judgement.[2]
Any study of Lloyd's work must consider how far this
unfavourable judgement is justified.

The point has been made that Lloyd came to the Foreign
Office after a relatively short period of ministerial and
particularly Cabinet experience. But a man is not equipped
for positions of high responsibility in politics simply by
his narrowly political experience; and indeed it seems
that Lloyd's rapid promotion owed something to what was
known of his record before he entered the House of
Commons.[3] At the time of his entry into politics, in fact,
he had already demonstrated his capacity in two other
fields - the Law and the Army. Born in Liverpool, the son
of a doctor, he had had a conventional upper-middle-class
education at boarding school, followed by Cambridge,
thereafter practising law successfully on the North-Western
Circuit. In the war, after joining up as a Territorial,
he had a distinguished record of service, ending up as
deputy Chief of Staff, Second Army, with the unusually high
rank for a 'non-regular' of brigadier. Afterwards he had
entered the House of Commons, embarking relatively late at
the age of forty on a political career. As a back-bencher
he caught the eye of R.A.Butler, who recruited him to work
in the Conservative Research Department and used him as
his principal lieutenant in drafting the Conservative
election manifesto of 1951; and also of Anthony Eden.
When Churchill formed his government in October 1951, both
Eden and Butler asked for Lloyd's services, at the Foreign
Office and the Treasury respectively. Lloyd went to the
Foreign Office as minister of state and served a fairly
prolonged apprenticeship in foreign affairs, lasting for
about three years. He did well, at the UN and elsewhere,
established a close relationship with Eden, whom he much

admired, and was promoted to be Minister of Supply in 1954.

In 1955 Eden brought him into the Cabinet as Minister of Defence. In that office he confirmed the favourable impression which the premier and most of his colleagues had formed of him,[4] but was not there long enough to achieve much: after eight months he was further promoted and became foreign secretary, at the age of fifty-one.

These facts are worth reciting, because the picture has sometimes been presented of a junior and essentially second-class figure promoted suddenly and beyond his capacity to one of the highest offices, mainly because Eden desired a more malleable foreign secretary. But a man who achieves some success in three different careers by the time he is fifty and whose services are sought by the two leading figures in a government when he has had only backbench experience is surely something more than is implied by such a judgement.

The contrary is in many ways true. Lloyd had emerged from the ruck of his contemporaries by displaying ability and application. He had done very well as minister of state, making a good deal more of that office than many subsequent holders of it managed to do. It must be remembered that unlike later periods, when there were a number of ministers of state at the Foreign Office, he was the only one at that time; moreover, towards the end of this period his chief, Eden, was a sick man, and away from the Office for long periods. At these times the running of the Office devolved upon Lloyd, who also attended Cabinet meetings. Even before this he had had the important task of representing the British Government at meetings of the United Nations General Assembly, where he had played a major part in the negotiations which eventually led to the winding up of the Korean War. He had also played a considerable role in getting disarmament negotiations under way with the USSR, rather against the wishes of his official advisers, who were afraid unrequited concessions might be made to the Russians. He was fully aware that really major progress in this field was unlikely, since the Russians would not accept an effective system of international control. The Soviet view was that such control would merely provide a cover for Western

espionage. But Lloyd was aware also that a continuous
willingness to make constructive proposals in this field
could help to achieve two ends, both important. On the
one hand, the 'cold war' was by definition a contest which
was waged largely in and for the minds of men; it was important that the West should be seen as having constructive
and positive proposals for improving the international
climate in this field. On the other hand, by making such
proposals Britain could indicate to the Russians her continued willingness to talk and negotiate; and so perhaps
actually improve the climate of relations with them and
move a little towards the detente in the cold war which
Churchill, Eden and Macmillan all wished to achieve.

In short, Lloyd had a creditable record as minister of
state and he was undoubtedly during this period a major
figure at the UN where he was in general regarded with
respect.[5] He had proved himself to be a skilful negotiator, a capable administrator and a prodigiously hard
worker. He had established good relations with the Americans, including the difficult John Foster Dulles, and had
also acquired much experience and knowledge of foreign
affairs. He was not therefore surprised to be asked to go
back to the Foreign Office in 1955, and probably confident
of his ability to do the job.

II

Lloyd had quite definite ideas on most aspects of British
foreign policy, ideas derived from his close co-operation
with Eden. Except perhaps in disarmament, his role as
No 2 had necessarily been more that of an executant than
an originator, but there is no reason to doubt that he
shared the general views of his two predecessors, and
therefore saw no reason to depart from the major lines of
policy as laid down during the previous four years, during
much of which he had collaborated in its formulation. In
relations with the super-powers, therefore, in East-West
relations and the cold war generally the policy was to
maintain the American and Western alliance, while pushing
the Americans gently towards detente where possible, in
such fields as disarmament; no easy matter, since both
Dulles and President Eisenhower were highly suspicious of
the Russians. In European matters the first priority was
to strengthen the alliance by rearming West Germany and

integrating her closely with the rest of Western Europe.
Subject to that, the reunification of the whole of Germany
under a democratic system should still be pursued as the
ultimate objective, though German rearmament made it unlikely that the Russians would agree to reunification on
acceptable terms. Nonetheless it was essential to continue to pursue reunification, if only because of the
effects on German morale of any apparent weakening by the
West in this regard. Once West Germany was firmly linked
with Western Europe, it might just be possible to achieve
reunification in a climate of detente and in the context
of a general European security treaty including Russia;
such an arrangement including perhaps a measure of 'dis-
engagement' or thinning out of Western and Soviet troops
in Central Europe, as envisaged by, for example, the so-
called Rapacki Plan put forward by the Polish foreign
minister. Such proposals were seriously examined by the
Foreign Office throughout the fifties, though it was
clearly unwise to invest too much hope in such prospects.[6]

On the question of West European integration generally,
Lloyd shared the view of most of his Cabinet colleagues
and the majority of his Foreign Office advisers, a view
which was both sceptical about prospects in general and
lukewarm in relation to the particular matter of British
participation. That is to say, he doubted the prospects
for any immediate further step in this direction, as envisaged by the proposals for a European Economic Community,
or Common Market, which had come before the Messina conference of the Six in the summer of 1955; and he considered that Britain's world-wide commitments and in particular her special links with the United States and the
Commonwealth made it impossible for her to enter fully
into any supranational project, such as the European Coal
and Steel Community of 1950 or the EEC itself, both of
which called for some surrender of sovereignty in specific
fields.

Lloyd's views were not unreasonable at the time. In the
light of the very recent collapse of the 'European Defence
Community', with its plans for an integrated West European
army — a proposal which had finally been torpedoed by the
French who had originally proposed it — the prospects for
an immediate further advance in European integration did
not seem bright at this time to any informed observer.

What helped to transform the situation as much as anything was the French deduction from the Suez crisis a year later that the Americans could not be relied upon to protect or respect French national interests and that it was there-fore necessary to forge stronger links with the rest of Western Europe as soon as possible. Without this, it is doubtful if the EEC would have come to fruition when it did. But this could not be foreseen in December 1955. As regards Britain's worldwide commitments, a large part of the Empire still remained. Certainly Britain's imper-ial economic ties were gradually becoming less important, but the economic dependence on her of many Commonwealth countries was still considerable, and was to lead to some thorny problems of negotiation when Britain finally did apply to join the Community five or six years later. In addition Lloyd hoped that, if the EEC did materialise, it would be possible to establish links between it and a wider free trade association in industrial goods. He was given some encouragement, especially by the French premier, Guy Mollet, to think this might come about.[7]

Furthermore, anxious though many Europeans were for Britain to participate in the new integrated Europe, some of its most influential exponents, such as the Frenchman Jean Monnet and to some extent the Belgian Paul-Henri Spaak, had already concluded that it might be easier to take the most important steps first without Britain, in the expectation that later on it would be easier to admit her. They had been led to this conclusion both by the British attitude to earlier experiments in 'Europeanism', such as the Council of Europe (1949) and the Coal and Steel Community, and also by a realistic appreciation of the difficulties posed by the US imperial and world commit-ments already mentioned.[8] Monnet and others were afraid that the price Britain would demand for participation in their schemes would be the elimination from them of those very supranational elements which they themselves most valued, as paving the way for a federalist United States of Europe. In 1955 this seemed likely to be the case in relation to the EEC. It seems to have been intimated to Lloyd that a British attempt to join the EEC in 1955-7 might in fact make it far more difficult to bring the latter into being, or at the very least undermine its basic supranational conception.[9] In short that, if Britain insisted on being a signatory, there might be no

Treaty of Rome, at any rate in the shape that its most
ardent supporters wished. As against this it can fairly
be said that participation in the Messina talks would have
enabled the British government to find out what terms were
to be had, and that her willingness to do so would have
made it less easy afterwards for the critics to argue that
Britain lacked 'a European faith'.[10] It is the writer's
view, however, - at the risk of seeming more Gaullist than
de Gaulle - that Britain was not psychologically ready to
'enter Europe' in 1955; and that her interests and commitments were then probably irreconcilable with the essential
EEC concept. This was certainly the general view at the
time.

On the Middle East also, Lloyd's views were essentially
the same as the majority of the Cabinet, which meant that
they were less extreme and rightwing than those within
the Conservative parliamentary party who had opposed the
British withdrawal from the Suez Canal base - the so-
called 'Suez Group'. As minister of state, Lloyd had
played his part in negotiating the British evacuation of
the base and the granting of independence to the Sudan.
He shared Eden's hopes that from these events might
emerge a better relationship with Egypt and with Arab
nationalism generally, on which could be based a collective policy for Middle East Defence. He shared, too, the
false hopes engendered by the ill-fated Baghdad Pact. He
was, however, more cautious in pursuing the aim of enlist-
ing other Arab countries in the pact than Macmillan, and
in this context is known to have had doubts about the
Templar mission to Jordan which almost certainly did more
harm than good.[11] Moreover, he probably considered that
Britain's major and vital interest in the area - more
vital than the Canal - was the safeguarding of her oil
supplies, and that the key to this was the British position in the Gulf. At this time there were some pessimistic views in the Foreign Office about Britain's ability
to maintain her position in that area: with this view
Lloyd evidently disagreed.

On the most important international issue of the period
- the possibility of detente with the Soviet Union -
Lloyd had views which were definite and clear-sighted.
He had no illusions about the difficulties of negotiating
with the Russians and was totally opposed to making

unrequited concessions, especially at the beginning of negotiations: but, subject to the overriding necessity of
preserving the US alliance, he believed in the possibility
of detente, especially in such fields as disarmament and
the liberalisation of trade relations. In these matters
he was, like Churchill, Eden and Macmillan, in advance of
many of his colleagues and of the Conservative parliamentary party, and considerably in advance of the US administration, which viewed negotiations with the USSR with
fear and suspicion.

III

As foreign secretary, Lloyd had more assets than were always appreciated at the time. Apart from considerable
knowledge and experience of foreign affairs, he was tho-
roughly familiar with the administration and practice of
the Foreign Office and with the principal personalities
there both at home and abroad. He had good judgement,
though he was sometimes diffident in relying on it.[12] He
had the goodwill of the majority of his Cabinet colleagues,
with whom he was on excellent terms for the most part, and
a close and friendly relationship with the prime minister.
On the other hand he lacked, as has been pointed out, the
prestige and status which comes from years of Cabinet
office and service in the House of Commons, which his two
predecessors had possessed. Personal qualities of a
colourful or unusual kind - in today's jargon, the quality
of 'charisma' - would perhaps have compensated for this
to some extent; but, though generally respected for his
integrity, industry and ability, he lacked by common consent the offbeat personality, the touches of personal in-
dividuality which characterised a Macmillan or a Bevan,
and singled them out from their fellows. Although often
an effective speaker on the public platform, or in international conferences, he was apt to be flat and uninteres-
ting in the House of Commons. He had his moments of
success, but seldom a real triumph.[13] After Suez, too, he
had to struggle against a good deal of prejudice, both
from those of his own party who had regarded the initial
use of force with disfavour and from those who had been
infuriated by the subsequent withdrawal. He also had to
contend with the hostility of a substantial section of
the Labour Party which, reasonably enough, identified him
with the entire Suez policy. However, speeches on foreign

policy do not lend themselves to a vigorous, hard hitting and controversial approach, of the kind which rallies the faithful and puts down the opposition. Indeed both Bevin and Eden, though always listened to with respect, were regarded as rather flat and dull speakers in opening foreign policy debates.[14]

It was also a handicap to Lloyd that he was ill at ease with the press and the media and usually an unconvincing performer on television. Within the Cabinet he was listened to with respect, especially in the latter period of his term at the Foreign Office; but at the same time he was working with prime ministers who had strong views on foreign policy.

The problem of Lloyd's relations with his two prime ministers must therefore be directly addressed, since it is the key to much that was said and felt about him at the time as foreign secretary. There are undoubtedly some advantages for the foreign secretary in having a prime minister who is interested and knowledgeable about foreign affairs, especially if the relations between the two men are close and friendly and the premier respects the judgement and ability of the foreign secretary. Both of these conditions characterised Lloyd's relations with Eden and Macmillan, and he nearly always had the advantage of the premier's full support in Cabinet and with the party. There was never any likelihood of a breach between prime minister and foreign secretary.

On the other hand, Eden's known desire to keep a grip on foreign policy and Lloyd's relatively junior status and previously subordinate role to Eden, together with his somewhat diffident manner in the early days, combined to give an impression of greater subservience to Eden than may actually have been the case. This was a disadvantage to Lloyd at first in his relations with his officials and some of his Cabinet colleagues.[15] The view that he was not in sole charge, that foreign policy was made from 'No 10', lessened his authority in the Office, in the Cabinet and to some extent in the House, particularly with the Opposition, with whom the idea persisted into the Macmillan era.

That Lloyd had a close relationship with Eden, and a

respect and even deference to his judgement going beyond
the normal respect for the ultimate authority of the prime
minister, need not be questioned. It would have been
strange if it had not been so. Eden's prestige and reputation were such in his chosen field of foreign affairs
that even Churchill had deferred to him, and in these circumstances most other ministers hesitated to oppose him.
It would have required a very high degree of self-confidence, even arrogance, for a newly-appointed and relatively
junior foreign secretary to have challenged that judgement:
especially since, on the major problem which dominated the
field during the remainder of Eden's premiership – namely
the Middle East – the premier's views were supported by
the highly experienced Macmillan and the overwhelming
majority of the Cabinet.[16] Nevertheless, Lloyd did express
disagreement with the premier on a number of occasions, one
of which, concerning the Suez Canal Users' Association, is
recorded by Eden.[17] On that occasion Lloyd yielded to
Eden's arguments, influenced no doubt equally by personal
loyalty and by respect for Eden's judgement. But a more
experienced and senior minister in that situation would
have been quite as likely to do the same.

   On the general point of Lloyd's relationship with his
two prime ministers, there is of course one crucial difference. Lloyd served under Eden for little more than a
year, and that year dominated by the long-drawn-out crisis
of Suez. With Macmillan he had a partnership extending
over three and a half years. The two men not only worked
closely together at home but travelled together to many
international conferences, including the important 'reconciliation' conference with the Americans at Bermuda in
March 1957, and the equally celebrated Moscow conference
with Khrushchev in February 1959, which Lloyd himself had
advocated as a necessary contribution to detente and as an
indication to the British public and world opinion of
Britain's genuine desire to pursue it. They had time to
get to know each other well, and there is no reason to
doubt Macmillan's high regard for Lloyd's work as an executant and administrator of foreign policy. The premier's
judgement in February 1958 was that 'he is so good in his
work that I really cannot think of anyone who would be
more efficient' – as high a tribute as one could possibly
desire from a prime minister. Macmillan also respected
Lloyd's creative capacity, describing him as 'fertile in

ideas and resourceful in proposing solutions' - a judgement which is relevant to the opinion expressed by some
that Lloyd made little creative contribution to the making
of foreign policy.[18] Throughout his memoirs, indeed,
Macmillan is generous in his tributes to Lloyd, and it is
of some importance that he not only asked Lloyd to stay on
at the outset of his government, when there must have been
a considerable temptation to make a change after Suez, but
on two subsequent occasions persuaded Lloyd to remain in
office when his resignation was freely offered. On the
first occasion, certainly, after Eden's departure,
Macmillan took the view that 'one head on a charger is
enough'. But this argument did not apply to later
occasions.[19]

   On his side, Lloyd undoubtedly acquired greater self-
confidence in dealing with his redoubtable chief as time
went by; also a greater understanding of the complex
nature of the man, and the way in which Macmillan concealed
a highly sensitive temperament behind a mask of languid
Edwardian assurance.[20] Thus the relations between them
altered imperceptibly, though always remaining cordial.
There was never any real tension between them: but there
may have been occasions, as tends to happen between all
foreign secretaries and prime ministers with strong views
on foreign policy, when Lloyd indicated to the prime
minister the undesirability of there being 'a rival Foreign
Office at No 10'. Such occasions were few, however, and
relations between the Foreign Office and No 10 were much
helped in this period by the presence on the prime minister's personal staff of a Foreign Office official. This
was Philip de Zulueta, who by common consent did an invaluable job in maintaining liaison between the two, both in
Lloyd's time and in that of his successor.[21]

   The subject of Lloyd's relations with the Foreign Office
requires further elaboration. It is generally conceded
that he was a hard-working and competent administrator.
There is less agreement about his ability to establish
easy personal relations with those who served him, whether
ministers or officials. There was an increase in the number of junior ministers at the Foreign Office at this time,
partly as a result of the proliferation of international
organisations and the increasing number of independent
states in the world. Eventually there were two ministers

of state and two under-secretaries, all of whom had to be
fitted in to the routine of the office. Lloyd made great
efforts to treat these ministers as a team, using them a
great deal, giving them considerable discretion, consul-
tine them widely and bringing them into office meetings
on matters where they were particularly concerned.[22] A
certain amount of specialisation developed, partly, as
later under Lord Home, by area, partly by subject.[23]
Junior ministers might be allocated mainly to European
concerns, to UN matters, to disarmament and so forth: an
understanding also developed that papers which officials
had minuted should go to the foreign secretary via which-
ever of the junior ministers was particularly concerned in
the particular area. In addition some ministers specialised more in the parliamentary side of the work and some
in the policy and administration side.

On the whole Lloyd handled these relationships well, but
inevitably the Suez crisis put a considerable strain upon
them, as upon those with the senior officials, and some of
them parted under the strain; notably in the case of
Anthony Nutting who carried his disagreement with Eden and
Lloyd to the point of resignation from his office of
minister of state.[24] In general, however, and particularly
once Suez was over, relations within the Office under Lloyd
were pleasant and amicable.

This also applied in the end, and considered generally,
to Lloyd's relations with his officials, but here he had a
more difficult task, and more obstacles to overcome. Partly this was due, as has been mentioned, to the circumstances of his initial appointment and the impression among
senior officials that he was very much Eden's subordinate:
and partly to the fact that Lloyd, a man basically shy and
at first unsure of himself, sought to conceal this under
a rather teasing facetious manner which did not go down
well with some of the polished and very high-powered officials with whom he had to deal. Some of these never
revised their first unfavourable impression. One at least
who served with Lloyd at the outset of the period held the
view that he was not well suited by temperament and experience to be foreign secretary, and lacked the imagination,
courage and decisiveness required to give effective leadership in the department and in Cabinet.[25] On the other hand,
those who served with Lloyd for any length of time, and got

to know him well, often revised first unfavourable impressions. Thus Sir William Hayter records that he eventually came to like and respect him, and formed the view that he was 'a very able Minister'.[26] Another who knew him well and served with him over a long period considered both that he was decisive — though careful and cautious in reaching decisions — and that he possessed ability and judgement. Yet another who worked with Lloyd afterwards wrote that he could seldom recall the flow of business being held up by lack of decision.[27]

The Suez period itself, of course, was an exceptionally difficult period, as it would have been for any foreign secretary, since the Office was divided: and the majority of the officials concerned with the Middle East were against the government's policy when, at a fairly late stage, most of them learnt of it.[28] This very fact, of course, rendered Lloyd's relations with the Office uneasy in the immediate aftermath of Suez. He worked hard, and in the end in most cases successfully, to overcome this handicap. He was much helped in this as in all his dealings with the Office by a succession of able private secretaries who listened to his problems, advised, counselled and generally did all they could to help him repair the breach.[29] Lloyd's pleasant terms with these younger men are evidence that he could also establish good relations with his juniors.

It has been argued by academic critics, and sometimes by politicians, that all departments, and particularly powerful departments like the Foreign Office and the Treasury, seek to bend the minister to their will and impose their policies through him on the government.[30] No doubt this is sometimes the case, but it does not seem to be a weakness which can be held against Lloyd. Indeed, in arguing that he was too much under the influence of 'No 10' his critics to some extent rule out the possibility of such an accusation; and on the first major issue that arose, the Middle East, Lloyd supported a policy on which he knew that official opinion was, to say the least, divided.[31] He for his part did not feel that he was constantly subject to 'corporate pressure', nor did his officials regard him as a 'rubber stamp'. The truth is, of course, that the degree to which a minister runs or is run by his department depends entirely on the character of the minister and the

130

ministry - in the case of the latter particularly the character of the permanent under-secretary. Lloyd was served by two permanent secretaries, Sir Ivone Kirkpatrick, who had the reputation of 'an Irishman, who never minded a fight', and Sir F. Hoyer-Miller (now Lord Inchyra), an able but discreet official who got on well with Lloyd.[32]

One further complication in the conduct of British external policy at this time must be mentioned. Since the 1930s British relations with certain self-governing Commonwealth countries had been handled by a separate ministry, the Commonwealth Relations Office (CRO). From 1945 onwards, countries such as Australia and Canada began increasingly to conduct their own foreign policy and to take initiatives in the field of foreign affairs; and the tendency for there to be different viewpoints within the Commonwealth on foreign policy was of course much increased by the advent in the 1940s of the 'New Commonwealth' countries, India, Pakistan and Ceylon. The point was vividly illustrated in the Suez affair itself by the markedly different initiatives taken by Australia and Canada, and the difference of view between many of the Asian members and the British Government.[33]

A further complication was sometimes caused by the fact that vast territories overseas were still administered by the Colonial Office and colonial problems sometimes impinged on the field of external relations. This situation was usually covered by a working agreement whereby internal colonial matters remained the prerogative of the colonial secretary, but the external aspects of both colonial and CRO matters were normally handled - at the UN, for example - by the Foreign Office. If a colonial problem raised international complications, as happened in this period with Cyprus, then there were obvious problems of dual responsibility; as also sometimes happened in the case of the CRO and Colonial Office, for example in relation to the Central African Federation, where two of the governors concerned were responsible to the Colonial Office and the third to the CRO. Clearly much depended on the personal relations between the three ministers concerned, and fortunately Lloyd was on good terms with Lennox-Boyd the colonial secretary - a tough, vigorous minister, but a good co-operator - and Lord Home the commonwealth relations secretary.

Lloyd would have liked to have facilitated co-ordination, through a greater degree of integration between the Foreign Office and the CRO, but there was some resistance from the officials in the CRO and it was not until a decade later that the two departments were amalgamated. A beginning was made, however, in Lloyd's time with a limited exchange of personnel. At this time, with extensive territories still under direct colonial rule, the question of amalgamation with the Colonial Office did not seriously arise, yet so great was the speed of the subsequent dissolution of empire that this too was to come within a decade.

In looking at Lloyd's record as a whole it is of course essential to remember that all governments and all ministers are limited by the given facts of their situation. These limitations are partly of a purely practical kind and have to do with the resources available, both human and material. In Lloyd's time the process was rapidly advancing whereby these resources were to shrink to those available in these islands; and the consequences of this in terms of access to vital raw materials and manpower for the armed forces were already becoming apparent. The task of a British foreign secretary in this period was not helped by the growing dependence of the British economy on supplies of imported oil from particularly sensitive and volatile parts of the world. In addition ministers are limited by domestic political factors - the size of the government's majority, the degree of co-operation with the Opposition, the extent of public support, the attitude of the media, personal relations with colleagues and the premier, etc. Most of these have been touched on already as they affected Lloyd. Some could be manipulated or managed to some extent, though, as has been noted, Lloyd was not particularly gifted in some of these fields. But for a foreign minister the most important factors are external ones which are not ultimately manageable except by superpowers - and not always by them, even when in agreement. In the post-war era this has been particularly true of Britain, by reason of her economic weakness, her loss of empire, and the changes in the technology of war. The last is the most important. In a nuclear world Britain had become very vulnerable; and British dependence on the Anglo-American alliance, then as now, derived more from her need of the American nuclear umbrella and US naval protection for her shipping routes than from economic factors.

   On the whole, British public opinion had not faced up
to the realities of this situation in the 1950s, nor had
political leaders of either party. It is easy, with hindsight, to say that with the decline of empire the stark
choice for Britain was either continuing dependence on the
United States or entry into Europe. But in 1955 few politicians or officials believed this.[34] The Labour Party
and its leaders showed even less readiness to abandon
their insularity (and their desire to retain control of
the British economy) than the Conservative Party. Nor was
there any great public support for such a move — and, as
Disraeli pointed out, 'in a democratic country it is sometimes necessary to defer to the opinions of the people'.
The fashionable view at the time was still 'the three con-
centric circles' — the Atlantic Alliance, the Commonwealth
and Europe — with Britain at the point of intersection,
belonging to all three, uniquely able to serve as a link
between them and as the interpreter of one to the other.
This was Lloyd's view, as it was the view of almost every-
one who counted, though within this general context he was
not averse to forming closer links with Western Europe,
and on the institutional side fathered a personal 'grand
design' which was intended to produce a streamlining of
Western Europe's proliferating institutions.

IV

Viewing Lloyd's career at the Foreign Office as a whole,
it is clear that it must be divided into pre-Suez and
post-Suez. The present writer shares the common view that
the Suez operation was politically a blunder, that it
failed largely because of American opposition, and that
the crucial mistake therefore was the misjudgement of
American intentions. Some maintain that this was largely
Britain's fault, and in particular that she should have
guessed that US support would not be forthcoming in an
election year, in which President Eisenhower was being
presented as 'a man of peace'.[35] Others, of whom the
present writer is one, consider that the blame for the
misunderstanding must be put equally on the shoulders of
the Americans, and particularly Dulles. The latter's
ambiguous phraseology and habit of blowing hot and cold
on the use of strong measures were calculated to mislead,

and indeed were part of a carefully thought out delaying action, designed to prevent Britain and France from resorting to force. It had precisely the opposite effect, since it eventually goaded Eden and his colleagues into action. At the same time Dulles and President Eisenhower more than once undermined the Anglo-French position vis-a-vis Egypt by public and often unnecessary statements at times when silence on their part might have led Nasser to adopt a more emanable line. This happened, for example, at a crucial period of the mission led by the Australian premier R.G.Menzies to Cairo (August 1956), again after the creation of the Suez Canal Users' Association (September 1956), and again during the UN negotiations in October. A greater degree of frankness with Britain on the part of the US and a greater degree of firmness with Egypt, would have produced infinitely better results.[36]

Whether the Suez operation, even if successful, would have produced the right results for Britain is uncertain. The answer depends to some extent on one's view of possible Arab reactions, which were unlikely to be helpful in the long run. The moral aspect, too, turns on a number of disputed questions: whether, for example, it is always wrong to use force to defend vital national interests (most people did not think at the time that it was necessarily wrong to do so); and whether Nasser's action in taking over the canal was in breach of international law. Whatever may be the verdict on that score, there was an element of hypocrisy in the attitude of the United States, in view of American actions before and since in Latin America, and subsequently in Vietnam; not to mention − the final irony − a more recent US threat to use force to safeguard Middle East oil supplies. On the subject of contemporary Soviet strictures, delivered from the vantage-point of a subjugated Hungary, nothing needs to be said.

One of the most weighty and deeply felt arguments against British policy in the Suez crisis was, however, that it encouraged the Soviet Union to take the crucial decision to suppress the Hungarian revolt, prompted by the disarray in the Western camp. The evidence seems to suggest that this was not the case. A further weighty charge relates to the element of deliberate deception involved in relation to 'collusion' with Israel. But Suez was an operation of war: and in war, as Churchill put it, 'truth needs to be

attended with a bodyguard of lies'. On the 'rule of law'
argument, on the other hand, it is difficult not to feel
that Britain tried to have it both ways, condemning Nasser
but justifying her own actions.

Of Lloyd's own part in the crisis it must be said that
he shares full responsibility and has never sought to evade
it. It is known that he had some doubts and reservations,
as any sensible man would have had in his position against
the background of Foreign Office doubts.[37] He favoured
telling the Americans frankly what was intended, and worked
hard to arrive at a settlement at the UN. Perhaps in
retrospect the government should have accepted the so-
called 'six principles' of settlement worked out at the
UN, as the best Britain was likely to get; coupling this
with a political gesture to France which might have saved
the Fourth Republic and enabled Britain to 'get in on the
ground floor in Europe'.[38] But this is speculation; and
one cannot blame Lloyd for not seeking to convince a
sceptical prime minister and Cabinet that the 'six principles' would really offer adequate safeguards to Britain,
or represent anything other than a surrender, particularly
in view of the fact that it would have been difficult to
convince a substantial part of the Conservative Party or
the French of this. By this stage Lloyd must have felt,
like others, that the die was cast.

What is generally conceded is that Lloyd displayed remarkable stamina, industry and patience during this gruelling period and kept his head and his temper to an admirable degree.[39] On the personal level he also managed to
keep on good terms with a wide cross-section of the parliamentary party and retain their respect - a considerable
achievement at such a time.[40]

It is agreed too that Lloyd managed the Suez London
conferences and the UN negotiations as well as anyone
could have done: and that he has been given too little
credit for the skilful and determined way in which he
handled the negotiations following the collapse of the
Suez policy, in extraordinarily difficult circumstances.[41]

In the aftermath of Suez the two major concerns of the
Macmillan government, which was formed in January 1957 -
and therefore of Lloyd who remained foreign secretary -

were the rebuilding of the Anglo-American alliance and the restoration of the British position in the Middle East. Anglo-American relations had been very unsatisfactory for some time before the Suez crisis, owing to the personal antipathy between Eden and Dulles. As a result British and US policies in the Middle East had diverged.[42] It is no small tribute to the skill of Macmillan and Lloyd that the first objective was largely and the second partially achieved by the end of 1957. The first step along both paths was in fact taken as early as January 1957 by the American announcement of the so-called 'Eisenhower doctrine' directed against aggression and subversion in the Middle East - an instrument which could be used equally against the Soviet Union, or, with a little flexibility, against any Arab state which could be regarded as aligned with Moscow; for example, Egypt or Syria. The United States thus served notice of her intention to fill the power vacuum in the Middle East which she herself had helped to create. Not unnaturally Lloyd and Macmillan regarded this as to some extent a vindication, though unacknowledged, of Suez; and it confirmed their view that whatever the pros and cons of that operation, its results were not all bad, since the shock of the Anglo-American breach and the revelation of the full dangers of a Soviet move into the Middle East undoubtedly combined to bring about this new and more positive American attitude. There was indeed a not unnatural mood of contrition in Washington over the brutal treatment of a loyal ally, necessary though it was thought to have been. Macmillan and Lloyd took full and skilful advantage of this, the latter re-establishing very quickly and even strengthening his former good relationship with Dulles. Dulles, in fact, who had been ill in hospital at the most crucial moment of the Suez crisis, always subsequently argued that Anglo-American relations would have been more gently handled if he had been in charge at this period: and even indicated to Lloyd that he personally wished the Anglo-French expedition had not been halted when it was. Lloyd is said to have behaved with remarkable restraint on this occasion.[43] At the Bermuda conference with the Americans in March 1957 the reconciliation was sealed and a new constructive phase in Anglo-American relationships inaugurated.

The benefits were felt first of all in the Middle East where, in contrast with the previous two or three years,

Anglo-American policies were co-ordinated in dealing with
a difficult situation which arose between Syria and Britain's ally Turkey in August of that year: and in the
British dispute over Oman with Saudi Arabia, at about the
same time, the US attitude was not unhelpful. The full
benefit of the change in the US attitude was, however,
most forcibly demonstrated in the Middle East crisis of
the following year, centred on the Lebanon to begin with,
but subsequently involving Jordan and Iraq. In the Lebanon
the pro-Western regime of President Camille Chamoun was
threatened by internal revolt, fomented by the newly formed United Arab Republic, embracing Egypt, Syria and the
Yemen. In Iraq a successful revolution overthrew Britain's
staunchest remaining ally, Nuri-es-Said, and his master
King Feisal, while a similar fate seemed only too likely
to overwhelm Feisal's cousin, Hussein, in neighbouring
Jordan. To meet this crisis American and British policies
were closely co-ordinated by Dulles and Lloyd, the latter
visiting Washington at Dulles's suggestion at the crucial
moment, to concert their policies. In July US troops were
landed in the Lebanon and British troops in Jordan and the
position restored. The whole episode was deftly managed
to the point of ultimate withdrawal, with Anglo-American
objectives largely achieved, in an atmosphere of general
international approbation. Both in terms of the building
up of Anglo-American relations which preceded it, and in
terms of the actual 'crisis management' itself, it can be
regarded as one of the most successful episodes in Lloyd's
career at the Foreign Office; and it was followed by an
American move towards a closer association with the Baghdad
Pact - a step which Britain had wished for over a long
period.

It was largely because of this Anglo-American concord
that British policies in the Middle East achieved reasonable success during the remainder of Lloyd's term at the
Foreign Office; and while it could certainly not be said
that by the end of it the British position in the area had
been restored, more progress had been made than could have
been expected in the immediate aftermath of Suez.[44]

The restoration of Anglo-American harmony was, of course,
even more important for Britain in the context of East-West
relations. For Macmillan and Lloyd this was particularly
important in relation to their efforts to move towards

detente with the Soviet Union, both by progress on specific
issues such as the control of nuclear testing and through
the holding of regular conferences with the Russians at
foreign minister or heads of government level.[45] It was
also of major importance when a serious crisis over Berlin
occurred towards the end of this period.

Lloyd was aware, having been concerned with the disarmament problem on and off since 1951, that very little progress could be made in general disarmament so long as the
Soviet attitude remained hostile to effective measures for
inspection and control. In 1958, however, both Macmillan
and Lloyd came to the conclusion, and Dulles also with
some persuasion from Lloyd, that progress might be made in
a limited but vitally important sector, the agreed suspen-
sion of nuclear tests, in relation to which there was already much concern on the score of atmospheric pollution.
It seems that Lloyd's continuous pressure on the Americans
played a considerable part in getting them to agree to an
international conference on this issue.[46] With the support
of their respective chiefs, Lloyd and Dulles persuaded the
USSR to begin the long-drawn-out negotiations which began
at Geneva in October 1958. Dulles, however, naturally
suspicious and reserved in his dealings with the Soviet
Union, and influenced by the hostility of the US Defence
Department to any such agreement, was slow to make the
kind of concessions which would have made rapid progress
possible, and after his initial agreement was apt to 'drag
his feet'. It was Lloyd's persistent and skilful handling
of Dulles, no less than Macmillan's consistent support for
the policy, which prevented the negotiations from breaking
down altogether. As it was, Lloyd laid the foundations,
but was prevented from seeing it through to the ultimate
successful conclusion of a test-ban treaty in 1963.

In the same way Macmillan and Lloyd consistently nursed
an often reluctant and dubious Eisenhower and Dulles along
the path towards detente and (though this was more Macmillan's special concern) towards a 'summit' meeting.
Neither can be held responsible for the collapse of that
edifice in May 1960, a collapse for which Soviet obduracy
and American maladroitness were equally to blame.

The difficulties inherent in pursuing these objectives
were much enhanced by the prolonged crisis over the Allied

position in Berlin, precipitated by Khrushchev's threat in November 1958 to sign a separate peace treaty with East Germany and so, according to the Soviet argument, bring to an end the post-war agreement on which the four-power occupation in that city rested. As in the previous crisis over Berlin in 1948-9, the Western position was that they could not afford the psychological defeat and the blow to Western morale which would have resulted from being forced out of Berlin. It became Lloyd's concern therefore to join with the Americans and the French in resisting the Soviet ultimatum, and to defend Allied rights in Berlin, while maintaining a sufficiently flexible posture to ensure that any favourable opportunity to defuse the crisis should not be missed. To achieve this nice balance while maintaining Western unity vis-a-vis the USSR called for all Lloyd's skill as a diplomatist, particularly since the personalities involved included the difficult and now ailing Dulles; the aged and often touchy Adenauer; and the prickly de Gaulle. That the West was able to maintain a reasonably united front owed a good deal to Lloyd's efforts, particularly in the Foreign Ministers' Conference between Britain, the US, France and Russia, which lasted from 11 May to 5 August 1959. At that conference the Russians were particularly unforthcoming, and it was difficult to maintain Western unity over this prolonged series of meetings. The general verdict at the time, however, was that Lloyd handled the situation very well. Indeed, it was Macmillan's judgement that it was largely owing to him that the conference even got under way.[47] At this conference there were considerable difficulties about the seating of the two delegations from East and West Germany, leading to arguments about the number of tables to be used, their position, and even their shape. Lloyd played a major role in solving these apparently trivial, but in fact important problems; important because they were tied to the question of recognising the East German government, which the West had always refused to do. Certainly, Lloyd's reputation was much enhanced by the episode, and the effort was not in vain, for the Khrushchev ultimatum (on a separate Soviet treaty with East Germany) was now extended for a year, and subsequently to eighteen months. Eventually, in fact, the Soviet government solved its problem over Berlin — the stemming of the flood of refugees escaping from East Germany — by the brutal but effective expedient of the Berlin Wall; and the question of a separate peace treaty was quietly dropped.

Apart from these major problems of East-West relations
and those connected with the Middle East, Lloyd's main concern during the latter years was the question of Britain's
attitude towards the evolving European Community. The crucial decision, namely to refrain from participating in the
original Messina conference, had already been taken by
Macmillan during his brief period at the Foreign Office.
But, as has been noted, Lloyd shared the views which led
to the decision and continued the policy of British absten-
tion from the successive negotiations which led to the
Treaty of Rome in March 1957. The British Government's
attitude, though sceptical, was not in fact actively hostile, though unguarded remarks occasionally suggested the
contrary, and there was certainly some concern about the
possibility of being completely excluded from a powerful
European bloc. The Government was cautiously favourable
towards any development which would serve to strengthen
West European unity, and it was hoped that if the Community
materialised it could be linked with a wider free trade
area in industrial goods - the so-called 'Plan G' of the
Macmillan government.[48]

It was perhaps naive to think that Britain could obtain
in effect the advantages of membership of the EEC without
its disadvantages or commitments - for so Plan G appeared
to many Europeans. Nevertheless the proposal was accepted
by the Organisation for European Economic Co-operation,
which included the six prospective members of the EEC;
and the French attitude seemed favourable at that time.
However, when the Treaty of Rome came into force in January
1958, and the question of Plan G was brought up again, that
attitude changed, and de Gaulle's return to power later
that year did not help. In November 1958 discussions on
Plan G were finally terminated by an official French statement to the effect that it was not possible to create a
free trade area between the Common Market and the rest of
the OEEC.

British policy then turned to the creation of a more limited free trade area, including only those West European
states left outside the EEC, and agreement was reached with
those six states in November 1959 to set up the appropriate
organisation, known as EFTA (the European Free Trade

140

Association). Many people would now consider that this scheme, completing as it were the division of West Europe into two competing blocs, was misconceived and did Europe, and Britain's own cause, more harm than good. It appeared to many Europeans to be designed as a wrecking exercise – hostile, that is, to the EEC – though it does not seem to have been intended as such. Macmillan himself states that he regarded it as 'a temporary measure pending the final unification of the economy of Europe' and this also seems to have been Lloyd's view. In a memorandum to Lloyd at that time, Macmillan also stressed that Britain should not try to disrupt the EEC, and he certainly hoped that some kind of bridge could be created between the two organisations.[49] It was not perhaps unreasonable in the face of the creation of a powerful economic bloc in Western Europe to look for some such alternative, if only to create the possibility of 'negotiating from strength' which in other contexts was considered a virtue. But both Macmillan and Lloyd came fairly quickly and at about the same time to the conclusion that EFTA, though valuable enough in its own limited sphere, was insufficient for Britain's needs. It had become clear to them that Britain's proper course was to apply to join the EEC. The decision to do so, however, was not finally made until after Lloyd had left the Foreign Office.

V

To sum up the character and achievements of Selwyn Lloyd over nearly five years is not easy. Perhaps, indeed, no one who has held the office of foreign secretary in the post-war era presents like difficulty. There were then, as there still are, conflicting views about the man and his work. Some of these have already been glanced at. Both of the prime ministers under whom he served have paid him glowing tributes in their memoirs; his junior ministers, with some exceptions, mostly connected with the Suez crisis, regarded him with respect and liking: his senior officials include some who never saw cause to revise early and unfavourable judgements; but most, as they came to know him, also came to respect him and to admire certain of his qualities very much.

Most of the foreign statesmen, too, with whom he negotiated regarded him with respect; and he was able to

141

form valuable personal relationships with foreign ministers as different as the American Dulles, the German von
Bretano, the Dutchman Luns, the Greek Averoff and others.
Of the Americans, the formidable Dean Acheson formed a low
opinion of him, but Acheson was a pretty severe judge.[50]

   It is hardly in dispute that Lloyd was an exceptionally
dedicated and industrious administrator, and a skilled,
patient and effective negotiator. On what might be
called the executive side of his work he was clearly
strong, as Macmillan testifies, and his officials and junior ministers for the most part regarded him as prudent,
courageous and generally decisive; though in his early
days, a little slow and diffident in reaching decisions.
He was effective too on the plane of personal diplomacy,
in international conferences and in overseas missions.
It is clear, for example, that his handling of the crucial
Anglo-Greek-Turkish conference on the difficult and potentially explosive problem of Cyprus in 1959 was one of his
major triumphs and that Macmillan's tribute to his 'consummate skill' is justified. Eden also pays tribute to
his ability in personal negotiations.[51] He was less effective in Parliament, and so great a part does effectiveness
in that forum still play in shaping a man's public image
that his reputation has probably suffered more than it
ought on that account. But he certainly had the qualities
necessary for success in some important aspects of his
work and did in fact enjoy a considerable measure of suc-
ces in those fields. Was he, however, sufficiently quick
to adapt his thinking to a rapidly changing world and
Britain's changing place in it? It can fairly be argued
that both in the Suez crisis and subsequently in his attitude to European unity Lloyd revealed deficiencies in this
respect. Yet so did Eden and Macmillan, neither of whom
was usually thought of as lacking imagination, judgement
and flexibility in relation to foreign affairs. It could
however also be argued that Lloyd would have been in a
stronger position to take on the Foreign Office a few
years later than he did; and that Eden did him a disservice when he appointed him in 1955 — apart from the
fact that Lloyd thereby became 'the Foreign Secretary of
Suez'.

   A final and important question must be considered, namely how far Lloyd possessed original ideas and how far his

142

contribution to foreign policy was creative. The question is more than usually difficult to answer in Lloyd's case, precisely because he worked so closely with his prime ministers, and particularly with Harold Macmillan; it was difficult even for his contemporaries to be sure as to whether the basic ideas and particularly the new ones came from him or from Macmillan. But it is clear that Lloyd did have creative ideas, particularly in the broad sphere of disarmament and detente with the USSR; and it is probably for his part in these matters that he would most wish to be remembered. In more detailed matters of negotiation he was undoubtedly capable of being resourceful and imaginative, for example in the Cyprus negotiations, where some of the more important elements of the 1959 settlement, particularly the 'sovereign bases' idea, came from him; and again in his handling of the rather awkward problem posed by the Formosa Straits crisis of 1958, that of reconciling a public posture of support for the United States with a private desire to avoid too great an appearance of commitment to the US policy of support for Chiang Kai-shek.[52]

Finally, one should say of Selwyn Lloyd that he had to a marked degree the quality of dogged persistence, of keeping on in the face of arduous and discouraging experiences which would have deterred most others. It was a quality which sometimes enabled him to salvage something from an apparently hopeless situation. This is always an admirable quality, and one the British people generally admire, partly indeed, though one hopes not mainly, because it is thought to be particularly British. Future historians will probably consider that he was a dedicated, capable and efficient foreign secretary, if not a great one, and may well conclude that he was underestimated and undervalued by his contemporaries.

CHAPTER 7

LORD HOME

I

No appointment to the Foreign Office in the postwar period
was greeted with more surprise or received more immediate
criticism than that of Lord Home.* The objections rested
partly on the view that he was an obscure figure - 'insuf-
ficiently distinguished' as The Times put it. Certainly
he was not well known to the general public, partly for
the very reason that membership of the Lords had kept him
out of the limelight; and partly because he had for five
years held an office - that of commonwealth relations
secretary - which was not often the centre of political
controversy or the focus of public attention. But the
main objections centred around Home's status as a peer.
It was argued by the critics, particularly the Opposition,
that it was politically and constitutionally objectionable
for the principal foreign affairs spokesman not to be
available for questioning in the Commons, and for major
statements on foreign policy to be made in the Upper
House.[1]

As sometimes happens, the critics spoilt a good case by
over-stating it. It was true that there had not been a
foreign secretary in the Lords for twenty years; true
also that Eden has passed over Salisbury for the Foreign
Office in 1955 on the ground that he was a peer.[2] Nor

---

* The title by which he is now known. As Lord Dunglass
he was MP for South Lanark 1931-45 and 1950-1; as the
fourteenth Earl of Home, minister of State, Scottish
Office 1951-5, commonwealth relations secretary, 1955-60
and foreign secretary 1960-3: as Sir Alec Douglas-Home,
prime minister 1963-4, leader of the Opposition, 1964-5,
foreign secretary 1970-74. Now Lord Home of the Hirsel,

was it unreasonable to assert that the objections to a
prime minister in the Lords applied almost as much to the
foreign secretary. But whatever the political objections
to the appointment, it was certainly not unconstitutional;
and on the other side of the controversy there were, of
course, some good arguments, including that used by Macmillan himself, that an able man should not be debarred
from the highest offices simply by birth. Also there were
advantages of a practical nature to be gained from such an
appointment. In the Commons a minister's burden is made
heavier by an MP's parliamentary and constituency duties.
Relieved of divisions, late-night sittings, committee work
and constituency business, a peer has more time for the
work of his department and is a good deal fresher. The
advantage is particularly great in the case of the Foreign
Office, where the sheer volume of work involved is acknowledged to be particularly heavy and unremitting, with very
little 'let-up' even at weekends, a fact acknowledged by
many recent holders of the office. The burden of travel
alone now imposed on all foreign secretaries is considerable.

   Home, however, took the view that it need not be a killing
job if one decentralised effectively and there was no doubt
in his mind, nor in that of the officials who served under
him, that he gained greatly from being in the Lords. One
essential requirement, though, was that the Foreign Office
should be represented by a competent 'No 2' in the House
of Commons, who in these special circumstances would need
to have the status of a cabinet minister. The novel procedure of 'double-banking' the Foreign Office in the Cabinet was therefore adopted by Macmillan, apparently at the
suggestion of the outgoing minister, Selwyn Lloyd.[3] Edward
Heath was appointed to the Foreign Office under Home, with
special responsibilities for European affairs. The fact
that these were soon to bulk very large,with Britain's
application to join the EEC,helped, with other things, to
take the sting out of the objections to the foreign secretary's own absence from the Commons.

   More important, however, was the fact that it very soon
became clear that the new foreign secretary was fully up
to his job. Home took over control with a competence and
authoritativeness which were quickly apparent, and to
which both his background and character contributed.

Indeed his wealth, and status probably contributed to a
certain sense of detachment about office and the rewards
of political life which was a source of strength.

Home was born in 1903, the heir to one of the senior
Scottish Earldoms. From Eton and Oxford he had entered
Conservative politics, but his close association with
Neville Chamberlain in the Munich period had been a disadvantage to him in the post-war years, when he returned to
public life after a long and critical illness. He had concluded from the failure of Chamberlain's appeasement policies, however, that it did not pay to conciliate dictatorships, and he was one of the first critics of the Yalta
agreements in 1945. This independence of mind probably
recommended him to Churchill, who brought him back to
office in 1951. In 1955 he entered the Cabinet for the
first time as commonwealth relations secretary and in 1957
became leader of the House of Lords. It is clear that not
only Eden but also Macmillan formed a favourable opinion
of his diplomatic gifts and administrative ability during
this period.

On Selwyn Lloyd's transfer to the Treasury in 1960,
therefore, Macmillan had little doubt that Home was fitted
by character and experience for the Foreign Office. Home
himself had some doubts about his qualifications, but was
afterwards to judge that the CRO with its opportunities
for contacts with a variety of political leaders of different races and viewpoints around the globe, had been in fact
an excellent preparation for foreign affairs. The Premier
himself had some reservations about Home's health and membership of the Lords, but these were outweighed by his belief that Home was the right man.

Judgement of character was clearly as important a factor
as experience in Macmillan's decision and that of the colleagues he had consulted. Home was popular and respected,
primarily for his integrity and straightforwardness,[4] and
because he had the moral courage to say unpopular things.
He had, too, a natural shrewdness and a sense of judgement
which, though sometimes narrow, was usually penetrating.
In addition he had acquired, after nearly ten years in
office and five in the Cabinet, an instinctive authoritativeness and self-confidence. Also, and most important
for a foreign secretary, he had good nerves and a relaxed

146

approach to the problems of power and decision-making. He did the day's work in the day, refused to worry about de-decisions once made,[5] and wisely tried to avoid being con-stantly at full stretch. He had learnt over the previous decade the wisdom of decentralising and delegating as much as possible, and this not only contributed to his effec-tiveness as an administrator but also helped him to keep something in reserve, both physically and mentally.

On the other hand, he was perhaps a little short of cre-ative imagination and intuitive sympathy with other people's patterns of thought, especially when motivated by what seemed to him unreasoning emotion, as in relation to Spain or South Africa. Level-headed judgement was his strong suit, rather than intuition or imagination. But this very fact made him a particularly useful foil and complement to a prime minister who was both imaginative and creative, but temperamentally a man of moods.

Home's judgement on most of the major problems of inter-national politics was as fully formed by 1960 as his chara-cter. As a realist, he was pretty well aware after Suez, and with the liquidation of empire, that British power had declined sharply. This meant - and here he shared the gen-eral view of foreign secretaries of the period - that so long as the cold war continued, the American alliance was paramount.[6] Only the United States could provide the gua-rantee of our shipping lanes which was still vital so long as Britain had worldwide interests, as in 1960 it still did, and worldwide commerce and trade. It is clear that Home throughout his term at the Foreign Office tried always to avoid public disagreements with the United States, while at the same time being prepared to talk frankly and toughly to American leaders in private, when he thought they were in the wrong. Such occasions were sometimes to occur in the 1960s, for example in relation to US policy in the Congo, the development of nuclear weaponry and the Berlin crisis.[7] Moreover, desirable though an independent British deterrent and perhaps ultimately a European deterrent might be, it would be some time before Europe could do without the American 'nuclear umbrella' in its dealings with the USSR. Home had no doubt that it was the 'balance of terror' more than any other factor which had kept Europe at peace since 1945 and induced the Russians to back down in a num-ber of situations where there was a real risk of war.[8]

147

This view clearly influenced him in his reactions to the
second Berlin crisis of 1958-62 and later in the Cuban
missile affair.

Towards the Soviet Union, indeed, his attitude was simple and uncompromising, but not narrowly ideological. He
saw the Soviet Union as a vigorous, aggressive and expansionist state, in a phase of growing power, already controlling half of Europe and with avowed objectives threa-
tening British interests there and elsewhere. It was
these facts, more than the nature of the Soviet state or
the ideological content of its policy, which were important. Russia should therefore be confronted as a state in
whose policies realpolitik was likely to be more important
a factor than ideology. In dealing with such a state vigi-
lance and firmness were the first prerequisites: then a
clear indication to Soviet ministers that one was under no
illusion about their objectives and tactics. Conciliatory
gestures were useless, unless given in the context of an
immediate quid pro quo; otherwise they would simply be interpreted as a sign of weakness. Concessions from the
other side could only be expected if it seemed clearly in
the Soviet interest to make them.[9]

Home was not, however, opposed to detente and an improved
climate of relations with the USSR. But he was less optimistic and more sceptical than Macmillan in his approach.
Detente he seems to have felt would probably at best be
partial: and if it came, it would come as a result of
Soviet appreciation of the situation created by such factors as the 'balance of terror' and the Sino-Soviet dispute,
rather than from genuine goodwill. Progress was only likely in areas where an agreement was of equal advantage to
the Russians as to the West, and where that fact was sufficiently obvious to be accepted by the most suspicious member of the Politburo.

Home also differed to some extent from Macmillan on the
tactics to be followed in pursuing detente. 'Summit meetings', had no appeal to him. He thought, and remains of the
same opinion today, that the consequences of a failure such
as 1960 were disastrous, both for public morale and for the
morale of the participants themselves.[10] Therefore one
should never have such a meeting, unless it had been so far
prearranged that there were at least two significant

achievements certain to emerge in the final communique.
Otherwise 'summit' meetings were a trap.[11]   In this he
held similar views to his predecessor, Selwyn Lloyd, but
Home's distrust of 'summits' was if anything greater.
Both were probably influenced to some extent by Foreign
Office doubts about the value of such meetings. But there
was also a personal feeling that great and intractable
issues which had not yielded to the normal processes of
diplomacy were unlikely to be solved in a few days by discussion among heads of government. Such a meeting might
still be helpful, even without concrete achievements, if it
contributed to an improved international climate or enabled
the leaders of great states to know and understand each
other better. But Home considered that the risks of such
meetings were always considerable and apt to outweigh the
gains.

   He recognised, however, that 'personal diplomacy', in
the sense of regular contacts between ministers below head
of government level, could be valuable. Home felt that informal contacts in such meetings had enabled him to establish useful relationships with the Americans Christian
Herter and Dean Rusk and in his second term of office with
William Rogers and Henry Kissinger; Rusk indeed thought
him 'one of the ablest foreign ministers he dealt with'.[12]
Home also established good relations with the German,
Walter Scheel, and even to some extent with the Frenchman
de Murville.   In general, however, he preferred to work
by means of the traditional processes of diplomacy,
through contacts with and messages to ambassadors; occasionally summoning an ambassador home for consultation,
and regularly having all the envoys from each of the main
areas back for the conferences which were a regular part
of Foreign Office routine. It was the judgement of at
least one of his colleagues that Home's success at the
Foreign Office stemmed partly from this firm reliance on
the traditional methods of diplomacy.[13] It certainly added
to his popularity with his senior officials. It seems
agreed, however, that Home was usually very good in personal negotiations; and that while he might not succeed in
reaching solutions to intractable problems, 'he never made
a position worse,' as a ministerial colleague put it, 'and
he often made it better'.[14]

   For reasons which will be evident, Home was not disposed

to be particularly yielding on the main East-West issues, particularly that which was the most troublesome in the early sixties, namely Berlin and the related questions of relations with East Germany. On the other main European question, that of Britain's relations with the EEC, Home's views had gradually, like those of his principal colleagues, been moving in favour of membership. He did not see such membership as necessarily incompatible with the American Alliance, provided French suspicions could be assuaged by bringing them into that alliance as equal partners. When it came to the point, however, de Gaulle, though demanding closer consultation with Britain and the US, tended to reject such overtures. He did not really wish to 'get closer to the Americans'.[15] Characteristically, having come to the conclusion that Britain should probably join the EEC, Home expressed his view firmly in a speech to the Lords in 1961, even before Macmillan had announced the British application for membership. Home was influenced to some extent by his experience at the CRO, which had, he felt, shown that increasingly both old and new members of the Commonwealth were taking their own path economically and politically: and since this process might be expected to continue, Britain must also look more to her own interests, while safeguarding Commonwealth interests where she could.

So far as the other main centres of Britain's interest were concerned, the Middle East was in 1960 relatively quiescent. Home had no doubt that he should continue to preserve Britain's position in the area, which had recovered somewhat thanks to Macmillan's and Lloyd's 'rescue operation' after Suez, and that to do so, it was essential not to permit any divergence with the Americans. He considered also that the British position east of Suez should be maintained and supported by a naval presence in the Indian Ocean — which meant keeping the links with South Africa through the Simonstown agreement.[16] The realism of this scenario is in fact open to some question, since British naval forces could have made relatively little impact on the situation vis-a-vis the USSR; and in the event of a full-scale global war much would be happening elsewhere to reduce the significance of this area. Nevertheless a belief in the 'east of Suez' policy was not confined to Home. It was continued by the succeeding Labour government, until economic pressures forced its abandonment

For Home, however, the cardinal feature of British policy
was the American alliance, though it remained important to
restrain any American tendency to become militarily involved in the Far East, to the detriment of the Western
'Watch on the Elbe'. But Home also recognised that one
could not expect American co-operation in Europe unless
British co-operation were offered in other parts of the
world.

II

In achieving his objectives as foreign secretary, Home had
the advantage of the kind of standing in the party and in
the government which derived from years of continuous service at cabinet level. This, added to the respect felt
for his personal qualities, was a considerable asset. His
position on the right of the party did him no harm in this
regard. He owed his stature with the party to his personal
qualities, not to his right-wing views; but the latter
were seldom a handicap.

Home therefore had little difficulty with the parliamentary party on the whole. When he did it was usually over
some issue where he was rather less right-wing than some
of his party desired - for example, over the Congo and
even more over Rhodesia.[17] Certainly a substantial section
of his party were disappointed that he did not after 1970
impose a settlement in the interests of the white population and that, after his failure to reach an agreed settlement, he continued the Labour government's policy of sanctions and adherence to the famous 'five principles', designed to provide safeguards for African advancement in the
context of Rhodesian self-government.[18] In the Congo
crisis, too, in the sixties there was some feeling that he
acquiesced too readily in UN actions. On the other hand,
there were members of the liberal wing of the party who
were occasionally critical of his defence of British ties
with South Africa or Portugal, and thought him sometimes
too inflexible and unyielding vis-a-vis Russia. But these
issues caused him little difficulty, and on the whole
brought him into confrontation with the Opposition rather
than with his own party. This also applied to his views
on Israel in his second term of office, expressed in a
characteristically unequivocal fashion in a speech at
Harrogate in 1971, when he advocated the evacuation of

much of the occupied Egyptian territory in return for a
more satisfactory Israeli frontier and iron-clad guarantees of Israeli security. It was the Labour Party, in
which pro-Israel sentiment is greatest, which reacted most
strongly, though Home had some pro-Israel members on his
own side to deal with. Yet he was advocating a realistic
and sensible policy, as others were later to see.

   In general Home was held in high regard by the bulk of
the party, and assured of their support. This was even
more the case in his second period of office than his
first, after he had gained additional respect by his surrender of the leadership and his willingness to serve under his successor. His prestige thereafter was supremely
high, and it is generally agreed that no one else could
have persuaded reluctant Conservative backbenchers to
accept the sanctions policy against Rhodesia year after
year.[19]

   For one whose views were often anathema to a large section of their members, Home also had surprisingly good
relations with the Opposition, particularly after his return to the Commons in 1963 brought him into closer contact
with them. He was therefore able in general to maintain a
fairly high degree of 'bipartisanship'. This was achieved
partly through his essential likeability - he was almost
invariably courteous to the Opposition - and partly by his
accessibility to Opposition spokesmen on foreign affairs.

   Home, as has been noted, was also in a strong position
in the Cabinet from the beginning, and this too became
stronger as time went by. His colleagues liked and respected him personally, and came to respect his judgement
in foreign affairs more and more. One minister who sat
beside him in Cabinet thought that in general 'once he had
spoken the matter was decided', a judgement which suggests
that his authority in Cabinet on his own ground was comparable to that of Anthony Eden at his peak. Partly this
was due to the fact that he was careful to discuss issues
with his prime minister before Cabinet decisions. Home
was, of course, occasionally opposed in Cabinet, for
example over the Congo intervention, and later over the
policy of relying on the US to help Britain out of the
dilemma caused by the cancellation of the Skybolt missile
in 1962, when the minister of defence, Peter Thorneycroft,

152

wished to adopt a tougher line with the US than Home
advocated.[20] However, those who already were, or subsequently became, his colleagues soon came to recognise, as
Lord Hill has put it, 'a tough and penetrating mind'.[21]
At an early stage of Home's first period at the Foreign
Office his conduct of the Laotian crisis and especially
his handling of the Americans in that crisis commanded
their respect.[22] His authority was increased by the evident fact that he had Macmillan's full support as prime
minister in the 1960-3 period and that Heath generally
appeared to defer to his judgement on foreign affairs in
the 1970 government - or at least seldom openly dissented
from it in Cabinet. This relationship is always important,
and on this point it is clear that Home was on generally
good terms with both prime ministers and enjoyed their confidence and support.[23] But the two relationships were
different, if only because Home's stature as an 'elder
statesman' and former prime minister was much higher in
1970 than ten years earlier; and Macmillan's prestige
and experience as a successful prime minister was at its
height in 1960, while in 1970 Heath still had to create
his.

It helped considerably in the first case that both
Macmillan and Home were aware from their own experience of
the difficulties which could arise from any divergence
between premier and foreign secretary and of the importance
of avoiding it. Home had observed at close quarters the
unhappy results of Neville Chamberlain's breach with Eden.
He therefore made a point of insisting that he saw the
prime minister alone about once a week for a brief discussion of current foreign issues.[24] As a result partly of
this sort of precaution, and partly because on most issues
their views were not too far apart, no serious divergence
ever emerged between Home and Macmillan. There were, however, occasions when they differed. Apart from the issue
of 'summitry', on the major issue of Berlin and the German
problem Home was chary of concessions and more cautious
than Macmillan in recommending them to the Americans.
Home indeed was adamant on the status of West Berlin; and
on other German issues took his customary position that
concessions should only be made in return for a substantial
quid pro quo.[25] Home, however, was loyal to his political
chief, even where he differed from him, and on certain
issues recognised that the prime minister would 'make the

running'. This particularly applied to the nuclear test-
ban treaty and the application to enter the EEC, where he
recognised that Macmillan's heart and mind were deeply engaged, and which to some extent were handled directly between Macmillan and Kennedy or de Gaulle. Nevertheless
his junior ministers who were engaged in the detailed negotiations on these issues always felt that he knew what
was going on and was fully 'in the picture'.[26]

Much the same might be said about European issues and
entry into the Common Market in the 1970 government, where
Home likewise recognised not only Heath's ultimate authority as premier, but also his dominant concern and expertise in this field.[27] Here again he took care to insist
on frequent and regular meetings with the premier, so that
he was always fully informed; and the two men were in fact
agreed on the necessity of entry.

Home's relationship with Heath was, as has been indicated,
different from that with Macmillan, though in both cases a
fairly close identity of view was preserved throughout on
most issues, and Home, it is clear, felt he could rely on
the support of both. Heath, however, had the reputation
of not being the easiest man to work with and the circumstances were difficult for both men, as they are bound to
be when a former subordinate becomes the senior. It is to
the credit of both that they worked well together for three
and a half years. Heath was very conscious of his authority as prime minister – few men have been more determined
to exercise it to the full. But he was equally conscious
that Home's prestige and experience were considerable
assets to his government, and that some of the party had
an even higher respect for Home than they had for him. It
is clear that he was always anxious to maintain a cordial
relationship with Home.[28]

Some differences of opinion there undoubtedly were.
Over the issue of arms for South Africa, for example, Home
was as strongly in favour of the policy as Heath, but was
more conciliatory than the latter in his handling of pro-
tests from the African Commonwealth members. There also
seems to have been some difference between the two over
British policy towards the Indo-Pakistan war of 1970.
Heath was rightly concerned to repair British relations
with India, which had deteriorated under the previous

154

government. He was prepared to accept the independence of
Bangladesh, even if it meant Pakistan leaving the Commonwealth; as in fact it ultimately did. Home however had
always felt that the partition of the Indian sub-continent
had been a tragedy, and that further partitition should be
avoided if possible. He may also have been influenced in
his attitude a little – he would not have been human if he
had not – by his recollection that India had always seemed
to him to have had an unrealistic and unhelpful attitude
in the cold war, and had shown a tendency towards the
'double standards' of which he so much disapproved, by
using force to annexe Goa, while condemning Britain for
using force at Suez. It was argued by defenders of the
Indian action that the use of force is justifiable in a
good cause. But that argument, Home felt, is almost invariably used to justify the use of force, whatever the
circumstances. Basically, Home wished to keep links with
both countries and to try to build bridges between them.
But Britain was not in fact in a position to intervene to
any effect in the conflict; and eventually Home seems to
have decided that Heath as premier must have the last
word.

   In his relations with the Foreign Office itself there was
never any doubt from the beginning who was in charge. Home
was a good listener, and respected the expertise of advisers, who he recognised were very good in their own field.
He recognised, too, that it was the duty of officials to
put the arguments before him, if their views differed from
his, and his to listen to them. Equally, he had the clearest possible idea of what the functions of the civil servant and the minister were, and had no difficulty in exercising the minister's function to decide. Since the best
civil servants prefer a minister who knows his own mind –
provided it is a sensible mind – he very soon won their
respect and regard. For his part he regarded the Foreign
Office as probably the best department he had worked in,
and staffed by the ablest men; and he approved of the way
in which juniors were brought into office meetings on sub-
jects they specialised in and enccuraged to speak their
minds.[29]

   There were, of course, occasions when he had differences
of opinion with his advisers. On the highly controversial
matter of a Rhodesian settlement after 1970, he recognised

no doubt, that he himself was prepared to go further in the direction of conciliating white opinion in order to get a settlement than many of his advisers thought wise or desirable. Indeed Sir Hugh Foot, the British representative at the UN, resigned on this issue. In this context his officials were more inclined to worry about Commonwealth reactions, especially in Africa; particularly since by 1970 the Foreign Office had absorbed the Commonwealth Relations Office, and thereofre its advice reflected Commonwealth opinion more strongly.

Much the same was true on the issue of arms for South Africa, where the sale of frigates to that country by the UK in 1970 was also opposed by the weight of official advice, largely because of African reactions. On the crucial question of detente with Russia, on the other hand, there were in the sixties different views within the Office, some leaning more to Macmillan's flexibility, some towards Home's cautious approach. Home always felt, however, that whatever the differences of opinion with them, once the decision had been made, he received the most complete co-operation from the officials.[30] He never felt in danger of being unduly 'managed' by them: and they found him a decisive and authoritative minister, who they felt could be relied upon to put a case clearly in Cabinet and to foreign governments, and whose high standing was an advantage, both in commanding attention for his point of view and in convincing foreign diplomats that what he said would be supported by the government as a whole. Moreover, they appreciated the fact that he was unlikely to commit himself to any initiative which his colleagues would not support or which for other reasons the British Government could not perform.[31]

In his management of the Office, as in other matters, Home was not temperamentally an innovator. If the machine was running well he saw no reason to tamper with it. He recognised, however, in his first period, that the eventual amalgamation of the Foreign Office with the CRO and Colonial Office was probably inevitable and desirable in the long run. As commonwealth relations secretary he had experienced the disadvantages of the dual and conflicting responsibilities of the two ministries, for example in relation to the Central African Federation.[32] In his second term of office, after the amalgamation of the three departments, he found that it had the incidental disadvantage of increasing the foreign secretary's burdens, since he had more countries and more envoys to deal with. He himself had now returned to the Commons after relinquishing his hereditary title, and consequently had an MP's normal parliamentary duties to perform. He also had less junior ministers to help him than had been the case in the previous Labour government — three instead of five — but he made full use of them, continuing, as in his previous tenure, to allot a wide area for each to deal with, and giving them a good deal of discretion, relying on their common sense to know when to consult him.[33] This sensible policy both lightened his burdens and made him a popular minister to work for.

Though successful in so many fields — with his colleagues, his juniors, his officials and his backbenchers — Home was less successful, at any rate in his first term, in putting himself over to the public. He was not very effective on television, and was not the kind of colourful character who provided good copy for reporters: nor did he specialise in the kind of meaningful ambiguities and occasional indiscretions which made R.A.Butler, for example, popular with the press. This did not matter much between 1960 and 1963. Home in the Lords supervised the detailed conduct of foreign policy and controlled the Office, while that superb performer Harold Macmillan looked after the problems of public relations and public opinion with consummate mastery of the necessary techniques. In this respect, as in others, the two men admirably complemented each other. A poor 'public image' was more of a disadvantage to Home later, as prime minister; but by the time he returned to the Foreign Office in 1970 he was better known to the general public, and his qualities were more widely appreciated.

In his conduct of British foreign policy spanning a period of nearly fourteen years, Home was of course subject to the same constraints as other foreign secretaries. The diminishing power and authority of Britain through her persistent economic weakness and the shrinking of empire lessened the choices open to a foreign secretary and diminished the effectiveness of his initiatives. The contrast in this respect between 1960 and a decade later was very marked. In the earlier period Britain still controlled

large areas of the globe and was active in Europe, the
Middle East, South-East Asia and Africa, where imperial
problems still bulked large. In addition Britain was
still very much one of the 'Big Three'. Her policies
counted for a great deal in East-West relations, for example, in the disarmament negotiations and over Berlin and
Germany; and she was very active at the UN. The 'special
relationship' with the US remained significant, and although there were divergences between Britain and the US,
for example over the Congo, the US government was always
anxious to know Britain's views.[34] By 1970 much of this
had gone and Britain's effective sphere, as well as her
commitments, had virtually been reduced to Europe.

His appreciation of the lessening significance of the
Commonwealth has already been discussed. It stemmed both
from a realistic appraisal of the diminishing economic
ties and from the judgement that the Commonwealth, lacking
any kind of political unity or harmony of views, could
never really be an effective force in international affairs,
useful though it might be as a multi-racial forum for the
discussion of common problems. He saw that its members
frequently differed with each other, as well as with the
mother country. Moreover, the Asian members as well as
Canada had shown little sympathy for Britain in her desire
to protect her vital interests at the time of the Suez
crisis. On what Home probably regarded as the main issue
in the post-war world, the cold war, there was no Commonwealth unity whatsoever and the difference of view if anything increased with time. In 1971, indeed, India signed
a twenty-year treaty with the Soviet Union, Britain's main
antagonist in the world for the past twenty-five years,
while Pakistan had already moved close to China and in
1973 left the Commonwealth. South Africa was expelled
from the Commonwealth in Home's first period, yet the defence links with her remained stronger than those with new
Commonwealth members. One could not realistically feel
that Britain's shaky fortunes could be allowed to rest on
such an uncertain foundation.

In addition, by 1970 the Anglo-American 'special relationship' had declined considerably from the importance it
had had in the days of Macmillan and Kennedy, when the two
men corresponded regularly on a wide variety of common
international problems and talked daily to each other on

the 'hot line' during major crises such as that over Cuba.
In the seventies the United States showed little inclination to consult regularly or fully with the British government, even on issues where British policy had been made to
depend on US policy, such as the detente with Communist
China and the withdrawal of recognition from the Nationalist regime on Taiwan. There was in fact some feeling in
the Foreign Office that the US had stolen a march over
Britain on this issue, after originally asking her to hold
back.[35] There was also little consultation on the Middle
East, still of vital concern in Britain, with the closure
of the Canal and the threat of Arab oil sanctions.
Kissinger's celebrated initiatives were largely conducted
on a unilateral basis. Not surprisingly, British and
American policies sometimes diverged, for example in relation to the Indo-Pakistan war of 1971 and later in
Cyprus. Home drew the obvious conclusions from all this.
In 1960 he had already become cautiously convinced that
economics and politics both dictated that Britain opt for
Europe. By 1970 he was probably as sure as his leader
Heath that 'the three-circle concept of British foreign
policy was for all practical purposes eclipsed... there
could be no other circle for Britain than Europe'.[36]

III

In judging Home's conduct of British foreign policy it is
clear that a good deal of weight must be attached to his
handling in his first term of three major crises - Berlin,
Laos and the Congo. In the first two cases the US was
directly involved, and the respective balance of power
between the two countries meant that Home's ability to
make British policy effective depended mainly on his and
Macmillan's ability to influence the Americans. As it
happened, events favoured them in this task, though it
did not seem so at first. At the height of the Berlin
crisis and at the outset of that on Laos the Eisenhower
administration left office. A young and untried president
succeeded, with a secretary of state in Dean Rusk who, it
must be said, was a promoted civil servant who never
seemed quite to make the transition from an executive and
adviser to a policy-maker.[37] These two men succeeded
Eisenhower and Christian Herter, with whom Macmillan and
Home respectively had had very good relations - in the
case of the Macmillan-Eisenhower relationship, based on

an old friendship. Eisenhower, however, was a senior and
experienced statesman. Kennedy was not; but he was prepared to listen to anyone who seemed to have ideas, and
therefore to listen to Macmillan who had plenty. Fortunately the two men established a close and friendly relationship almost from the beginning, at meetings in Florida,
Washington and London in 1961.[38] Home too made a good
impression on the new administration during the Washington
visit.

Inevitably the Kennedy administration took a little time
to find its feet, and in the spring and summer of 1961 was
groping towards a policy on both Laos and Berlin. Kennedy
found the State Department under Rusk irritatingly slow
and weak, and was not helped by this. It was possible
therefore for skilful diplomacy by Home and Macmillan to
exert some influence on him, though it was probably greater on Laos than Berlin. In so far as it had effect, that
diplomacy probably served most usefully in strengthening
Kennedy against the 'hawks' in his own administration.[39]

As has been noted, the Berlin crisis dated from 1958.
The West was being pressured, as in the crisis of 1948-9,
to abandon Berlin, and to recognise East Germany - and
this with no effective Soviet concession in return. The
situation in the spring and summer of 1961 was certainly
a dangerous one, as Kennedy strove to find some middle
way between the tough line, virtually ruling out negotiations, advocated by Dean Acheson, and the belief of others
in his administration in a 'negotiating position', though
without a very clear idea of what it should be. In this
situation Macmillan, afraid that the US without a clearly
defined policy might blunder into war, urged various possible concessions as bargaining counters, with a view to
getting detente moving again after the collapse of the
1960 summit meeting with Khrushchev. Negotiations over
Berlin might form part of a general German and European
settlement, and help towards progress on disarmament,
particularly in the area of test-ban treaty negotiations.[40]
Home, however, felt that there should be no yielding on
the crucial point of Western rights in Berlin and the
essential freedom of Berliners to have what political and
other links with the West they wished; and that the Oder-
Neisse line should only be recognised as the frontier
between Germany and Poland in return for a substantial and

160

concrete quid pro quo. He was not in fact very optimistic
about the prospects of general negotiations on German problems, embarked on under threat, though prepared to negotiate on the limited issue of Western access to Berlin, if
the Russians looked like being reasonable. He was perhaps
not very far from de Gaulle's position, which was that
general negotiations with the Russians could only lead to
the erosion of Western rights. De Gaulle and Adenauer,
indeed, were if anything more inflexible than Home, as
were some of Kennedy's advisers such as Acheson.[41] Home
took the view that if one stood firm, the Russians usually
backed down, and they could be expected to in this case.
Macmillan, anxious to secure a real detente and as its
first-fruits a test-ban treaty, was more flexible in his
approach. No major divergence between the two opened up,
perhaps because West German obstruction and Soviet unres-
ponsiveness prevented a deal on Berlin. So Macmillan's
theories were never really put to the test.

Throughout the crisis Home was content to try to exercise a restraining influence on the US, while remaining
firm in the fact of Russian threats. This he thought
might eventually lead Khrushchev to back down. Perhaps
negotiations might then be worthwhile, to get the Russians
to reaffirm the status quo in Berlin: but basically there
was very little to negotiate about. His skill was shown
mainly in reconciling the slightly different points of
view of himself and his chief in dealing with the Americans and in helping to maintain a united front in facing
the Russians, in spite of differences of view within the
camp of the Western powers. At the Western Foreign Ministers' conference in August 1961, he was prepared to support a four-power conference with the Russians if necessary, but was probably not unduly perturbed when French
objections and American hesitancy ruled this out.

Finally Khrushchev broke the 'log-jam' by building the
Berlin Wall and so staunching the massive flow of refugees
to the West through this outlet - the main concern of both
the Soviet and the East German governments in the whole
business. It seems possible that the firm Western posture
which Home had played his part in maintaining was beginning to convince the Russians that the West was not going
to give way, and that continued pressure involved the risk
of nuclear war. Having, at all events, secured his minimum

objective by this expedient, Khrushchev was able to retreat a little on the maximum aims, and in October 1961
withdrew his threat to sign a separate peace treaty by
the end of the year. With this volte-face, the crisis
began to diminish, though the situation remained dangerous. Occasional harassment of Western air-traffic continued, and on one occasion in 1962 Home and Rusk had to
talk in very strong terms to Gromyko, the Soviet foreign
minister, and impress on him the risks of this course.[42]
It was clearly the Cuban missile crisis of 1962 which
finally jolted Khrushchev into a more cautious attitude,
in Berlin and elsewhere,[43] and one should not exaggerate
the influence of British policy in all this, or the particular role of Home himself. But undoubtedly Home played
a valuable and steadying part.

In the Laotian crisis, which came to a head at the beginning of 1961, rather similar factors obtained, in that
initial US doubts and uncertainties about policy enabled
Britain to exert some leverage. Here Home had a particular instrument to hand, in that Britain was co-chairman
with Russia of the International Control Commission for
Indo-China, set up by the Geneva Conference of 1954, but
persistently hamstrung in its work by the vetoes of the
Communist members. In Laos the right-wing royalist government, backed by the Americans, was threatened by
Communist insurgency in the north, likewise supported by
the Russians with arms. American policy under the Eisen-
hower-Dulles regime had made things worse by undiscrimina-
ting support for right-wing groups, which had driven the
neutralist elements into the arms of the Communists.
Kennedy, in fact, fairly soon came to the conclusion that
a neutral Laos, rather than a Laos committed to the US,
was the right objective to aim at. But the position was
not simple. US prestige had to some extent become committed, and there was a risk of a complete Communist take-
over in Laos: it might not be possible to win the neutralists back and persuade them to join in a government
acceptable to both the US and Russia. The problem was to
warn off the Russians by giving the impression of possible
massive US intervention in Laos, without in fact becoming
committed to such intervention.[44]

Home sympathised with the dilemma and with the objective.
But British military advice was that intervention was not

'feasible or likely to be successful':[45] and, as always, Britain wished the US to avoid too deep a commitment in the Far East which might open up opportunities for Russia in Europe. The best answer seemed to be to reactivate the International Control Commission and hope that the Russians would allow it to work and co-operate in encouraging the formation of a neutralist government. It seemed likely that they might, since there was some evidence that the USSR was no more anxious to become heavily committed in Laos than the US. But it would probably help in urging the Soviet leaders in this direction, if the impression were given that US intervention would otherwise be inevitable, supported by her allies. Accordingly, Macmillan, summoned urgently to meet Kennedy in Florida in March, gave a conditional but cautious promise of British support,[46] and Home, always convinced that it was best to talk bluntly to the Russians, simultaneously made a forthright speech at the SEATO conference in Bangkok, pointing out that the security of Thailand, a SEATO member, might be threatened by a Communist Laos, so that all SEATO members were affected.[47]

At the Florida conference and the subsequent Anglo-American meeting in Washington in April, US and British policy towards Laos was harmonised – all being well, the immediate aims were the re-convening of the ICC plus an agreed cease-fire in Laos, followed by a fresh international conference of all the interested parties, including the USSR; the object, a neutralist Laos. At worst, if the policy failed, limited US intervention might then follow, to stiffen Laotian resistance and Thai morale. It is clear that the president was under heavy pressure from some of his advisers to intervene on a large scale and in effect continue the Eisenhower policy of unconditional support for the right-wing contender Phoumi; clear also that, as with Berlin, the new president and his administration were taking time to find their feet and work out a new and more effective policy. Macmillan and Home were able to strengthen Kennedy's hand in resisting more extreme counsels and it is probable that it was partly because of their diplomacy that he took the line he did, overruling a powerful body of State Department and Pentagon opinion.[48] At all events, the medicine worked and at the end of April the Russians accepted Anglo-American policy, joined with Britain in calling for a cease-fire,

163

which was accepted, and supported the re-convening of the ICC and the summoning of a conference. The major crisis was now over, though it took a year's negotiation to bring about a coalition government (in June 1962) and permit the withdrawal of the limited US forces which had been sent. Even then Laos continued to be divided by internecine rivalries, and the conflict between Communist and anti-Communist factions was to continue, until engulfed in the larger Vietnamese war. But the major threat, of a direct US-Soviet confrontation in Laos, had been averted. Because of this, and the fact that two-thirds of Laos remained non-Communist, Home considered the settlement fairly satisfactory.

Home was afterwards to regard this as one of the two or three occasions when Britain was able to influence US policy significantly through Kennedy, the others being the signing of the Test-Ban Treaty and the 'Polaris' agreement in 1962.[49] This was less true of the other major crisis of the period over the Congo. Indeed, Home felt this was one of his failures, since he would if anything have preferred to see an independent Katanga, which seemed to him the most stable element in the situation. He eventually concluded, however, and Macmillan agreed, that to support Katanga would mean an enormous loss of goodwill so far as African leaders were concerned.[50] Nearly all of them were concerned for the security of their frontiers in what were to a large extent artificial states, their limits defined originally by the impact of European colonialism: they regarded attempts to split up the Congo as indirectly a threat to themselves.[51] In these circumstances it seemed wise to accept the idea of UN intervention – even military intervention, as authorised by the Security Council resolution of 14 July 1960 – as the best way of avoiding any pretext for Soviet interference. Home hoped that a unified but federal Congo would emerge. He was equally positive in his view that UN military action should be limited to keeping the peace between rival factions and should not be used to impose a settlement. This qualification, however, was not to be observed.

In the case of the Congo, the Kennedy administration had a clear and definite policy from the beginning, and this limited possible British influence. President Kennedy recognised from the outset that the Congo was the most important African problem and took the same initial view as the British Government, namely that the UN was the best assurance against great-power conflict in the Congo. As his assistant Arthur Schlesinger puts it, 'From the start the new President had a simple and constant view: that unless the UN filled the vacuum in the Congo, there would be no alternative but a direct Soviet-American confrontation... but this would not work unless the central government in Leopoldville possessed authority... a unified Congo therefore seemed the condition for the success of UN policy.'[52] Congolese unity should therefore be preserved.

Holding this view, Kennedy did not share Home's reservations about forceful UN action to preserve that unity and was prepared to support UN forces in their military action against Katanga in September 1961 - action which Home regarded as disgraceful and which he opposed, partly because he thought the UN might be taking on responsibilities which it was inherently unfitted to bear. There was a clear difference of opinion between him and the US, as he subsequently conceded - and in this instance it was US policy which prevailed.[53] Home might still have been able to salvage some elements of British policy objectives from the situation - a reasonably autonomous Katanga under Moishe Tshombe in a federal Congo - but these objectives were vitiated by the unreliability of Tshombe himself. The latter could never be trusted to honour an agreement with the central government, though on more than one occasion Home by patient diplomacy helped to secure one.[54] The British Government therefore had reluctantly to acquiesce in further UN action against Katanga in December 1962, as a result of which Katanganese resistance collapsed and Tshombe finally fled the country. Home regarded the affair as a minor defeat, demonstrating once again that Britain could not prevail in direct opposition to US policy. His prime minister, Macmillan, conceded that US policy in this matter had at least the advantage of being clear and effective. One might add that it was probably the right policy, and certainly what most of the African states and the Western powers were prepared to support.

It was not the case, however, that the UK could never act independently of the US. In the Middle East, for example, Britain was able in July 1961 to intervene militarily to defend Kuwait against the threat of annexation by Iraq, in spite of US doubts; and two years later Britain pursued her own policy of establishing a pro-British federation in Aden and the neighbouring territories of the Persian Gulf and defending the new federation vigorously against attacks from the republican government of the Yemen. In the latter case there was a clear divergence from the US policy of recognising and conciliating the Yemeni republic, but British policy was pursued nonetheless.[55]

Similarly, in South East Asia, towards the end of Home's first term at the Foreign Office, the British policy of creating a federation of Malaysia embracing Malaya, Singapore and the British colonies in North Borneo was pursued in the face of US objections. The Kennedy administration was concerned in this case by the opposition of both the Philippines and Indonesia to the proposed federation. The former was a long-standing US client and SEATO ally, the latter potentially a powerful and wealthy state, whoe movement towards the Communist camp under President Achmed Sukarno should if possible be checked. In this instance Macmillan tended to brush aside US objections; and the policy of vigorous military resistance to Indonesian attacks was pursued from the moment these began, in April 1963, to the end of Home's term of office. But it is perhaps noteworthy that both in relation to the Yemen and Malaysia, Home was, it seems, more concerned not to offend the US than was Macmillan.[56]

A word must also be said about the most dangerous crisis of all - the Cuban missile crisis of October 1962. In this study of Lord Home's work at the Foreign Office it is justifiable to deal with it summarily, if only because, as Home himself recognised, it was largely a matter for American decision; and the British role, though not completely unimportant, was confined largely to providing reassurance and support at the end of the 'hot line'. It is probable that the more cautious attitude of the British helped Kennedy to combat the 'hawks' in his own administration,[57] but in general it was clearly a crisis which the US had to resolve by its own actions. Home's most valuable contribution personally was probably to make it clear to the Russians that Britain would not be led into attempting mediation. He was satisfied at all events not only that US policy was right, but that Britain had been adequately consulted.[58]

166

In October 1963 Home unexpectedly became prime minister, only to lose the 1964 election after a year in office. Soon afterwards he retired from the leadership and magnanimously agreed to serve under the new leader Edward Heath as foreign affairs spokesman. When Heath in turn unexpectedly won an election victory in June 1970, Home again accepted the Foreign Office.[59] Something has already been said of the major preoccupations of this second period. What dominated everything was the renewed application to join the European Economic Community. In this matter de Gaulle's resignation had transformed the scene, though there is some evidence that even that inflexible statesman had been having second thoughts on the issue. Germany had not proved quite the reliable ally that de Gaulle had wished. With Brandt as foreign minister she was already showing disturbing signs of flirting with the concept of an 'Ostpolitik', involving fundamental concessions to the Soviet bloc on such issues as the Oder-Neisse line and recognition of the East German regime. There might be something to be said for having Britain in Europe after all, especially with such an exponent of realism in one's dealings with the USSR as Home at the Foreign Office. De Gaulle's successor Pompidou, with his more pragmatic, businesslike approach, had apparently no difficulty in coming to this conclusion.

Home had little doubt that Britain now had no sensible choice but to enter the EEC if at all possible.[60] All that had happened since 1964 helped to confirm this view. During that time Britain's power had further declined, and the basic cause, the economic malaise, had persisted. The Commonwealth had been further strained by the prolonged arguments over Rhodesia. In addition, Commonwealth economic ties had also become weaker. With the United States the close ties of the Macmillan era had not been continued to the same extent under Presidents Johnson and Nixon. So far as detente with Russia was concerned, that had to some extent been achieved. As one commentator has put it, 'The new mood in Soviet-American relations... seemed to be based in both their minds on a tacit mutual acceptance of the status quo in Europe, including the division of Germany, as for all practical purposes a permanent state of affairs.'[61] But one result of the partial Soviet-American

detente after the Cuban missile crisis had been that the
two super-powers tended more and more to deal <u>a deux</u>. In
spite of the talk of 'seats at the top table' there seemed
little room for Britain in this partnership of the super-
powers.

 The conclusion was inescapable. Britain needed to be
part of the EEC both to rebuild her economic strength within the confines of a larger market and to have any chance
of exerting some influence comparable to that of the two
super-powers. A divided Europe could not hope to do so.
Home therefore supported Heath's policy of renewing the
bid for negotiated entry, while leaving the detailed conduct of the negotiations to another minister, and the
occasional initiatives, designed to overcome difficulties
with the French, to the prime minister. It was Heath who
finally established with Pompidou the Anglo-French entente
which was a necessary prerequisite to a satisfactory outcome of the negotiations. Home was content to keep himself fully informed of all the stages of the negotiations,
but seems to have had no doubts about supporting the acceptance of the terms finally agreed in the summer of 1971.
His influence was necessary, for more than thirty Conservative MPs remained opposed to entry - about the size of the
government's majority. Indeed the Treaty of Accession was
approved in January 1972 by a bare majority of twenty.

 Home was no doubt confirmed in his view by various developments already referred to in Anglo-American and Commonwealth relations. He probably felt, as did Heath, that
Britain had been inadequately consulted by the Americans
about their approach to Communist China in July 1971 and
the consequential withdrawal of recognition from the Chiang
Kai-shek regime on Taiwan; and he shared his leader's
doubts about the American policy of support for Pakistan
in the conflict with India and Bangladesh which began in
November 1971. Here again he regretted the divergence of
Anglo-American policies; but, while not courting a public
breach with the United States, saw this, no doubt, as
further proof that the 'special relationship' was largely
a thing of the past. On the Commonwealth side he found
the Afro-Asian members not only unhelpful on the vexed
Rhodesian question, but also on the necessity, as he saw
it, to build up Britain's position in the Indian Ocean and
strengthen links with South Africa. Though he accepted

their criticisms with his usual courtesy, they probably
helped to confirm his view of the Commonwealth as a waning
asset. Even more, perhaps, the Indian decision to sign a
treaty of alliance with the Soviet Union reinforced this
view.

   Home's main concern, in fact, in the early years of the
Heath government, was not so much Europe as Rhodesia and
southern Africa. He was aware that the party looked to
him to achieve a settlement of the former problem, which
had been a potent source of Conservative disunity since
1964 - a settlement which would safeguard the interests
of the white population, while containing sufficient safeguards for African advancement to make it acceptable to
the Rhodesian Africans and the African Commonwealth, and
so perhaps to the UN also. He may well have thought that
he was possibly the one man who had a chance of success.
He was trusted by the Rhodesian leaders, had the confidence of his party, and was familiar with every aspect of
the issue.[62] As prime minister, Home had tried to persuade Ian Smith in September 1964 to refrain from pushing
for absolute independence. But when Smith nonetheless
unilaterally declared independence in 1965, much though
Home doubted the wisdom of the Labour government's policy
towards Rhodesia, he had felt bound to say that the act
was illegal, and to advise the Conservative conference not
to vote against sanctions, since this might be taken as an
indication of support for UDI.[63] Now, five years later,
Home was faced with a problem of whose intractable nature
he was all too well aware. Nevertheless he was prepared
to risk his reputation to attempt a solution and was very
anxious to secure one. Such a result would, he felt, be
in the interests of both black and white and would put an
end to the damage which had been done for the past six
years to our relationships in Africa. Accordingly he visi-
ted Rhodesia and succeeded in arranging a settlement with
Smith which envisaged a gradual though probably very slow
transition to black majority rule - not in itself a disadvantage, Home thought, since it would give Africans more
time to prepare for self-government. He was extremely
disappointed when the Pearce Commission eventually found
that the Rhodesian Africans' opinion was hostile. The
Africans did not like the settlement nor did they trust
Smith. Home himself probably felt that to impose the
settlement would have been a service to both Africans and

whites. But he was committed by his promise to respect
the findings of the Pearce Commission and was forced to
leave the Rhodesian problem still unsolved when he left
office for the last time in February 1974. He had felt
bound also in the meantime to continue to support the
'five principles' and the UN mandatory sanctions, little
though he probably believed either in the moral justifi-
cation or the practical effectiveness of the latter. He
felt, it seems, that the British Government was committed
to these policies and could not now abandon them without
doing grave harm to Commonwealth relations. But the failure to achieve a solution was one of the biggest dis-
appointments of his political life.

As is so often the case in international politics, one
issue here was linked with others. The raison d'etre of
Home's South African policy was the necessity of naval
bases for the West, to safeguard the routes for oil and
other supplies, after the closure of the Suez Canal in
1967; but he also seems to have hoped, with some reason,
for South African assistance in bringing about a Rhodesian
settlement. Certainly South African policy has been more
helpful in this regard in recent years. But the oil problem also made it desirable to repair British links with
the Arabs; and the 1971 Harrogate speech on the Arab-
Israeli dispute was perhaps prompted by this consideration
among others. Home also considered, no doubt, that Israel
ought to give back some of the occupied territories; and
that it would be wise policy, for at this moment she had
the best opportunity for securing peace with Egypt. Dr
Kissinger's policy in this regard certainly had his support, though Britain now had little power in most of the
Middle East to influence the parties towards a settlement.

On the same flank the issue of security in the Indian
Ocean was linked to the question of policy in the Persian
Gulf and towards the Indian sub-continent. With India
moving towards closer ties with the USSR and Pakistan
with China, neither of Britain's main Commonwealth partners
could be considered reliable. The Central Treaty Organisation - the old Baghdad Pact - was largely dead, but of the
original partners Iran could be considered a firm ally.
The policy of winning her friendship and helping to build
up Iranian armed strength with supplies of modern weapons
was therefore adopted. By the same token it was necessary

170

to play down to some extent the policy, to which both Home
and Heath were committed, of rebuilding the British 'presence' on the other side of the Gulf. The British-supported
minor sheikhdoms of the area were encouraged to form a
closer union, but in deference to Iranian and Saudi Arabian
opinion no attempt was made to recover the position surren-
dered by the Wilson government in Aden and South Yemen. A
powerful Iran seemed a more secure ally to rest on than the
sheiks.

V

To sum up satisfactorily Lord Home's work at the Foreign
Office in one respect presents great difficulty, since so
short a time has passed since he left office. The contemporary historian always has the disadvantage of being close
to the events in question, so that a proper perspective is
difficult to achieve. In the case of Lord Home, anyone
writing only a year or two after his departure from office
must be particularly conscious of the difficulty.

Some aspects of contemporary judgement, however, are not
likely to be reversed by future historians. They will probably accept the contemporary verdict on Home's character
and ability. His competent and authoritative management
of the Foreign Office, his patience and skill in directing
the traditional processes of diplomacy, are not likely to
be denied. That his character commanded the respect of
both officials and colleagues at home and of foreign statesmen abroad is clear. The latter particularly found him always explicit and clear in his exposition of policy, so
that they knew where they were with him: and moreover knew
that he had the support of his government and could usually
deliver anything that he promised. This straightforwardness and refusal to be ambiguous or over-elaborate in his
exposition of foreign policy undoubtedly made that exposition more effective and was generally an advantage in diplomacy. As a public man he never lacked courage; his
decision in his second term of office to expel over a hundred Soviet diplomats for espionage was an example of this.
He was not especially creative: as his biographer puts it,
'he seldom bubbled with new ideas and fresh initiatives'.[64]
But this very quality made him in many ways the ideal foil
for Macmillan's creativeness and imaginativeness, supply-
ing a sometimes useful touch of cold common sense. As a

colleague put it, 'he always kept his feet firmly on the ground'. He was apt, perhaps, to over-simplify, but that also could be an advantage.[65] Certainly the simplicity, even bluntness, of his utterances was often a healthy thing. Whether his views were right or wrong, he helped to clear the air of cant. He himself thought that one of his most valuable services to Britain during his public life was his determination to defend Britain's colonial record, particularly with regard to the grant of self-government, against unfair attacks, and to draw attention to the double standards of those who, at the UN and elsewhere, criticised Western imperialism while turning a blind eye to the Soviet variety.[66]

On his views on some aspects of foreign policy there was and will be less unanimity. Though aware that British power was in decline, he was a little slow to recognise the full implications of this, and continued in the sixties to talk of Britain being in 'the first four batsmen', when the question was whether we could still make the first eleven. In this respect as in relation to some other matters discussed here, his views could sometimes be considered old-fashioned to the point where they became unrealistic. It is still in doubt whether he was right in thinking that a policy of firmness, rather than over-conciliatory appeasement, was the best course in the central issue of our time, the cold war. The fruits of detente are still uncertain and the question is still arguable. But he recognised that there were times when flexibility was appropriate. He was not, that is to say, blindly intransigent, or unwilling to negotiate where there seemed any point in doing so. He was more open to criticism in his attitude towards racialist regimes in southern Africa and Fascist dictatorships in Spain and Portugal, sometimes showing, too, a lack of appreciation of the force of deeply felt moral objections to these regimes. Yet in practice he did in fact realistically often allow Britain's policy to be influenced by considerations of regard for African and world opinion, even when he regarded that opinion as wrong-headed - in relation to Rhodesia for example, or the Congo - and it is, after all, on the policies he actually pursued in the light of all the relevant factors that a foreign secretary must be judged.

There is also a case to be made at least for his views
on some of these issues (one that does not rest solely on
strategic grounds), though, on balance, not a case that
is accepted by the present writer. It could at least be
argued that years of boycotts and moral disapproval had
made comparatively little impression either on South
African apartheid policies (of which Home in fact disapproved) or on the Franco dictatorship. Home was in
fact consistently opposed to trade boycotts, against Cuba
no less than against South Africa.[67] A more conciliatory
attitude might, he thought, have more effect at least in
producing a more helpful policy externally. An examination of the development of South African policy in recent
years, externally if not internally, suggests that there
may perhaps be something in this view; but also that the
weight of international and Commonwealth opinion is not a
factor that any British foreign secretary can or should
ignore.

One final point should perhaps be made, which applies
to Home, as it does to most of those whose work at the
Foreign Office is described here. Wellington once said
that the most difficult test of generalship was the conduct of a successful retreat. To preside over a country's
foreign policy in a period of rapidly declining power is
equally perhaps the acid test of a foreign minister's
capacity, and one from which Lord Home emerged in general
with credit.

CHAPTER 8

R A BUTLER

It is never a very rewarding task to fill a high office of state at the end of a government's term of office, with the knowledge that it will not be very long before one has to vacate it. This was the experience of R.A.Butler, the last of five Conservative ministers who conducted Britain's foreign policy between 1951 and 1964. Butler came to this office following Macmillan's resignation from the premiership, at a time when it seemed that the succession lay between himself and Viscount Hailsham. But it was Lord Home who unexpectedly took over the premiership, and Butler accepted the Foreign Office.[1]

He was well qualified for the post. None of his predecessors had had a wider variety of ministerial experience. He had served in a number of junior ministerial offices, including the Foreign Office, in the thirties and as Minister of Education during the Second World War. From 1951 onwards he had been continuously a member of the Cabinet, holding a succession of high offices, including the Treasury and the Home Office. He also had his liabilities, however; his association with the 'appeasement policies' of Neville Chamberlain and his supposed opposition to the Suez 'advanture' in 1956 had not endeared him to the right wing of the Conservative party. It was this, probably, added to his part in winding up the Central African Federation which decisively cost him the Premiership in 1963.

Throughout his political career, in fact, Butler was something of a puzzle even to his closest associates. Few questioned his intellectual and administrative ability or his constructive contribution to politics. Loyalty to his party and to the government of which he was a member may well have prevented him fron considering resignation over Suez and certainly induced him to serve under Lord Home. Yet his critics still considered that there were flaws in

174

his character and record. They accused him, not of lack
of integrity, but of lack of toughness and decisiveness
and a certain tendency to ambiguity in thought and deed.[2]
They were not always sure where they were with him, and,
so far as the Right were concerned, when they were sure,
they did not always like it. He was certainly by temperament a natural conciliator and mediator, and a man of the
'Establishment', who preferred, when unsuccessful in his
aims, to remain within the fold and try to influence
events, rather than to stage a dramatic resignation. These
characteristics, too, did not appeal to those of his party
who preferred to see both domestic and foreign politics as
a contest to be waged to the death.[3]

   On the other hand, Butler had considerable assets at
this stage of his career. Not only was he able and experienced, but there was much sympathy for his position in
the parliamentary party, many of whom (including some of
his cabinet colleagues) thought that Butler should have
become first minister. His willingness to serve under
Home was applauded; and these factors ensured a sympathetic hearing in the Commons. His officials, too, respected
his ability and expertise and he had good relations with
them.[4] In his actual management of the office, Butler had
little time or instinct to make changes, but he took the
opportunity to implement the recommendations of the Plowden report, improving the conditions and allowances for
staff; and he noted how much more important a factor
economic matters had become in foreign policy, and how
since his previous term in the thirties, a large economic
section had come into being in the Foreign Office as evidence of this fact. In his relations with other departments and particularly in dealing with the Commonwealth
and Colonial Office he had the invaluable assistance of an
able minister of state in Lord Carrington,[5] who spent much
of his time on problems of interdepartmental liaison.
Like previous foreign secretaries, Butler found that the
overlapping responsibilities of the two departments could
occasionally cause difficulties, especially as Cyprus,
Malaysia and Arabia were all trouble-spots during this
period. Fortunately there was little friction between the
two departments.

   Butler came to the Foreign Office, which he would much
have preferred to have achieved earlier in his political

175

career,[6] under the disadvantage of knowing that an election must follow within at most a year and that his party
would probably lose it. In addition Butler had accepted
office as a matter of loyalty, and at the end of twelve
arduous years of ministerial service.[7] Not surprisingly,
he gave the impression to some of his colleagues of a
tired and disappointed man, whose heart was not really in
it.[8] Although his duties were adequately performed he
sometimes gave the impression of being inadequately
briefed and uninterested. One senior official recounts
the story of how a new French ambassador went to see
Butler to obtain an up-to-date picture of British policy
towards France. The ambassador returned after a long and
enjoyable talk of an hour, but on sitting down to write
his report, realised that he had been told exactly nothing.
Perhaps on this occasion, however, Butler was merely repay-
ing Couve de Murville in his own coin. Another senior
official, however, thought Butler ineffective, for two
basic reasons - tiredness after more than a decade in high
office and a short tenure of the post. On the second
point, it is the nature of foreign policy that it takes a
year or two to initiate decisive changes and to set a firm
imprint on its course.[9], Moreover, foreign governments
tend to 'wait and see' and hold back from commitments,
when a government is not expected to remain long in office.
This affected particularly relations with the US and
Russia, both of which for different reasons were during
this year apt to be non-committal in their foreign policies. In Moscow the internal struggle which was to result
in the fall of Khrushchev was already under way and Butler
found the Soviet leaders unresponsive to suggestions that
a further relaxation of tension could be achieved by progress in nuclear disarmament, perhaps by means of a more
comprehensive test-ban treaty or a non-proliferation
treaty. Surprisingly, the Russians were quite anxious for
him to visit Moscow in July 1964, but though he found
Khrushchev and the other Soviet leaders friendly and not
unsympathetic to certain aspects of these proposals, no
immediate progress could be made.

   In Washington the Johnson administration, after the
shock of Kennedy's assassination, was still preoccupied
largely with the task of binding up the domestic wounds
and creating a climate of reassurance at home. Butler
was anxious to test the reality of the 'special relationship'

under the new administration, but did not find his visit
to Washington in May 1964 particularly reassuring in this
respect, though he was well-received, as the prime minister
had been a few months earlier. But in a meeting with the
president, which he did not particularly seek, Butler received the distinct impression that the former's mind was,
to put it mildly, on other things. It was fairly clear
that in their relations with Britain the Americans, like
the Russians, were 'marking time' pending the result of
the 1964 election.[10]

So far as Western Europe was concerned, the outlook was
not much more promising. It was too soon after de Gaulle's
brutal cutting off of the Common Market negotiations to do
very much towards getting the advance towards greater unity
in Europe and British membership moving again. With a view
to improving Anglo-French relations, Butler took the opportunity that occurred of attempting to melt a little the
glacial Couve de Murville. But nothing much could be done
so long as de Gaulle stood like a giant road-block in the
way, and in this as in other respects, de Murville was the
perfect instrument of his master's will.[11]

British policy had more importance in relation to three
lesser but difficult problems which persisted during
Butler's year in office - those relating to Malaysia,
southern Arabia and Cyprus. It will be evident from the
previous chapter that American and British policy had diverged somewhat over Malaysia. The US had continued to
give Indonesia aid, even after the latter's President
Sukarno had launched a policy of harassment and guerrilla
activity, designed to break up the British-sponsored
Malaysian Federation and annexe the North Borneo Territories which belonged to it. American pressure had been
brought to bear unsuccessfully on Britain to soften her
policy of vigorous resistance to Indonesian attacks, which
the US thought might drive Sukarno further into the Communist camp. Home's visit to Washington, during which he
talked plainly to the Americans, had helped in this respect,
and produced a communique in which President Johnson publicly identified the US with 'the peaceful national independence of Malaysia'. What helped more, however, was
Sukarno's steady progress towards close links with communist China and his domestic reliance on the Indonesian
communist party. Eventually the US, disillusioned,

withdrew its support, but during Butler's year in office
it was always necessary for him to maintain pressure on
the Americans. A settlement did not come until some time
later, and in the meantime British troops and ships continued to fight off Indonesia at considerable cost.[12]

In relation to southern Arabia also, British and US policy had diverged somewhat towards the end of the Macmillan
era. In the civil war in the Yemen between republican and
royalist factions, which broke out in 1962, the former
supported by Egyptian troops and the latter by Saudi
Arabia, the US had sought to conciliate President Nasser
of Egypt by recognising the republican government, while
at the same time trying to satisfy its Saudi Arabian
friends by persuading Nasser to withdraw. Britain, having
little faith in Nasser's goodwill and anxious for the security of its Aden base and the friendly Gulf sheikhdoms if
the republicans won, had adopted a more pro-royalist stance,
which had the incidental advantage of restoring more
friendly relations with Saudi Arabia, after previous difficulties over the Buraimi Oasis and Abu Dhabi. Arguments
between London and Washington had continued, with Britain
still withholding recognition, but here too the Johnson
administration began to show signs of disillusionment with
its protege President Nasser, who like Sukarno seemed to
be turning more and more to the communist world for aid,
though to the USSR rather than China. Moreover, US policy
had not produced the withdrawal of Egyptian troops, which
had indeed attacked Saudi Arabia. The Egyptian presence
in the Yemen seemed therefore to threaten the vast US oil
interests in that quarter.[13] This put a different complex-
ion on the matter. By 1964, therefore, US policy in the
area had shifted to the point where Butler could subsequently write, 'The Americans were usually, but not invariably sympathetic about areas where British troops were
involved in action.'[14] But on this matter too, it was
always necessary for the Foreign Office to maintain pressure through the US ambassador.

It was Cyprus, however, which seemed likely in this period to prove the most dangerous, involving the risk of a
direct confrontation between two NATO allies, Turkey and
Greece. Since Cyprus had become an independent Commonwealth country in Selwyn Lloyd's settlement of 1960, the
question of 'Enosis' or Cypriot Union with Greece, which

178

Turkey violently opposed, had dropped for the time into
the background. On the other hand, the treatment of the
Turkish minority by the Greek majority under the government of President Makarios had not been wise, though
again there had been provocation on both sides. In the
early months of 1964 violence broke out and Turkey threatened to invade Cyprus to protect its minority; fresh
troops had to be dispatched to British bases on the island.
During the crisis Butler worked closely with the US ambassador, with whom he saw the Turkish ambassador almost
every day.[15] Their combined pressure averted the threatened invasion, and the dispatch of a UN peace-keeping
force in March 1964 defused the crisis. The importance
and scope of this achievement can be measured by the
events of 1974 when, with Britain weaker and US policy
less helpful, the catastrophe of a Turkish invasion actually occurred.

Overall, in spite of the factors which tended to weaken
British influence in Washington, the essential unity of
the Anglo-American alliance was maintained. On defence
and economic matters Butler was personally less involved,
and he played little part in the abortive discussions on
the American proposal for a multilateral force,[16] designed
to give NATO countries, including West Germany, some access
to the nuclear deterrent. He remained in office, however,
just long enough to see the conference begin at Geneva on
the 'Kennedy round' of trade talks, designed to reduce
world tariff levels.

In all his dealings with Washington, Butler had the support and help of the prime minister, Sir Alec Douglas-
Home, and a word should be said about this relationship,
always so important for a foreign secretary. For obvious
reasons the situation could have been a difficult one, but
Home's tact and the call of other matters on his mind in
this period, most of all the necessity of making himself
known to the British electorate, prevented any friction.
Home's natural good sense precluded unnecessary interference, and he was no doubt satisfied to leave the day-to-
day conduct of foreign policy in experienced hands. Home's
biographer suggests that Butler welcomed a lead from the
prime minister in foreign policy matters, but Lord Home's
natural preference was always for the avoidance of unnecessary interference.[17]

As Butler has himself said in his memoirs, his aim in the limited time he had in this post was 'not so much to achieve, as to probe'.[18] Indeed, there were few achievements on the cards in the international and domestic circumstances described. He was able to keep relations with Washington on even keel, to indicate to Moscow and Paris that doors were still open, to continue the defence of British interests in South-East Asia and southern Arabia, and to help avert real dangers in Cyprus. With that he was probably content. His standing in the history books will rest on other and more substantial achievements than his conduct of British foreign affairs for a brief period at the end of his political career.

CHAPTER 9

PATRICK GORDON-WALKER

Patrick Gordon-Walker was not even a Member of Parliament
when he became the first Labour foreign secretary for
thirteen years in October 1964. Along with Harold Wilson,
the prime minister, and James Griffiths, the secretary of
state for Wales, Gordon-Walker was a survivor from the
Attlee cabinet and still active on the Labour Party front
bench. He had been the secretary of state for commonwealth relations from 1950 until the Labour government
left office in October 1951. Prior to that he had been
under-secretary at the same office for three years and,
in 1946, only a year after his election to Parliament, he
had become the parliamentary private secretary to Herbert
Morrison. After the loss of office, he remained a Member
of Parliament for the whole of the period in Opposition.
He was elected to the Parliamentary Committee (shadow
cabinet) of the Parliamentary Labour Party in November
1957 and had from that date held the shadow portfolio in
home affairs and defence before becoming, in 1963, the
shadow foreign secretary. It was ironic that at the moment when the Labour Party returned to power and Gordon-
Walker found himself once more a cabinet minister he
should lose his Parliamentary seat in Smethwick, a seat
which he had held for nineteen years.

   Gordon-Walker was both by background and temperament
very different from the two other post-war foreign secretaries which the Labour Party had provided. He was neither
a trade union leader nor an experienced political opera-
tor in local government. His background was almost exclusively in education and then in politics. Even after
Labour's defeat in 1951 he was active in the conduct of
the Opposition as a young former cabinet minister, although he had to wait some years before he was elected to
the shadow cabinet. His experience in government was limited to commonwealth relations, but his scope had been
broadened during his years in opposition. In the run-up

to the 1964 general election, Gordon-Walker had spent some
time preparing to become the secretary of state for defence
should Labour be victorious. However, with the death of
Hugh Gaitskell and the subsequent election of Harold
Wilson to the leadership, Gordon-Walker was invited to fill
the vacant post of shadow foreign secretary. This promotion was a considerable personal achievement for a man who
had no identifiable personal following within the Parliamentary Labour Party. As a man who was probably right of
centre he could not expect left-wing support, nor was he
assured of the support of trade union members. It was,
thus, a measure of the respect he commanded within the
parliamentary party that he was elected to its Parliamentary Committee, which was the subject of annual, highly
competitive, elections. However, outside Parliament, he
never really made a mark in the Labour hierarchy. A
little over a year after this appointment, he found himself established as the first Labour foreign secretary for
thirteen years.

The fact that he was not a Member of Parliament does not
seem to have substantially affected Gordon-Walker's position as foreign secretary except in the rather obvious way
of preventing him from speaking or answering questions in
the House of Commons. Indeed, there was a lot of sympathy
for him from his fellow ministers and from Labour supporters generally. This sympathy was based on a dislike of
the methods used by the supporters of Mr Peter Griffiths,
the Conservative candidate who won Smethwick from Gordon-
Walker with a swing of 7 per cent, very much against the
national trend. It was widely believed that the introduction of the immigration issue into his campaign had affected the result.[1] The tactics used in the campaign were
roundly condemned and the prime minister was in the forefront of those who reacted strongly against them. In his
speech during the debate on the Government's legislative
programme, Harold Wilson referred to the absence of the
foreign secretary after 'a squalid campaign' and ended by
warning that the new member for Smethwick might find himself being treated as a 'parliamentary leper'.[2] Many
Opposition members took exception to this remark which
clearly demonstrated the strength of government feeling
over the issue of race in British politics. Although
Gordon-Walker could expect a reasonable honeymoon period,
it was clear than an early return to Parliament was

essential for the new foreign secretary. The simplest
solution would have been to ennoble him, as Wilson was to
do to another minister, Alun Gwynne Jones, who as Lord
Chalfont became minister of state at the Foreign Office.
This solution appears not to have been considered feasible,
Harold Wilson recorded in his memoirs that Gordon-Walker
'would be looking for an alternative seat'.[3] In addition
Labour was in a cleft stick on the question of having a
foreign secretary in the House of Lords as a result of its
vitriolic attacks on the appointment of the then Lord Home
as foreign secretary by Harold Macmillan in 1960. Hence
Gordon-Walker had to combine his activities as foreign
secretary which involved a fair amount of travelling and
a full-time commitment with the equally arduous task of
seeking and winning a parliamentary seat. Ultimately this
task proved beyond him, and, having failed on a second
occasion, this time at Leyton, to gain a seat at Westminster, Gordon-Walker resigned as foreign secretary three
months after his appointment.

Despite the shortness of his period in office, Gordon-
Walker did play an active role both in the conduct of
foreign policy and in the introduction of a number of new
ideas. However, he was not a believer in the idea of
'socialist' foreign policy, in so far as it implied a
radical change in the content of the foreign policy to be
pursued. Neither the ideas of neutralism nor those of unilateral nuclear disarmament appealed to him; he accepted
the view that the immutable facts of geography meant that
little change was possible.[4] On the other hand, he was
determined to widen the basis of foreign-policy-making not
only by improving the planning machinery but also by the
introduction of a process of high-powered discussions between Foreign Office officials and outside experts, a process which was extended by George Brown when he took over
the Foreign Office. In addition to this, Gordon Walker
set out to change the emphasis given by the Foreign Office
to various parts of the globe. For instance, he sought to
increase the importance of the ambassadorial posts in
Eastern Europe which he regarded as 'true nations, not
satellites',[5] thus foreshadowing a period when relations
with that part of the world would become increasingly significant to the Western alliance. He was also responsible
for the appointment of Sir Paul (now Lord) Gore-Booth as
the successor for Sir Harold (Lord) Caccia as permanent

secretary at the Foreign Office, even though the former did not take up his appointment until after Gordon-Walker had left office. Gore-Booth was in some ways a controversial appointment in so far as he was not the person whom many of the Foreign Office establishment had expected would get the job. Gordon-Walker had known and liked Gore-Booth from his previous ministerial experience and his qualifications were clearly acceptable.

In general the relations between Gordon-Walker and his officials were quite good and the change from a Conservative to a Labour administration went as smoothly in the Foreign Office as it did in other departments of state. One reason for this was clearly the fact that although he was intent on changing some of the emphasis within the Foreign Office, no fundamental changes were expected or contemplated by him in the overall strategy of British foreign policy. Whilst it was probably true that the idea of Britain being at the focal point of the Churchillian interlocking circles had ceased to be the underlying philosophy of British foreign policy, it was not clear at this time what had taken place. The application to join the European Economic Community (EEC) had been opposed by Labour in opposition, but Gordon-Walker does not seem to have gone to the Foreign Office with any real alternative 'grand strategy'. He was, like many Labour ministers, prepared to modify the existing policies whilst carefully avoiding any more fundamental reform. This is not to place the blame exclusively on Gordon-Walker; indeed the Labour Party itself had few well-conceived ideas about changing British foreign policy. The Labour manifesto,[6] for example, concentrated much more on domestic policy and domestic reform. On foreign policy there was little more than the usual trite phrases. The major areas of difference seemed to be in the primacy to be given to relations with the Commonwealth whilst still seeking to 'achieve closer links with our European neighbours'[7] and the dispute over nuclear defence. The manifesto promised the appointment of a minister for disarmament, promised a new lead at the United Nations and outlined a number of policies to be pursued to reduce cold war tension. All these proposals, however, were made within the general parameters of the bipartisan foreign policy strategy and no attempt was made at reformulating Britain's long-term foreign policy goals.

Despite the fact that it may have lacked a clear long-term strategy in foreign policy, the Labour Party in general and Gordon-Walker in particular had given some thought to more immediate questions. In addition to the changes mentioned above, Gordon-Walker had also suggested in an article published before he became foreign secretary[8] a number of policy areas which a future Labour government would regard as being of high priority. Whilst much of this article could be regarded as being common ground between the two main parties, there were some areas of distinction. Whilst the Labour Party shared the Conservative Party's acceptance of the importance of the Western alliance and the necessity to maintain British interests around the world including east of Suez so that Britain would be 'the most significant of (the) great powers',[9] they differed from them in their interpretation of how to achieve these ends. The most significant areas of difference lay in the approach to the future development of the Atlantic Pact. The need for change was accepted by all parties because the demands from Western European states for a share in the control over the alliance's nuclear strategy had to be met.

The initial proposal was President Kennedy's 'grand design' for an Atlantic partnership consisting of two equal pillars: one American, the other European. The rejection of Britain's EEC application by de Gaulle, who was becoming increasingly maverick in his attitude towards NATO in general and the United States in particular, marked the final demise of the 'grand design'. It was against this background that the United States proposed the multilateral force (MLF) as an alternative. The Labour Party rejected both the proposals for the MLF, a device for spreading control of nuclear weapons without spreading the weapons themselves to NATO members including West Germany, and the maintenance by Britain of a nuclear strike force. Gordon-Walker promised that new arrangements with Washington would be negotiated in an effort to give all the Alliance partners a real say 'in the formulation of the ideas, policy and strategy'[10] of the Alliance. This, the Labour Party believed, was a preferable alternative to the MLF. Before undertaking this task, the Labour Government conducted a review of defence and foreign policy and found that despite its promise to phase out the British nuclear force, 'production of the (Polaris) submarines was well past the point of no return'.[11] The discovery that the Nassau Agreement could not be fundamentally renegotiated and that the phasing out of the British deterrent was unlikely to occur for the foreseeable future, led to the floating by the Labour Government of the idea of an Atlantic nuclear force (ANF). Under this plan Britain would pledge her nuclear submarines along with a number of US nuclear submarines to NATO for as long as the Alliance lasted. These vessels would thus be under the control of the NATO supreme commander. This proposal had, from the Labour Government's viewpoint, several advantages over the MLF. Firstly, it made it clear that Britain had no intention of retaining possession of her own nuclear deterrent; secondly, it avoided the spread of nuclear weapons to West Germany, which many critics had seen as likely to have adverse consequences for relations with the Soviet Union and her allies. Finally, it still gave a more equal share to all NATO members in decisions about the future strategy, tactics and deployment of nuclear weapons and a definitive US commitment to Europe.

The British plan was the basis of the talks which took place early in December 1964 in Washington between the American president, Johnson, and the new British prime minister. Before the meeting the British had been under considerable pressure to modify their opposition to the MLF,[12] but this was stoutly resisted by the Labour Government despite a division of opinion between the Foreign Office and the Ministry of Defence over the proposal.[13] The Washington meeting was cordial and highly successful. The British, after initial discussion between Defence Minister Healey and Gordon-Walker for Britain and Secretary of State Rusk and Defense Secretary MacNamara, achieved their objective. Wilson pursuaded Johnson to drop his support for the MLF and back the British counter-proposal of the ANF. In addition the British resisted an attempt by President Johnson to get a British contingent sent to Vietnam; 'even a token force so long as the Union Jack is there'.[14] The trio of Labour ministers thus returned from Washington with a considerable degree of success and a vindication of their views on both the MLF and the fact that they were still 'welcome at the top table',[15] despite their willingness to give up possession of nuclear weapons.

186

In other areas as well the new Labour Government sought
to differentiate its policy from that of its predecessors.
In the article, referred to above, Gordon-Walker adopted
a fairly cautious policy towards the EEC, and the Labour
Government followed suit. 'A Labor Government would not
risk a second failure of negotiations to enter the Common
Market; that would have catastrophic consequences...
Our general policy would be to create as close relations
as possible between ourselves and the European Community.
We would seek to proceed by pragmatic steps.'[16] In addition he pointed out the need to resolve the fundamental
question of whether Britain could join the EEC and still
retain her traditional relations with the United States
and the Commonwealth. However, he concluded that a Labour
Government 'would want to take part in any discussion of
steps toward a closer political union in Europe'.[17] These
questions had not been resolved when he left office, nor
indeed were they when the Labour Government itself left
office five years later. Generally, the relations with
Britain's European Free Trade Area partners began rather
badly with the decision by Britain to impose a 15 per cent
import levy, and Gordon-Walker had the task of defending
this decision and promising an early review of the situation at the EFTA meeting in Geneva early in November 1964.
This decision had been made unilaterally and caused considerable anger among the remaining EFTA members. The
unilateral decision had been forced on the Labour Government by the gravity of the economic situation facing them
at home and abroad. The initial decision to maintain the
parity of the pound sterling was to act as a major con-
straint on foreign policy in the early years, just as the
devaluation of the pound was to force major reversals of
foreign policies in the later years of the Wilson government. The decision to raise the import levy was hardly
an auspicious start in the Labour government's relations
with the rest of Europe.

The final areas of difference lay in the attitude of the
Labour Party to the question of 'North-South relations'[18]
and the granting of aid without strings, which many in the
Labour Party regarded as being equally important to East-
West relations. To this end, Harold Wilson created a separate department of state, the Ministry of Overseas Development, with Barbara Castle as the minister in charge. He
also gave her a seat in the Cabinet. This appointment was

part of a process whereby a number of functions in the
general field of foreign affairs were assigned to individual ministers: Lord Chalfont was appointed to lead the
British attempts at disarmament and Lord Caradon was
appointed as permanent representative at the United
Nations; both men held the rank of minister of state at
the Foreign Office. This arrangement seemed to work well,
although at a later date the presence of two Foreign
Office ministers in the Cabinet was regarded by many as
highly unsatisfactory. The need to delegate work in
foreign affairs is, however, generally accepted by foreign
secretaries. This delegation of authority works within
the understanding of the constitutional principle that it
is the foreign secretary who retains overall authority as
the minister ultimately responsible for the conduct of the
affairs of state.

   The relationship between the foreign secretary and the
prime minister was, at this time, close and Gordon-Walker
discussed most important issues of foreign policy with
Wilson as often as was necessary. In addition, he would
normally report orally about once a week to the Cabinet.
This sometimes created problems as not all ministers received copies of Foreign Office documents or at best received edited summaries. The normal procedure was for the
foreign secretary to make an oral report and then answer
questions on it. There was rarely much discussion except
of major foreign policy decisions such as the MLF which
was discussed over a weekend at Chequers. This lack of
discussion is hardly surprising, given the urgency of the
domestic situation at this time. The normal procedure for
a major foreign policy decision was the circulation of a
paper by the foreign secretary and a full Cabinet discussion of the matter. All foreign policy decisions except emergency or routine decisions were discussed by a
Cabinet sub-committee normally chaired by the prime
minister. A good working relationship between Gordon-
Walker and Wilson was particularly important at this point,
especially as the former was outside Parliament. Although
they occasionally disagreed,[19] the two men seem to have
got on well together, although Wilson's relations with his
ministers were clearly tempered by his views of the role
of the prime minister as the 'managing director as well as
(the) chairman of his team'.[20] In turn Gordon-Walker's
relations with his senior Foreign Office officials were

generally cordial and, again, the fact that he was not in Parliament does not seem to have affected his relationship with them. The fact that he was a Labour minister seeking to make changes in one of the more conservative institutions may have been resented by some people in the Foreign Office, as indeed was his selection of the new permanent head, but this is only to be expected and in no way affected the professional relationship between the minister and his advisers.

Gordon-Walker's tenure at the Foreign Office ended almost before it had begun. It is clear, however, that even at this early stage in the life of the Labour government the prime minister was seeking to play an important role in foreign-policy-making. 'What is clear is that Harold (Wilson) himself is taking a predominant interest in foreign affairs and defence.'[21] This was not merely a consequence of Gordon-Walker's absence from Parliament, but also a reflection of a trend which had started when the Conservatives were in power, and it was clearly a trend which Wilson wished to continue.

The brevity of Gordon-Walker's tenure of office makes it difficult to make a firm judgement of his potential. Some critics have suggested that he arrived at the Foreign Office 'too late' and with an air of one who 'knew it all'.[22] Others have gone further and suggested that the whole of the Labour government's foreign affairs team of Gordon-Walker, Douglad Jay (president of the Board of Trade) and Arthur Bottomley (commonwealth secretary) were 'really all pretty hopeless', and that Gordon-Walker had been 'no good' as foreign secretary.[23] These judgements appear to be rather harsh, for Gordon-Walker certainly appeared to be well-qualified for his post and to have thought out at least some of the things he wished to do. He was not there long enough to make a real impact, and a general conclusion based on such scant evidence would seem rather unfair. He was not, for instance, able to carry out some of his ideas for creating a better relationship between Parliament and foreign-policy-makers. In a book published in 1970 after he had left the Labour government Gordon-Walker suggested that: 'the Foreign and Commonwealth Office should, for a period, be subjected to investigation by a select committee. In all fields of policy a Cabinet needs the backing of an informed public opinion, but particularly so in foreign policy, which has too long and too impenetrably been wrapped in secrecy'.[24] It is, of course, not clear whether he held these views before or after he had been at the Foreign Office. What is clear is that he did not have an opportunity to put them into practice. In some respects it would be fair to say that Gordon-Walker was unlucky; his career at the Foreign Office was prematurely curtailed and Britain lost a potentially sound, if not particularly outstanding, foreign secretary.

CHAPTER 10

MICHAEL STEWART

What is most surprising about Michael Stewart, who was
twice foreign secretary during the Wilson governments, is
that he was seriously considered for the office immediately
Harold Wilson won the 1964 election.[1] The circumstances
of his subsequent appointments were in some respects similar in that on both occasions he replaced a minister who
had resigned. In the first instance it was following the
defeat of Gordon-Walker at Leyton and the second following
the resignation from the Cabinet of George Brown. Michael
Stewart rose to prominence during the 1964-70 period although he was an influential figure in the Labour Party
before that. His appointment on the first occasion did
not come as a great surprise to him,[2] although he apparently had some regrets at leaving the Department of Education and Science.[3] The basis for his lack of surprise
can be seen from the fact that he had accompanied Harold
Wilson and Gordon-Walker as part of the official Labour
Party delegation to Moscow in 1963 shortly after Wilson
had won the leadership of the party. However, in terms
of seniority the appointment was a little unexpected.
Some members of the Cabinet were keen to see Dennis Healey,
the defence minister, transferred to the Foreign Office,
but Wilson would not consider this.[4] The decision to move
Stewart was clearly also taken because it was a relatively
painless change. Few ministers would be keen to move from
an appointment after three months and at a time when they
were beginning to find their feet. In this respect Michael
Stewart was no exception. On the day that Gordon-Walker
was losing the Leyton by-election, Stewart 'enjoyed a
triumph such as few enjoy in a lifetime in Parliament'[5] in
answering an attack on his policy for ending selection in
secondary education. At this moment of triumph he was
whisked away to the Foreign Office because the prime minister regarded him as 'a wise and authoritative figure capable of filling any position in the Government'.[6]

Certainly, Stewart came to the Foreign Office with a
wealth of experience in a number of junior posts in
government and front bench experience during Labour's
opposition years. He entered Parliament for Fulham East
in 1945 and was soon appointed to a post in the Whips
Office of the Attlee government (first as vice-chamberlain
and then controller of His Majesty's Household). In 1947,
he became under-secretary for war, a post which he held
until 1951, when for the last few months of the Attlee
government he was parliamentary secretary at the ministry
of supply. During the first years in opposition, he spoke
often on foreign and defence issues but later was given
front bench briefs on education and, in November 1959,
housing and local government. He was, however, not elected to the Shadow Cabinet until 1960. This was evidence
of the lack of a 'power base' within the Labour Party as
a whole, but he was a highly influential and respected
member of the Parliamentary Labour Party. It is perhaps
important to make this point because Stewart's public
image was by no means as high as the reputation he had
among his parliamentary colleagues.

When Stewart came to the Foreign Office in January 1965,
his appointment was welcomed by senior officials because
it meant that an end had been reached to the rather artificial situation which had prevailed under Gordon-Walker.
He arrived at the Office as the first effective Labour
foreign secretary for almost fourteen years. As noted in
the previous chapter, Gordon-Walker had been able to get
things done, but his absences caused by his need to return
to Parliament meant that there was 'no firm top-level
Ministerial direction of day to day foreign policy'.[7] As
a stop-gap measure, the then permanent under-secretary,
Sir Harold Caccia, instituted a regular daily meeting for
top officials. This process, although regarded as a temporary measure, was continued after Stewart became foreign
secretary.[8] In general the smooth working relations which
had begun with Gordon-Walker continued with Michael Stewart
and there is little doubt that a situation of mutual trust
and confidence grew up between the minister and his senior
advisers.

Stewart came to the Foreign Office believing that
Britain had to adjust to her new position of being a
'major power of the second rank'.[9] By this he meant

'Britain's former dominating position is gone.   But...
Britain retains a position of considerable influence all
over the world.'[10]   This view, which became much more popular at a later date, was also shared by his advisers.[11]
The fact that the thinking of the minister and of his top
advisers was so similar, not just on this issue but on
other issues which were to rise to importance over the
years, goes a long way to explain the existence of a high
level of rapport between them.   The question clearly arises
as to how far the process was one between equals and how
far the advisers, who all appear to have thought very highly of him, were allowed to have their own way.   Stewart
was certainly well liked by the Foreign Office.   He was
also a formidable debater, questioning all advice, not
just in relation to British interests but also from the
viewpoint of what was morally right for Britain and the
world.   This was particularly true on the question of
Biafra, where he was opposed not only by a large section
of the Labour Party but also by a substantial section of
the Conservative Opposition.   As noted below, Stewart
refused to be moved from his policies and was fortunate
to have the support of Sir Alec Douglas-Home on the issue,
otherwise he and the Government might well have been
placed in an untenable position.   This example tends to
bear out the view that although he was never a 'pushover',
once convinced of the validity of a case, Stewart was prepared to fight all the way to get his position accepted by
his colleagues and, having achieved that, he would defend
the policies to the best of his ability against all-comers.
However, in comparison with George Brown he appears to
have been a much more 'manageable' minister.   'Michael
Stewart spoke and thought like an official himself;   consequently his officials had little difficulty in guiding
him.'[12]   This latter point is perhaps borne out by a
comment made by Harold Wilson in his memoirs that Michael
Stewart had the right temperament to give a department
'a period of quiet and orderly administration'.[13]

   In the course of both the periods when he was at the
Foreign Office, Stewart dealt with many very thorny problems and presided in October 1968 over the amalgamation
of the Foreign and Commonwealth Offices, a reform which
had been first mooted by the Plowden Committee in 1964.
Another report suggesting change in the administration of
the Foreign Office was also made during Stewart's second

term. This was the Report of the Duncan Committee, charged
with examining the structure of the Diplomatic Service and
the requirements of Britain for overseas representation.
Although the Commonwealth and Diplomatic Services had been
amalgamated in 1964, this further review was necessitated
by the economic circumstances of the day and the need to
economise in every aspect of government expenditure. It
was clear that Britain's terrible economic position was
not just having an effect on the policies to be pursued
but also on the officials who were to carry them out. The
Duncan Report was published in 1969 and caused a considerable stir not just among diplomats but also in academic
circles.[14]

   Although these changes and proposals for change were
long in the future in 1965, the seeds, particularly the
economic seeds, had already been sewn. However, despite
Stewart's view of Britain's role, the Labour Government in
general and Harold Wilson in particular seemed to be committed to the idea of not reducing Britain's world position
or its sphere of influence. Although some Labour back-
benchers favoured a large readjustment of the areas of
British interest, particularly east of Suez, such changes
were not acceptable to the Government and only became so
when the measures necessary to make devaluation effective
were taken in 1967. In a sense there was no conflict of
view between Wilson and Stewart on this issue. Both men
felt that Britain still had an important role to play,
first in relation to the Commonwealth and the remnants of
Empire, second as permanent members of the United Nations,
an organisation which all Labour politicians feel obliged
to support strongly, and finally as an important member of
the NATO alliance. In line with this Stewart regarded
Britain as the 'pivot' of NATO forming a useful bridge between the European members and the allies on the other
side of the Atlantic; a British withdrawal from NATO
would, in his view, have been fatal for the organisation's
future, although it was able to survive French withdrawal.[15]
In general, therefore, the relations between the prime
minister and foreign secretary were very cordial during
both periods under consideration. Stewart rose steadily
in influence in the Cabinet and was, in 1966 when he transferred to the Department of Economic Affairs, third in
order of precedence in the Cabinet. After the resignation
of George Brown he became the established 'number two' in

the Cabinet, although Brown remained as deputy leader of
the party.[16] The good relationship between the two men
did not mean that they always agreed, or indeed that
Wilson would always back up the foreign secretary in
Cabinet. When, for instance, Stewart circulated a paper
to the Cabinet which was highly critical of French policy,
particularly with regard to the future of the EEC and relations with the Soviet Union, a group of Cabinet colleagues led a revolt against the line taken in the paper and
successfully had it dropped. In winding up the debate
Wilson indicated that his sympathies lay with those who
were critical of the paper.[17]

Another issue which divided the Cabinet at this time
and about which Stewart felt strongly was membership of
the EEC itself. The Foreign Office were very favourable
to renewing the British application for membership, although they were very hostile to de Gaulle and his policies, particularly since the veto in 1963. The longer he
remained at the Foreign Office the stronger became
Stewart's conviction that Britain would prove a valuable
member of the EEC and act as a counterbalance to both
France and Germany.[18] Another leading member of the
Government, George Brown, was also in favour of renewing
the application, and one estimate is that by January 1966
there was a majority of the Cabinet in favour of pressing
the application.[19] However, despite a request from the
foreign secretary that a paper advocating this course
should be circulated in December 1965, Harold Wilson refused to allow it to go forward for Cabinet discussion.[20]
The reasons for this are fairly clear. Firstly the effect
of changing course so soon after roundly condemning the
original application made by the Macmillan government
would be tremendous, and, more important, the effect on
the Labour Party would be dynamite and could have easily
disturbed the unity of the party at a time when the narrow-
ness of the Parliamentary majority indicated that an election was imminent. Furthermore, it was not clear that at
this time the prime minister was fully convinced of the
desirability of membership. The Labour manifesto in 1964
had clearly come down against British membership and had
emphasised the importance of relations with the Commonwealth, particularly trade relations.[21]

By 1966, however, the position had changed substantially.

The new manifesto published for the election on 31 March
stated that 'Labour believes that Britain, in consultation
with her EFTA partners, should be ready to enter the European Economic Community, <u>provided essential British and
Commonwealth interests are safeguarded</u>'.[22] This point was
amplified by Harold Wilson who told an Election Meeting in
Bristol: ...'given a fair wind, we will negotiate our way
into the Common Market, head held high, not crawl in. <u>And
we shall go in if the conditions are right</u>... Negotiations?
Yes. Unconditional acceptance of whatever terms we are
offered? No. <u>We believe that given the right conditions
it would be possible and right to join EEC</u> as an economic
community.'[23] Although this marked a major shift in policy,
it was also phrased in such a way that all Labour members,
whether in favour of membership or not, could support it
because the phrases could be interpreted to mean all
things to all men, as indeed they were. 'For my own part,
I felt that during the 1964-66 Parliament I could not,
consistently with party and government policies, make a
positive approach to the EEC; but after the 1966 Election
it was right to do so.'[24] Stewart's view, however, was
not the unanimous view of the Cabinet, several of whom
were opposed to entry, and Crossman, one of the leading
opponents, sought to bring 'into the open the contradiction
between the speeches of George Thomson and George Brown
and the assurance given us in private that there is no
real prospect of getting into the Common Market'.[25] When,
just over a year later, the Government decided to pursue
the application for membership, Stewart was not at the
Foreign Office. However, these negotiations were not
successful,[26] and Stewart had the task of initiating further talks which were successfully concluded by the Heath
government in 1972.

Despite the promise in the manifesto on relations with
the Commonwealth, and the amalgamation of the two offices
in 1968, there was no marked improvement in relations between Britain and the former colonial peoples. As noted
in the previous chapter, there was much concern among
ministers over the problems of developing countries, and
modest efforts were made to improve their plight. Stewart
saw the United Nations as playing an important role in
this work.[27] During the whole of the period of the Labour
government there were frequent rumours that the Commonwealth was on the point of breaking up, especially after

196

the Rhodesia problem had developed. However, none of
these rumours had much substance and the Commonwealth continued in existence. Trade between Britain and the
Commonwealth continued to decline and, as we have seen,
Britain looked elsewhere for her future economic relations. Although Stewart did not hold particularly strong
views on the Commonwealth, there was a natural propensity
in the Labour Party to favour the Commonwealth over other
groups. This was a result of a combination of factors.
Firstly the fairly close personal friendship which existed
between leaders (particularly in the New Commonwealth) in
Commonwealth countries and Labour Party members; and
secondly, the Labour Party's traditional suspicion of the
conservative (and Catholic) leadership in Western Europe.
Nevertheless, whatever their personal sympathies, Labour
leaders were forced to re-examine their views because of
the economic situation and reluctantly came to the conclusion that Britain's future could be better safeguarded
in Europe than in an attempt to revive flagging Commonwealth trade. This view was also gradually, if grudgingly
accepted by most of the members of the Commonwealth.

A further issue on which the Government felt under increasing strain during both Stewart's periods at the
Foreign Office was Vietnam. Britain was a co-chairman
with the Soviet Union of the Geneva Conference on Indo-
China and Harold Wilson was anxious to play an important
role in any moves to end American involvement in Vietnam.
The American commitment increased dramatically in the
early years of the Labour Government, although after 1968
the US Government was anxiously trying to extricate itself. This desire to play a role in the Vietnam situation had several difficulties. Firstly, there was a
clear conflict of loyalties between Britain and her relationship with the United States on the one hand, and the
apparent need as co-chairman of the Geneva Conference to
appear impartial over Vietnam on the other. Secondly,
the Government by refusing to condemn all but a few of
the American actions or to disassociate itself from American policy in Vietnam found itself under increasing
pressure from a substantial number of members of the
Labour Party both inside and outside Parliament. The
policy of the prime minister was actively supported by
his foreign secretary who felt strongly that there was
a case for the American presence there, a view which was

shared by many in the Foreign Office.[28]   Although a num-
ber of members of the Government shared the view that the
Americans did have a case, they were equally convinced of
the need for Britain to take the initiative in seeking to
end the war. For almost the whole of his periods at the
Foreign Office, Stewart was involved in diplomatic moves
to get a settlement in Vietnam, as was the prime minister.
It is not within the scope of this essay to detail Harold
Wilson's role in the attempts to reach a settlement in
Vietnam, except in so far as it reflected upon the role
of the foreign secretary or involved the Foreign Office
in general and Michael Stewart in particular.[29]   This was,
however, clearly an issue which the prime minister regarded as being of sufficient importance to warrant his personal attention. This is not to downgrade the role of
either the foreign secretary or the Foreign Office. As a
loyal minister, Stewart was prepared to allow the prime
minister to take any credit from the situation, whilst he
took any brickbats.

One of Stewart's first actions on taking office was to
fly to Washington for talks with the American leaders,
talks which took place against the background of growing
American military involvement in Vietnam. Despite Wilson's
fear that the Foreign Office might persuade Stewart to
offer unqualified support to the Americans, he roundly
attacked the American use of gas in Vietnam and the idea
that America had placed no limit on potential escalation.
His forthright opposition was applauded by the press, and
Wilson records that 'with his firm, persuasive and often
underrated authority, he had a marked effect in helping
domestic US pressures to steer American thinking away
from negative attitudes to negotiations'.[30]   Two months
later, after the failure of proposals for a Commonwealth
Prime Ministers' mission to Vietnam, which Stewart and
the Foreign Office had viewed with favour, the prime
minister proposed to send Harold Davies, a left-wing
Labour MP on a personal mission to Hanoi. This proposal
was supported by Stewart, but when, because of a leak,
the Foreign Office man, Mr Donald Murray, had to drop out,
the official advice became more negative. 'One could but
advise, with all respect due to Mr Harold Davies' personal
qualities and knowledge of the area, that his mission
could... only be a failure.'[31]   Stewart tried again on
his visit to Moscow in December 1965 but this also was

unsuccessful. A renewed attempt by Wilson to get a more amenable attitude on the part of the Johnson administration was frustrated more than somewhat by the renewal of the bombing of North Vietnam, an action which had, unbeknown to Wilson, brought a favourable response from the British Foreign Office.[32]

These were not the only times during the labour governments that information was either 'leaked' or given out in such a way as to cause embarrassment to the Government. Later, in 1969, another and much more damaging leak occurred while Stewart was foreign secretary when the substance of a conversation between Christopher Soames, British ambassador to France, and the French president, de Gaulle, was circulated by someone in the Foreign Office. 'L'affaire Soames', as it became known, did little to improve Anglo-French relations and further reduced the possibility of a successful application for EEC membership. However, Stewart saw circulation of the British version as a necessary move in order to show the other members of the EEC that 'we sincerely wanted entry to the EEC - that this was the firm objective of our policy and that we would not accept any substitute for entry'.[33] On the more general point about the Foreign Office, George Brown has been reported as saying: 'We were very leaky. Things were in the press and it was being used... to mould decisions in the Cabinet Room.'[34] The ultimate responsibility for such things clearly lies with the minister, although it would be unfair to criticise the foreign secretary too much on this score.

On Vietnam, the chapter of failures and 'near misses' continued after Stewart left the Foreign Office, although when he returned to the Foreign Office in March 1968 the problem seemed to be nearing a solution when President Johnson announced the cessation of bomb attacks on North Vietnam, called for renewed talks at the Geneva Peace Conference, and, finally, announced his retirement from the presidency.

A second issue which, although not strictly within the jurisdiction of the Foreign Office until its merger with the Commonwealth Office in 1968, was to cause the Government much anguish was Rhodesia, which declared UDI in November 1965. This action was to have increasingly

severe diplomatic consequences for Britain, particularly
in regard to relations with the New Commonwealth. The
Rhodesia issue was the first real test of the Labour
Government's view of the role the UN should play in the
world. Whilst insisting for some considerable time that
the Rhodesian problem was 'a British problem', the Government nevertheless sought UN backing for the implementation
of economic sanctions against the rebel regime. The Labour
Party view that a Labour government would 'reassert British
influence in the United Nations'[35] and would 'continue to
give full support to the authority and efficiency of the
United Nations'[36] came under considerable strain as a result of the attitude of many Third World countries in the
General Assembly not only towards the Rhodesia question
but also on the other 'colonial' issue of Gibraltar and
the Falkland Islands. This came about despite the decision
to appoint a Foreign Office minister to lead the British
delegation. One of the first acts of Lord Caradon on
taking up this appointment was to begin work on proposals
to fulfil the promises made in the 1964 Labour manifesto
to improve both the conciliation machinery and the effectiveness of peace-keeping forces. Despite the good work
of both Stewart and Caradon and a fairly well received
speech by Wilson at the General Assembly late in 1965 in
which these proposals were made explicit, these efforts
came to nothing. Indeed, after this time they were almost
forgotten, but 'will go on bobbing up as long as countries
take the UN seriously'.[37]

With regard to other promises made in the manifesto, the
Labour Government was somewhat more successful. The promise to appoint a minister for disarmament was honoured.
However, his work seemed to be at an end when the Geneva
Disarmament talks broke down in the summer of 1965. It
was fortunate that the prime minister and foreign secretary
shared the same holiday retreat, the Scilly Isles, because
this enabled Stewart to propose and have approved the idea
that Lord Chalfont should be permitted to attempt to revive
the talks with a new initiative. This led ultimately to
the signing in 1967 of the Nuclear Non-proliferation Treaty,
and therefore was a decision of considerable importance.
In other areas, too, Stewart's first period at the Foreign
Office was marked by success. Two long-running disputes
were resolved. Firstly, the confrontation with Indonesia,
which had made claims to sovereignty over parts of Malaysia,

200

was satisfactorily ended. Furthermore, relations between
Britain and Indonesia improved quite considerably and
Stewart had even been able to make a gift of food to the
Indonesian government during the confrontation. 'It was
made, partly as a matter of common humanity (because there
was a drought in Indonesia), and partly to demonstrate to
Indonesia that, although we felt obliged to help Malaysia,
we still desired to be on friendly terms with Indonesia.'[38]
Secondly, in 1966, an end appeared to be in sight to the
Aden problem when Britain announced her intention of with-
drawing from the base in 1968.

   During his second period of office, from March 1968 to
June 1970, Stewart found less success. Taking over from
George Brown he found that some issues were no nearer
solution than they had been almost two years before. The
Rhodesia problem remained unsolved; Vietnam, although
seemingly moving towards a solution, was still presenting
problems, and the EEC application was still 'on the table'
but lying dormant following the unsuccessful attempt to
join that had been initiated in 1967. In addition to
these continued problems were the economic difficulties
of Britain and the consequential effect of the devaluation
of sterling on foreign policy objectives, the amalgamation
of the Foreign and Commonwealth Office already discussed,
the aftermath of the 1967 Middle East war, the diplomatic
consequences of the Northern Ireland problem, and the war
in Nigeria. All these problems combined to give Stewart
a difficult time at the Foreign Office. On some of these
issues, such as the EEC application and the amalgamation
of the two offices, progress was made. A renewed attempt
to join the EEC was made in 1970 and the reorganisation
of the Foreign Office went relatively smoothly; on other
issues such as Northern Ireland and the Middle East little
was achieved. The remaining issues were in one way or
another resolved. In addition, the British took action in
the Caribbean when trouble arose over the future of
Anguilla, which had formed part of the Federation with
St.Kitts-Nevis. At the request of the Commonwealth states
in the area, the British sent a squadron of police to the
island to restore order. This action was subsequently
attacked as 'imperialist' by the very people who had invited it. The abrupt change of attitude caused considerable
annoyance both to the foreign secretary and to the Foreign
Office.[39]

By far the most serious issue, however, was the war in Nigeria. The plight of the Biafrans was skilfully used in a propaganda exercise to arouse sympathy for the cause. There was also considerable disagreement within the Labour Party as to the policy to be pursued by the Government in relation to the question of arms sales to the Federal Government. There was a broad measure of opinion outside Parliament and on the back-benches that the arms trade should stop.[40] Despite the considerable pressure to change policy, the Government stuck firmly to its view that support should be given to a Commonwealth government in trouble and that the supply of arms gave Britain a more effective say in Lagos. This argument suggested further that Britain's influence could still be effective and would act as a counterbalance to the growing influence of the Soviet Union, which was the other main supplier of arms to the Nigerian Government. Most important of all, however, was the argument concerning what the effect on Africa would be if Ojukwu's rebellion was to succeed. It was feared in many quarters but most particularly in Africa that such a success might trigger off a series of secessions which would turn Africa into a continent of tribal warfare. Such a turn of events would have meant that all efforts to defeat white racialism in Africa would have been doomed to failure. This was the reasoning behind the support of Ojukwu from South Africa, Rhodesia and Portugal and the opposition to him from 'the great majority of black African States... The other considerations (British influence in Nigeria, the desire to prevent the growth of Russian influence etc) were only makeweights in comparison'.[41] This was the basis upon which the Government's case was founded. It was strongly supported by the foreign secretary[42] and by ministerial colleagues[43] against vigorous and often bitter attacks. When the war finally ended in January 1970, the foreign secretary was swift to take action to ensure that relief aid became immediately available, although some in the Foreign Office were more cautious.[44]

Stewart saw the role of a British foreign secretary as being concerned with developing a more rational approach to change. He regarded change as inevitable and believed that all efforts should be made to ensure that changes came about peacefully.[45] In so far as few British soldiers were killed on active duty for most of the two

periods when Stewart was at the Foreign Office, this policy
was effectively carried out. However, it could be argued
that in many areas British policy was weak and ambivalent
and frequently lacking in success. In the area of detente
and disarmament the Labour Government, prompted partly by
idealism and partly by financial necessity, was most
active. Indeed, Stewart regards the work done by his
junior ministers on disarmament and the general contribution Britain made to the success of moves towards detente
as by far the greatest achievements of his period at the
Foreign Office.[46] The general moves towards detente took
a severe blow with the Soviet intervention in Czechoslovakia in August 1968, soon after Stewart's return to the
Foreign Office. As it happened, the effects of the crisis
were short-lived although an immediate effect was to make
the renewal of the NATO alliance almost automatic. Nevertheless Stewart was a strong supporter of policies designed
to reduce tension in Europe and in May 1970 urged the NATO
ministerial meeting to make a positive response to the
renewed Soviet offer of a European security conference.[47]
Regrettably, Stewart left office before he could see the
results of this initiative. In other policy areas,
Stewart was less successful in achieving his aim. He
accepted the view that with hindsight a change in the
attitude towards American involvement in Vietnam might
have been a more effective way of achieving the aim of
bringing peace to South-East Asia.[48] However, it is not
clear whether such a change would have been effective.
His successor and predecessor, George Brown, has blamed
Britain's failure to play a significant role in Vietnam
on lack of prior consultation with the Americans.[49] On
the other hand, a more vigorous condemnation of American
policy would certainly have been popular among a large
section of the Labour Party.

It would be true to say that Stewart was a moderate
foreign secretary operating in difficult times and seeking
to prevent the decline of Britain's effectiveness in the
world. He was, by all accounts, a good administrator but
he lacked any personal flair or desire to innovate. He
was a sharp contrast to George Brown and, in some respects,
just what was required. Opinions as to his effectiveness
are sharply divided. One colleague saw him as little more
than a subordinate: 'As for Foreign Affairs, I suspect
that under Michael Stewart, even more than under Gordon

Walker, the Prime Minister has been the prevailing personality.'[50] It was certainly admitted by most people that
Stewart worked hard and performed his duties in a conscientious if unenterprising way. He was 'sound' on the basic
issues such as relations with the USSR, the United States
and the EEC. Like all Labour ministers he was anxious to
reform the Oxbridge image of the Foreign Office, a task
which always proved difficult.[51] All in all, he was well
liked, by his officials, by his colleagues and by the
prime minister who paid a handsome tribute to him in his
memoirs: 'Recalling now the press vilification and the
violence of the demonstrations that marked Michael
Stewart's two periods at the Foreign Office, I have every
reason for saying that his critics were as wrong in their
misrepresentation of what he was seeking to achieve as in
their persistent under-valuation of his untiring efforts,
his influence - and his achievements'.[52] This view is
also shared by Lord Gore-Booth: 'With closer knowledge I
agree with Harold Wilson'. He adds that Stewart possessed
'a deep-seated idealism, a staunchness in difficult atmos-
pheres (politically speaking) and a crisp, choice use of
the English language',[53] all of which he regarded as important qualities in a foreign secretary.

   Although Stewart's occupations of the Foreign Office
were at difficult times, he carried out his task effi-
ciently and to the best of his ability. However, towards
the end of his period of office, he, like his fellow-
ministers, began to show the strain of six difficult years
in power. Furthermore, his second period at the Foreign
Office was to some extent marked by the legacy of George
Brown's personality and style, which was almost the complete opposite to that of Stewart. Nevertheless, history
will judge Michael Stewart as a competent if unspectacular
foreign secretary of clear views and sound judgement who
worked hard and gained limited successes.

CHAPTER 11

GEORGE BROWN

George Brown's appointment as foreign secretary was both imaginative and controversial. The controversy lay not so much in doubts about Brown's political strength and ability to do the job, but from doubts about his temperament and sobriety. The problem for an author writing about George Brown is to distinguish fact from fiction, especially when dealing with the innumerable anecdotes told by journalists, officials and other people about the period Brown spent at the Foreign Office.[1] This aspect of Brown's character was always to play an important part in his life and led ulti- mately to his downfall. However, in terms of political prestige as deputy leader of the Labour Party, it was un- doubtedly true that George Brown was the man for the job. Furthermore as a former trade union official, Brown had gained valuable experience, particularly in the field of negotiation which would prove a useful asset as Foreign Secretary.[2]

There were, of course, those who had strong reservations about Brown's suitability for the post. They recalled that, during the visit of the Russian leaders, Bulganin and Khrushchev, in 1956 he had been involved in an incident which had been sensationalised in the press. At a dinner given in honour of the two Soviet leaders, Brown audibly commented on the content of the speech by Khrushchev, who stopped and asked him to repeat the remark. It would appear that both men were angered by the comments of the other. Brown subsequently met the Russian leaders but his attempt to patch up the affair was snubbed by Khrushchev.[3] Nevertheless most people, including the press, felt that in the decade that had elapsed since this incident and especially since he had been in the Government, Brown had matured greatly, and his appointment was generally re- garded as an interesting move. Indeed the press welcomed the appointment and copy editors headlined the news 'Brown of the F.O.', alluding to a popular film 'Carlton-

Browne of the F.O.'[4] This honeymoon with the press did
not last long, however, and they were soon criticising him
unmercifully, as, for example, over the incident when he
'frugged' with the wife of a friend during a visit to the
Queen Mary whilst in New York.[5]

The appointment was welcomed by some of his fellow cabinet ministers[6] as well as the Foreign Office, since it was
thought that George Brown might aspire to be a second
Ernie Bevin. More important, perhaps, was the fact that
he was a senior member of the Labour Party, a highly influential character with a power base of his own. It was
this that attracted the attention of the Foreign Office.[7]
Brown also made it clear that he regarded his role at the
Foreign Office as that of the policy maker in the field
of foreign affairs. In an interview, published the weekend after his appointment, Brown, whilst still admitting
that 'none of this, of course, affects the fact that Prime
Ministers, as heads of government, are nowadays inevitably
bound up with the whole process of foreign policy making',[8]
stated clearly his views on the role of the Foreign Secretary: 'So long as I am Foreign Secretary, Foreign Office
policy will be made in the Foreign Office. That's what a
Foreign Office is for.'[9] This message was also relayed
to his officials when he arrived at the Foreign Office.[10]
Other features that endeared Brown to the Foreign Office
were his staunch anti-communism and his positive views on
the EEC. Brown had been a determined pro-marketeer even
during the days in opposition when Gaitskell had held a
strongly anti-market position as leader. Indeed, many
commentators believe that Brown made one of his finest
speeches to the 1962 Party Conference when he managed to
convey his pro-market convictions and remain loyal to his
leader.[11] Others have gone further and suggested that
this, coupled with his support of Gaitskell against the
left-wing unilateral disarmers two years earlier, and his
'reputation for impulsiveness, truculence and insensiti-
vity which more than offset his other qualities'.[12] cost
him the leadership of the Labour Party.

It was, however, his clear conviction on Europe which
enabled Brown to achieve his ambition to become foreign
secretary which he regarded not as a job but as 'the
job'.[13] The appointment would also clearly give conviction to the renewed application for membership of the EEC.

On the other hand, his view of the role of the foreign secretary and the political antagonism which he felt towards the prime minister meant that the relationship between the two men was at times strained. This strain was increased by the growth of the tradition that one of the Foreign Office officials was attached to Downing Street as a foreign policy adviser. This has been commented on both by Brown himself[14] and by his permanent undersecretary, Paul Gore-Booth.[15] Furthermore, the relationship was strained by the division between the two men over economic policy, Brown favouring devaluation while Wilson did not. This was another reason for Brown's move to the Foreign Office, the need to harmonise policy among the Labour government's economics ministers.[16] The matter had been brought to a head by the acute financial crisis in July 1966. The appointment thus killed two birds with one stone, and these reasons go a long way to explain the rather atypical appointment of a 'strong' foreign secretary by Harold Wilson.

The more vigorous conduct of foreign policy envisaged by Brown on his arrival in his new post was not the only change he wanted. He regarded the procedures of the Foreign Office as requiring reform. He instituted a change in the submission of recommendations in order to reduce the amount of paperwork and sought consultations with members of the Office of whatever rank in order to encourage a more fruitful discussion of the issues.[17] This view was not shared by all Foreign Office officials. 'People like Brown and Chalfont made the mistake of thinking that diplomatic problems could, occasionally at least, be solved.'[18] Nevertheless Brown's chief adviser, Lord Gore-Booth, sees some merit on this approach. 'Ideas come from below, from Committees, from Ministers (George Brown was very fertile). The tradition, fully observed, is no inhibition on the part of juniors arguing with seniors - except that of common courtesy.'[19] Brown himself was also aware of the great benefits and the pitfalls of the Foreign Office machine and seems to have been keen to avoid the trap of allowing the advisers to make decisions for him. It required a man of determination and strong will to do that! 'The Foreign Office is equipped to give the best information, the best of briefing on any international issue one cares to mention. But what bothered me, made as I am, was the thought that it was they who were deciding the areas I should be briefed about, and I quickly became aware that, unless I was very determined, I would inevitably become the purveyor of views already formed in the Office.'[20]

Furthermore, he made the Foreign Office more 'outward looking' by stimulating contacts with other ministries, particularly the Ministry of Defence with whom regular meetings took place to discuss matters of mutual concern. This might also have been a reflection of the fact that in an era of economic crisis both the Foreign Office and the Defence Ministry found themselves rather isolated. Never more so, perhaps, than on the vexed issue of trade with South Africa. Relations with South Africa always tend to be strained when the Labour Party is in office: the moral condemnation and repugnance of apartheid permeate the party both inside and outside Parliament. Brown was, however, on this issue 'a heretic',[21] being prepared to sell defensive arms to the South African Government. He was in favour of such a move for economic and political reasons. Economically the sale of Buccaneer aircraft and naval equipment could be regarded as a much-needed boost to Britain's external trade at a time of severe crisis; politically it would reinforce the defence of the Cape shipping routes which had gained in importance since the closure of the Suez Canal after the June war of 1967, and it might also 'buy' South African co-operation in resolving the Rhodesia situation. In at least some of these views, Brown was supported by the defence minister, Dennis Healey.[22] The outcome of the debate about this policy was a victory for those opposed to the resumption of the arms trade. The manner of the defeat had a profound effect on Brown who felt that he had been the victim of some prime-ministerial sharp practive.[23] Apart from this issue, and the more general feeling of isolation, there were other sound reasons for close co-operation between the Foreign and Defence ministries. It is to Brown's credit that he brought such meetings about. It is now clear that this co-operation has continued in recent years.

Other areas of change which he sought to achieve lay in the area of recruitment to the Foreign Service and the deployment of personnel. As noted in the previous chapter, efforts to widen the basis of entry into the Foreign Service proved less effective than had been hoped.[24] On the

other hand, Brown's approach to deployment was much more
successful. He was opposed to the idea of self-selection
by officials and believed that what should be done was to
'marry men and their abilities to particular posts'.[25]
This process resulted in the decision to appoint Sir Denis
Greenhill as Gore-Booth's successor. This method of selection was not without its problems, and some people were
aggrieved at not getting the jobs they expected. However,
they generally came to accept it. 'Once I'd explained
what I wanted done, they didn't try to obstruct me...
They were, indeed, very good about my whole approach to
diplomatic appointments.'[26] Since leaving the Foreign
Office both Brown and Gore-Booth have written of their
experiences; Gore-Booth effectively replying to several
of the criticisms made by the former foreign secretary.[27]

Despite his subsequent criticism of the Foreign Office
and the fact that relations with the prime minister were
not always easy, Brown's period at the Foreign Office was
far from disastrous. He set out for the Foreign Office
determined to steer Britain more closely towards Europe
and to change British policy towards the Middle East on
to 'more sensible lines'.[28] In both these fields he met
with limited success. His fall from power had nothing to
do with lack of success or the hostile criticism levelled
at him both by the press and by some members of his own
party but from a complete breakdown of his relations with
the prime minister. Nevertheless, these other factors
played their part. Brown's relations with his colleagues
were as subject to his whims as were all his other relationships. By his own account, he had lost the party
leadership in 1963 because his traditional base of power -
his fellow trade unionist MPs - had deserted him in favour
of Wilson.[29] This was, as we have seen, not the only
reason for his defeat, and he still had the support of a
large section on the right wing of the Labour Party. Criticism came mainly from the left and he was subject to a
two-pronged attack, as was Michael Stewart, over Vietnam
and the EEC application. He was quite capable of dealing
with these criticisms and was frequently at his best when
defending the policies he believed in.[30] It is perhaps
interesting to note that whereas his relations with colleagues both in Cabinet, in Parliament and in the party
outside were sometimes strained, he was very warmly regarded by many of the rank-and-file, and still is. He also

got on reasonably well with his junior colleagues in the Foreign Office, trying hard to get his advisers to accept their decisions on his behalf. This idea was frequently frustrated by the officials who naturally wanted the minister in charge to make the final decision in the event of disagreement and because he was the man ultimately responsible.[31]

In his general approach to Foreign Office work, Brown held the view that it was essential that decisions should be based on good and reliable information; he believed in the need for some measure of planning in foreign affairs, although he recognised that the techniques of internal economic planning such as those used at the DEA were not applicable to the Foreign Office. On his arrival at the Foreign Office Brown found the planning machinery 'very weak' and attempted, while he was there 'to step it up'. However, at that time career diplomats regarded the planning department as 'an interruption of their career'.[32] In common with Gordon-Walker and Stewart, Brown did not believe in a 'socialist' foreign policy although, also like them, he saw a Labour government placing different emphasis on some areas of policy.[33] As we have already noted, however, he took a far more pragmatic view of world affairs than did either of the other two.

It was both pragmatism and idealism that first led George Brown to espouse the cause of European union. He saw it both as a means of revitalising Western Europe and a way to 'stop the polarisation of the world around the two superpowers'.[34] The decision to renew the application for membership of the EEC was announced to Parliament in such a way that it was clear that the Government intended to 'test the water' before proceeding. It is clear that a majority of the Cabinet were in favour of this policy, but it is not clear what the outcome was likely to be. Certainly the appointment of the strongly pro-market Brown as Foreign Secretary had not harmed Britain's chances, but the question must be raised as to the seriousness of the attempt to join the EEC in 1967. This is not to call into question the sincerity of many of the pro-marketeers, but it is necessary to question their political judgement on this issue.

The real stumbling block to entry, as it had been in the

1960-3 negotiations, was the attitude of the French and of de Gaulle in particular. Anglo-French relations were no better in the post-veto period, although the Foreign Office had fought hard to preserve the Anglo-French 'Concorde' programme against the attacks from various quarters. This success did not extend to the continuation of British participation in the European missile project (ELDO). In more general terms, Anglo-French differences over a whole range of issues were very wide indeed. In 1965, France had announced her intention to withdraw from the military aspects of NATO, a decision greeted with some hostility by Britain and others. In addition, France had also decided to continue the development of her own independent nuclear deterrent, the force de frappe. This also led to considerable British disapproval. The French decision in both these matters was clearly the result of a major division of opinion between them and the other NATO allies over American intentions, and de Gaulle continued to view the British as the American 'Trojan horse' in Europe despite the change of government. But it was not just in the area of European defence and the role of Western Europe in the bi-polar world that divided Britain and France. They were also bitterly at odds over the question of policy towards the Middle East and especially the provision of arms to the two sides in that conflict. To that had later to be added the dispute over Nigeria, with the French openly siding with the separatist Biafrans.

Despite all these areas of apparent disagreement, some members of the Cabinet believed that the French veto on British entry into the EEC no longer applied. In 1965, for example, the then Foreign Secretary, Michael Stewart, had expressed precisely this view at a press conference.[35] Throughout 1966, the French attitude had been unclear, although Pompidou, on a visit to London, had allegedly made the dropping of the veto conditional upon the devaluation of sterling[36] a condition which Wilson and a majority of the Cabinet at that time had found unacceptable. Nevertheless, convinced that the remaining EEC partners were favourable to British entry, Wilson announced that he and Brown would tour the capitals of the Six early in 1967. The purpose of this tour was to establish the possible outcome of formal negotiations to enter the EEC. Prior to this tour, Brown had an unofficial and apparently cordial meeting with de Gaulle in Paris.[37] The tour of

the European capitals by the two men does not need a detailed discussion here;[38] it is merely important to
record that, despite a sympathetic hearing, they were not
able to convince the French that they should change their
minds. Indeed, the French Government refused to allow the
formal application by Britain to be considered, but Brown,
with the approval of the Cabinet, was able to circumvent
this obstacle by presenting the British case and the application at the meeting of the Western European Union in
July 1967. Although Brown was able to make Britain's
point, and the prime minister was able to claim defiantly
that the British application was 'on the table', negotiations on British entry did not begin until after Brown had
left the Foreign Office.

  While the decision to apply for membership was being
debated in the Cabinet and party, another debate was going
on over the future of Britain's role in the area east of
Suez. The debate lay between those who saw the decision
over the EEC and the acute economic crisis as indicating
the immediate end of a British presence in the Middle and
Far East and those who did not. Patrick Gordon-Walker, a
Cabinet colleague, has, however, pointed out that: 'The
movement of opinion in the Cabinet in favour of entry into
the Common Market marked an equivalent trend away from
support of the East of Suez policy: it temperamentally
implied a recognition that Britain was a European and not
a world power... But... the two things were not directly
or intellectually related. Each policy was being separ-
ately considered in the Cabinet.'[39] While this may be
true and a valid criticism of the way the Cabinet dealt
with this important issue, it is essential to realise that
this was an issue on which both the prime minister and the
foreign secretary were reluctant converts. Certainly
Brown was only a reluctant supporter of a change in policy:
'I cannot accept the proposition that our role East of
Suez has come to an end... Whether we like it or not, we
have still got responsibilities East of Suez.'[40] However,
the following year the Defence White Paper (published in
July 1967) marked the first public indication that the
Government was about to change its east of Suez policy.[41]
Although he disagreed with the 'speed and time-table to
which we subsequently decided to adhere',[42] Brown resol-
utely defended the policy at the annual conference against
demands for an immediate end to the British role east of

Suez.[43] Similarly the prime minister was only a late and reluctant convert to this changed situation, a mistake which he has subsequently admitted.[44]

This reluctance to drop the British role east of Suez, at least on the part of the prime minister, might well have been the result of a desire to add credibility to his attempts to reach a settlement in the Vietnam war. These attempts reached their height in the early months of 1967. The details of what happened during the visit of Mr Kosygin to London in February 1967 are beyond the scope of this essay.[45] It is sufficient to say that after what appeared to be a promising start the attempt at peace-making petered out into dismal failure. It is important to see what light this threw not just on the relations between Wilson and Brown, but also on the difficulties facing a foreign secretary when his prime minister decides that the issue is of such importance that it must be conducted at the highest level. In his account Wilson clearly places the blame for the breakdown of negotiations on the 'hawks' in Washington.[46] Brown on the other hand, places part of the blame on the lack of close liaison with the Americans, certain aspects of the American political system, the unreliability of the 'hot line' between London and Washington, and the fact that Kosygin 'never had any authority to do what he claimed to be doing'.[47] Added to these 'external' difficulties was the fact that although 'our Foreign Office officials worked magnificently over the whole period... we had No 10 Downing Street trying to maintain a private Foreign Office... We were all stultifying one another'.[48] This is a practical example of the difficulties discussed earlier in the chapter. A harsher verdict would be to agree with Joseph Frankel that this incident 'proved disastrous to Wilson's – and Britain's – standing in the eyes of the Russians, and, to say the least, was unhelpful for Anglo-American relations'.[49]

However, even when the prime minister and foreign secretary are involved in some kind of co-operative venture, this is still no guarantee of success. An example may be seen in the discussion of possible British action during the Middle East war of June 1967. Brown, as noted earlier, had regarded the Middle East as an area requiring specific attention. He had been, on his appointment as foreign secretary, keen to resolve the difficulties surrounding

213

Anglo-Egyptian relations. Relations had been highly unstable since the 1956 Suez adventure, and although official diplomatic relations had been resumed in 1961, they
had been broken off by Egypt in 1965 over the Rhodesia
question. Brown knew the Middle East quite well and was
acquainted with President Nasser. With what might be
regarded as an inspired piece of opportunism, he succeeded
in making contact with Nasser through one of his close
assistant, Field-Marshal Hakim Amer, when they were both
in the Soviet Union. As a result of this initiative, it
was agreed to restore diplomatic relations and to appoint
Sir Harold Beeley as British ambassador. The appointment
was welcomed in Cairo and 'it was largely due to him that
we were able to open a whole new chapter in British relations with Nasser'.[50]

It was thus a great surprise when, in the following year,
for reasons which it is not possible to discuss here, the
Egyptian President ordered the removal of the United
Nations emergency force from Egyptian territory. The
speed with which the Secretary-General of the UN accepted
the ultimatum has been criticised in many quarters, not
least by George Brown.[51] The decision also meant that
there was little time to take action to prevent the outbreak of hostilities, which was almost certain, given
Israel's repeatedly stated view that the closure of the
Straits of Tiran would constitute a casus belli. In a
desperate effort to avoid war, Brown 'with the approval
of the Prime Minister',[52] tried to organise a group of
maritime powers so that 'if necessary an international
naval force would be assembled to escort convoys through
the straits'. He adds that 'this operation never did get
under way, partly because of the reluctance of the Americans to support it, and partly because we got overtaken
by events'.[53] This issue is also briefly mentioned in
Wilson's memoirs.[54] However, in his book, The Cabinet
Patrick Gordon Walker produces a thinly disguised account
of these events,[55] which suggests that an additional reason for the failure of the Brown proposal was that the
Cabinet led by defence minister Dennis Healey[56] was not
prepared to support such a move. The account from this
source is dismissed by the former foreign secretary as
'distorted',[57] suggesting that a Labour foreign secretary
has particular difficulties with Cabinet colleagues and
with the Parliamentary Party: 'All (Cabinet Ministers)

214

are convinced that the Foreign Office is stuffy and preju-
diced... And so all the views of the Foreign Secretary,
however carefully considered, tend to be contested by
colleagues who cannot have the same access to all the
balancing arguments and may themselves have been exposed
to highly sophisticated pressures... But what is true in
the Cabinet is multiplied four-fold or more in the Parliamentary Party...'[58] Nevertheless, it would certainly
appear that on this occasion there is some evidence that
'Mr Harold Wilson and his Foreign Secretary were... once
overruled by the Cabinet'.[59]

Whilst Brown was unsuccessful in his attempts to prevent
war in the Middle East, he was primarily responsible for
the adoption of Resolution 242 of the Security Council,
which he regarded as one of his greatest achievements.[60]
The resolution was indeed a triumph and due credit must
be given to George Brown and his advisers for their efforts
to get it adopted. Although it could be argued that the
resolution was broadly based and inexact in its meaning,
this was necessary if it was to appeal equally to Israel
and the Arab states. Furthermore, it provided a basis for
further talks between those states most intimately involved, and this is still the case today. If it is true that
this was an outstanding success in Brown's career it is
equally to be regretted that he was not able to capitalise
on it. This is also a source of regret to him.[61] He was,
in his view, trying to do what Henry Kissinger has done in
more recent times in the Middle East and was concerned to
get talks going between the parties. However, Brown had
left the Foreign Office before he could capitalise on the
UN Resolution, and at that time there was no one to take
over the work which he had envisaged for himself.

It is commonly thought that a foreign secretary is constantly dealing with 'high politics' and affairs of state.
It is often forgotten that he is in charge of an extremely
large ministry and that much of what he does is routine
and very often the success which he achieves lies in small
areas of policy rather than in the settlement of major disputes. George Brown had his successes and frustrations
during his time. One area of policy which changed during
his period at the Foreign Office was the attitude to a
number of people who had been held at Sachsenhausen during
the war, but had been excluded from compensation on a

technicality.[62] He was greatly concerned with other
issues which were sometimes routine and sometimes almost
impossible to solve. The life of the foreign secretary
is, for example, concerned with problems of security, and
Brown was no exception, the Philby affair first coming to
light during 1967. Another decision of importance was
when Brown agreed that Gore-Booth should visit one of the
more neglected areas as far as Britain was concerned,
Latin America. This it was hoped would improve morale
among British diplomats in the area and possibly bring
'big dividends'.[63]

   However, much of the routine of the Foreign Office is
the result of inherited problems. Brown found added frustration in having to deal with perennial and almost insol-
uble problems such as Gibraltar. He was also forced to
deal with the tidying up of Britain's former imperial
role, particularly with regard to Aden and the Trucial
states of the Persian Gulf, a necessary consequence of the
decision to withdraw from the area east of Suez. In
addition there was the problem of Rhodesia which remained
unsolved despite an attempt at a negotiated settlement.
This failure had led to the imposition of mandatory UN
sanctions. Faith in the UN had been shaken by the action
of the UN Secretary-General following Nasser's ultimatum,
and by the failure to enforce the sanctions against
Rhodesia by some member states. Despite this, the future
of the UN and its improvement were a matter of great concern to Brown: 'Unless a British Foreign Secretary
emerges... who really thinks that we can return to the
days of gunboat diplomacy, then the creation of a world
authority, effectively able not only to decide but to
enforce its decisions, must be the aim of any occupant of
that post. Therefore, how we maintain the present United
Nations, keep it operating and seek to build up its authority must be present in one's mind at every point and in
every issue that arises.'[64] Nor was Brown particularly
successful in either his Middle East diplomacy or in his
efforts to get Britain into the EEC. In both areas he
moved policy forward quite substantially and deserves
credit for that, but he did not stay at the Foreign Office
long enough to see his policies mature into success.

   To the normal frustrations facing a foreign minister
dealing with the international system was added in

November 1967 the devaluation of the pount sterling.
Although such a policy had been long advocated by George
Brown, he could not have been enthusiastic about its consequences for Britain's position in the world. Devaluation marked yet another point at which British pretensions
to a world role could seriously be questioned. Although
some people might argue that this was the final straw,
this view was not entirely shared by the Cabinet. 'Even
the devaluation of November 1967 did not persuade the government openly and frankly to face up to Britain's diminished role in the world. Certainly major defence cuts
were announced in January 1968. But when it came to re-
assessing Britain's foreign policy in the light of her
deminished power, the Cabinet evidently decided it couldn't
face the task.'[65] Even though he was a convinved 'European', Brown still believed in Britain's world role. But,
to the attempt to enter the EEC and the consequential
measures needed to make devaluation effective, could be
added the decline of Britain's 'special relationship' with
America and the changing political and economic relationships with the Commonwealth. Together these all spelt the
end of an era for Britain and marked her transition into
a 'second-rank power'. This transition had not been and
indeed was not a very palatable one: 'Minds long inured...
do not readily accept the need for a downward revision of
expectations to what is required of a second-rank state
with strictly regional interests... (This led to a) tendency to be driven towards decisions and policies not
because they (were) the most desirable, or least undesi-
rable, options but because other options (had) ceased to
be available.'[66] The policy-making of the Labour Government in many areas, including foreign affairs, certainly
seemed to bear out this observation. Devaluation did,
perhaps, bring reluctant agreement that some changes in
Britain's foreign policy were necessary. Equally it was
agreed that it would take some time before the necessary
adjustments and reorganisation of resources could take
place, and it might well be thought that George Brown, a
man of great vision and drive, was the kind of minister
who would have made a success of such a job.

However, the time Brown needed was not available to him
because less than two years after his appointment he resigned from the Government. As noted earlier he had

217

considerable policy disagreements with the prime minister, added to which he became increasingly dissatisfied not so much with the decisions of the Cabinet, as with the manner in which they were made. It was a combination of factors which led in March 1968 to his resignation. The events of the evening of 14–15 March have been told by the two main protagonists, and although they offer a somewhat divergent account of what happened, the end result was that George Brown's ministerial career finished very abruptly.[67] Such an end was always on the cards, given Brown's temperament; it can be seen not just as a personal tragedy but in some respects a national one. Brown had so much to offer, which was of fundamental importance in his original appointment. 'The Foreign Office... could do with a shake-up and a little more dynamism... we would have to take a decision about Europe, and George Brown seemed to me the appropriate leader for the task which might lie ahead.'[68] In the words of another commentator, 'George Brown was determined to get things done, and he did'.[69] This view is shared by Harold Wilson's private secretary, Marcia Williams (Lady Faulkender) who, writing about George Brown's period at the Foreign Office comments that 'there is no doubt he achieved a great deal'.[70] A more critical appraisal has been given by Joseph Frankel:

> A forceful Foreign Secretary can command full co-operation for his initiatives as long as his own views are in basic agreement with those prevalent among the officials, as was the case with Ernest Bevin. George Brown, however, soon fell out with his officials and could not prevail against them.[71]

Perhaps a more accurate and balanced conclusion would be that George Brown did not achieve as much as he thought he did. He did not claim to be, nor was he, a second Ernest Bevin as some had hoped and expected, but equally he had exceptional insight into the nature and problems of a foreign minister:

> The fact of the matter is that foreign affairs, whether for Britain or any other nation, are not just a catalogue of unconnected events. They most certainly aren't just a question of relations with this or that foreign power. They are a kaleidescope of inter-related pieces, all of which must somehow

be juggled with, virtually at the same time and certainly in relation to each other.[72]

He even considered the idea of a parliamentary committee on foreign affairs but dropped it when he realised what it entailed.[73] It was not just for these reasons that his departure was so much regretted by his fellow party members:

> ... it was sad for all of us to see George Brown go. He was a man of first class ability, a forceful and indeed imaginative administrator, respected by his parliamentary colleagues, and commanding more affection in the wider Labour movement than any of us. His strengths far exceeded his weaknesses, but it was his weaknesses which ended his ministerial career.[74]

It is hard to disagree with this conclusion. Brown laid the groundwork for a successful career at the Foreign Office. He had arrived expecting it to be 'a bit of a rest'[75] after the DEA. In this view he was mistaken. His short period at the Foreign Office was packed full of activity. He arrived at the Foreign Office in an atmosphere of good will and enthusiasm. He was worn down by the constant press criticism. He believed that stories about him were being fed to the press by disaffected Foreign Office members who maintained close contacts with the diplomatic correspondents (often former diplomats themselves) and by the effect this had on his family.[76] This last point is strenuously denied by Foreign Office officials. 'The agony of the Foreign Office, which is a loyal place, was keeping loyally mum about episodes which the press knew to have occurred and preserving a more "don't know anything about it" exterior.'[77] When he left the Foreign Office some at least of the good will had gone, but he could look back on a job well done. He had brought a considerable amount of flair to it and had been responsible for the appointment of non-career diplomats to important posts. He had appointed Sir Christopher Soames to Paris and John Freeman to Washington. He thought that Soames had been a successful appointment but had his doubts about Freeman.[78] These doubts were not shared by Henry Kissinger.[79] He had also made the Foreign Office more aware of the economic aspects of foreign policy.[80]

There is no doubt that the flair George Brown brought
to the offices he held would have been of great value
during the later years of the Wilson government. According to one colleague he has a 'warm and imaginative mind
mind',[81] adding that 'whatever ministry he is in at the
moment is a booming, zooming ministry'.[82] His premature
departure from the government leads one to the ultimate
conclusion that he failed to achieve all that he wanted
and that, given more time, he might well have proved to
be one of Britain's better foreign secretaries.

POSTSCRIPT

It is one of the quirks of post-war British history that
two men, from different political parties, should have
two periods at the Foreign Office and that their second
terms should have been consecutive. This was the case
with both Michael Stewart and Sir Alec Douglas-Home, who
between 1968 and 1974 each enjoyed a 'second innings'.
Their careers and personalities have been dealt with in
separate chapters, but it is perhaps useful by way of
postcript to recall a few salient points about the years
1968-74 and to add one or two comments on Stewart and
Home during their second terms of office.

It is usually regarded as an advantage for a minister
to serve a second term in an office of state, particularly
in relation to one of the major and long-established departments which often have firmly entrenched policies on
major issues and tend to have the ablest civil servants
to recommend these policies to the unwary minister. Indeed one of the continuing themes which runs through this
book is the extent to which the various ministers considered were able to put a personal imprint on the course
of British foreign policy, placed as they are between the
often conflicting pressures from departmental advisers,
the prime minister and Cabinet and the wishes of their
party. To have had previous experience of the department,
to have become familiar with its policies, personnel and
machinery and to have had the opportunity to weigh up
each of them should be an advantage in this respect. The
careers of Palmerston and Salisbury in the nineteenth century and Eden in this seem on the whole to confirm this
proposition.

In the case of Michael Stewart and Lord Home, the former
had experienced only a relatively brief period of office
in his first term and had only just 'got into the saddle'

when he left. The gap, too, was a relatively short one,
so that it is easy to see Stewart's tenure of the Foreign
Office as one continuous term, broken by an interregnum.

The circumstances surrounding Stewart's reappointment
to the Foreign Office in March 1968 are of interest. As
soon as it became clear that George Brown was on the
point of resigning, Harold Wilson put into effect plans
already made to meet the eventuality.[1] This action effectively ruled out any alternative to the appointment of
Michael Stewart. By this account, George Thomson, the
commonwealth secretary, was not in the running; nor was
Dennis Healey, although the strength of his claim was
greatly enhanced by his successful period as defence minister and several colleagues thought he deserved promotion.[2]
Stewart's appointment perhaps gives an insight into the
prime minister's view of the importance of the foreign
secretary. Despite the fact that Stewart was high in the
Cabinet pecking order,[3] unlike Brown he had no clearly
identifiable support in the parliamentary party and could
therefore not be regarded as a threat to Wilson. The
decision to reappoint Stewart was clear evidence that the
prime minister was determined to maintain overall control
of foreign policy strategy during the difficult days
following the devaluation of the pound.

The failure of the British economy had a considerable
impact on the conduct of Britain's foreign policy, not
least in bringing about the premature end of the basic
premise of Labour's foreign policy to that date, namely
the pursuit of a world role. The scaling down of
Britain's position in the world could be traced directly
to the failure of the Labour Government to prevent the
collapse of sterling. The unpleasant measures taken to
make devaluation work had, of necessity, to include cuts
in defence expenditure, most notably in the area east of
Suez. The consequences of these cuts were also felt in
the Foreign Office in so far as they reduced the means
available for achieving the policy goals. The Foreign
Office was thus a rather different place from the one
which Michael Stewart had left in 1966.

A useful source of comparison can be found by reference
to a speech, made by Stewart in June 1966 during his first
period at the Foreign Office. The speech, given to

222

members of the Australian Institute of International Affairs,[4] is a careful documentation of the British position on most of the important issues in international affairs at that time. In his discussion of Asia, Stewart called for the admission of the People's Republic of China to the UN and condemned American bombing of North Vietnam. In addition, he offered some words of comfort to those who doubted Britain's interest in and ability to carry out a world role: 'There are, I think, those that fear that the United Kingdom... may be tempted to abandon her role in the Far East, evacuate Singapore, and go home. This is quite wrong... Far from opting out of a world role we will be very much still in business in the Far East as elsewhere... So you can take it from me that we have neither the wish not the intention to turn our backs on the world East of Suez.'[5]

When Stewart returned in 1968, British pretensions in the area east of Suez had been cut almost to nothing.[6] Furthermore, he returned to find that many of the problems he had left in 1966 were still unresolved. In Vietnam, for example, despite President Johnson's offer to negotiate, the war dragged on. Indeed, it was still an issue when Labour left office, as was Rhodesia, where despite the application of mandatory economic sanctions by the UN, the white supremacist regime of Ian Smith continued to hold effective power. The British application for membership of the EEC remained 'on the table' but little progress was made until shortly before the defeat of the Labour Government in the 1970 election. All Stewart could do in this direction was to ensure that the application did not lapse. To these areas of continuing concern had been added new ones. Civil war in Nigeria had broken out and British Government support for the Federal Nigerian Government came under heavy fire from many quarters, although the policy was supported by the Conservative front bench. Overshadowing all, however, was the situation in the Middle East in the aftermath of the 1967 war. Of these issues, only the Nigerian one had been resolved when Michael Stewart handed over the Foreign Office in June 1970 to his Conservative successor, Sir Alex Douglas-Home, to whom many of these problems also appeared familiar both from his previous experience as foreign secretary and, in the more recent past, as shadow foreign secretary.

Sir Alec Douglas-Home returned in 1970 to a department which he knew well and which respected him, and to take his seat in a Cabinet where he was very much an elder statesman, under a prime minister who had previously served him as No 2 at the Foreign Office. He had, too, great prestige in his party and a certain prestige and reputation internationally. There is no doubt that all these were advantages and strengthened his position. He carried very great weight in the Cabinet and in Parliament, and his views were heard with respect by foreign statesmen.

Nevertheless, Home's second term of office was not marked by any very outstanding achievements, competently though he guided British foreign policy between 1970 and 1974. The reason is twofold. Partly it lay in the fact that Home was not by nature a very creative minister. But mainly it lay in the fact that British power and consequently the scope and influence of this country's foreign policy had sharply declined since Home's previous term of office. Home recognised, to a greater extent than the preceding government had done, the limitations which this imposed on his conduct of affairs, and the fact that Britain now, for example, had little power to influence the course of events in Vietnam or in the Middle East conflict. He could indicate, as in the case of Israel and the Harrogate speech, which way he thought events should go, but that was all.[7] He recognised, too, the extent to which the 'special relationship' with the United States and the Commonwealth connection had become dwindling assets.

It was all the more evident to him, as to most of the political leaders on both sides and ultimately to the British people, that if this country was to play again any major part in the world's affairs, and indeed if British interests were to be adequately protected, it could only be as part of a larger political and economic unit, in other words through membership of the EEC. It is a truism to say that the one major achievement of the Heath government was to take Britain into Europe, and although Home, partly because of the prime minister's overriding interest, did not play a major part in the negotiations, he lent the full weight of his prestige and authority to the task of keeping the Conservative Party committed to the policy and securing its acceptance of

224

terms which were not widely regarded as favourable. When Home left the Foreign Office in 1974, therefore, it marked the end of a long era in British foreign policy and the beginning of a wholly new role for Britain, the nature and scope of which has yet to be determined, in Europe and perhaps in the world.

NOTES

CHAPTER 1: THE FOREIGN SECRETARY AND THE MAKING OF BRITISH FOREIGN POLICY

1   Hans J.Morgenthau, Politics among Nations (New York, Knopf, 2nd ed, 1954), 528
2. Hans J.Morgenthau, In Defence of the National Interest: A Critical Examination of American Foreign Policy (New York, Knopf, 1951), 242
3   For a different view see Joseph Frankel, National Interest (London, Pall Mall, 1970), 27
4   R.D.Snyder, H.W.Bruck and B.M.Sapin (eds), Foreign Policy Decision Making: An Approach to the Study of International Politics (New York, The Free Press of Glencoe, 1962), 65
5   Ibid, 67
6   The most useful and comprehensive account is F.S. Northedge, Descent From Power: British Foreign Policy 1945-1973 (London, Allen & Unwin, 1974). Another recent and outstanding survey which deals with the background to policy-making as well as the substance of policy is Joseph Frankel, British Foreign Policy 1945-1973 (London, Oxford University Press, 1975)
7   For a similar classificatory scheme see James N. Rosenau, The Scientific Study of Foreign Policy (New York, The Free Pres, 1971), 108-9
8   Kenneth Boulding, 'National Images and the International System', Journal of Conflict Resolution, 2 (June 1959)
9   Margaret and Harold Sprout, 'Environmental Factors in the study of International Politics', Journal of Conflict Resolution, Vol I No 4 (1957); see also Joseph Frankel, The Making of Foreign Policy: An Analysis of Decision-Making (London, Oxford University Press, 1963), 4-5
10 David Vital, The Making of British Foreign Policy (London, Allen & Unwin, 1968), 52
11 Harold Macmillan, Tides of Fortune (London, Macmillan, 1969), 529

12 William Wallace, <u>The Foreign Policy Process in Britain</u> (London, The Royal Institute of International Affairs, 1975)

13 For a detailed account of the relevant groups and agencies see Robert Boardman and A.J.R.Groom, <u>The Management of Britain's External Relations</u> (London, Macmillan, 1973)

14 For a fuller account of Parliament's role see P.G.Richards, <u>Parliament and Foreign Affairs</u> (London, Allen & Unwin, 1967)

15 Henry A.Kissinger <u>American Foreign Policy: Three Essays</u> (London, Weidenfeld & Nicolson, 1969), 95

16 George Brown, <u>In My Way</u> (London, Gollancz, 1971), 129

17 Kenneth Younger, 'Public Opinion and Foreign Policy', <u>British Journal of Sociology</u>, VI (June 1955), 169

18 Ibid, 171

19 F.S.Northedge (ed), <u>The Foreign Policies of the Powers</u> (London, Faber, 1969), 14

20 <u>Report of the Review Committee on Overseas Representation</u>, (HMSO, 1969, Cmnd 4107)

CHAPTER 2: ERNEST BEVIN

1   For an excellent biography of Bevin which covers his
    career up to 1945, see Alan Bullock, The Life and
    Times of Ernest Bevin, Vol I: Trade Union Leader
    1881-1940 (London, Heinemann, 1960) and Vol II:
    Minister of Labour 1940-1945 (London, Heinemann,
    1967)
2   Francis Williams, A Prime Minister Remembers: The
    War and Post-War Memoirs of Earl Attlee (London,
    Heinemann, 1961), 5
3   C.R.Attlee, As It Happened (London, Heinemann, 1954),
    69
4   Williams; A Prime Minister Remembers, 150
5   Ibid
6   Herbert Morrison, Government and Parliament (London,
    Oxford University Press, 1964), 50
7   Max Beloff, New Dimensions in British Foreign Policy
    (London, Allen & Unwin, 1961), 121 and 153
8   Quoted in Trevor Evans, Bevin (London, Allen & Unwin,
    1946), 210
9   Hugh Dalton, High Tide and After: Memoirs 1945-1960
    (London, Frederick Muller, 1962), 240
10 George Brown, In My Way (London, Gollancz, 1971), 57
11 Geoffrey Williams and Bruce Reed, Denis Healey and
    the Policies of Power (London, Sidgwick & Jackson,
    1971), 51
12 R.H.S.Crossman, The Charm of Politics (London, Hamish
    Hamilton, 1958), 76
13 Ernest Bevin, The Balance Sheet of the Future (New
    York, Robert M.McBride, 1941), 111
14 Sir William Hayter, A Double Life (London, Hamish
    Hamilton, 1974), 76-7
15 Lord Strang, Britain in World Affairs (London, Faber
    and Andre Deutsch, 1961), 344
16 Sir Roderick Barclay, Ernest Bevin and the Foreign
    Office 1932-1969 (London, published by the author,
    1975), 84
17 See, for example, Labour Party Conference Report, 1946.
18 Sir Ivone Kirkpatrick, The Inner Circle (London,
    Macmillan, 1959), 203-4
19 Hayter, A Double Life, 77

20 Letter from Lord Sherfield to the author, 6 May 1975
21 Lord Strang, Home and Abroad (London, Andre Deutsch,
    1956), 288
22 Lord Strang, The Diplomatic Career (London, Andre
    Deutsch, 1962), 110–11, and Lord Gladwyn, The
    Memoirs of Lord Gladwyn (London, Weidenfeld &
    Nicolson, 1971), 226–7
23 The Observer, 6 and 13 March 1960
24 Kirkpatrick, Inner Circle, 202
25 The Observer, 6 and 13 March 1960
26 Ibid
27 See, for example, Paul-Henri Spaak, The Continuing
    Battle (London, Weidenfeld & Nicolson, 1971), 143;
    Dean Acheson, Present at the Creation: My Years
    in the State Department (London, Hamish Hamilton,
    1969), 271; and Dirk W.Stikker, Men of Respons-
    ibility (London, John Murray, 1965), 285–6
28 House of Commons Debates vol 437 col 1965, 16 May
    1947
29 James F.Byrnes, Speaking Frankly (London, Heinemann,
    1947), 79
30 Quoted in the autobiography of Francis Williams,
    Nothing So Strange (London, Cassell, 1970), 244
31 Hugh Dalton's Diary, entry for 27 July 1947, in the
    Dalton Papers deposited in the London School of
    Economics and Political Science
32 Quoted in Harold Nicolson, Diaries and Letters
    1945–1962 (London, Collins, 1968), 49
33 Ibid, 107–8
34 Trygve Lie, In the Cause of Peace: Seven Years with
    the United Nations (New York, The Macmillan Company,
    1954), 31–2
35 Ibid, 309–13
36 Geoffrey L.Goodwin, Britain and the United Nations
    (London, Oxford University Press, 1957), 51–8
37 Francis Williams, Ernest Bevin: Portrait of a Great
    Englishman (London, Hutchinson, 1952), 262
38 Williams, A Prime Minister Remembers, 171
39 Williams, Nothing So Strange, 245
40 It is ironic that Bevin took the events in Greece as
    incontrovertible evidence of Communist intentions.
    Communist insurgency in Greece was the work of in-
    ternal forces; it was not Soviet-inspired. Indeed,
    Stalin instructed that 'The uprising in Greece must
    be stopped, and as quickly as possible'. See

Milovan Djilas, Conversations with Stalin (Pelican Books, 1969), 140-1

41   Millis, The Forrestal Diaries, 292
42   The Listener, 14 June 1956
43   Joseph M.Jones, The Fifteen Weeks (New York, Harcourt Brace, 1955), 36 and 255-6;   and Robert Murphy, Diplomat Among Warriors (London, Collins, 1964), 377
44   Herbert Morrison, An Autobiography (London, Odhams, 1960), 260
45   W.W.Rostow, The United States in the World Arena (New York, Harper & Brothers, 1960), 211
46   Jacques Dumaine, Quai D'Orsai 1945-1951 (Paris, Rene Juillard, 1956), 204-5;   and Vincent Auriol, Journal du Septennat 1947-1954, Vol I (1947), edited by Pierre Nora (Paris, Armand Collin, 1970), 311-12
47   Attlee, As It Happened, 170
48   Christopher Mayhew, 'British Foreign Policy Since 1945', International Affairs, October 1950
49   House of Commons Debates, Vol 445, col 1881
50   Attlee, As It Happened, 171
51   House of Commons Debates, Vol 446, col 383-409
52   Cmd 7212 (1947) Treaty of Alliance and Mutual Assistance
53   Spaak, Continuing Battle, 147
54   Cmd 7367 (1948) Treaty of Economic, Social and Cultural Collaboration and Collective Self-Defence
55   The Papers of R.G.W.Mackay, Group 7, File 2, deposited at the London School of Economics and Political Science
56   Viscount Montgomery of Alamein, The Memoirs of Field-Marshal Montgomery (London, Collins, 1958), 498
57   Harry S.Truman, Memoirs, Vol II: Years of Trial and Hope (New York, The New American Library, 1956), 280;   and George Kenna, Memoirs (London, Hutchinson, 1968), 398
58   Millis, The Forrestal Diaries, 372
59   Truman, Memoirs, Vol II, Years of Trial and Hope, 281-2
60   Lord Ismay, NATO: The First Five Years 1949-1954 (Paris, 1956), 10
61   Ibid, 37
62   House of Commons Debates, Vol 464, col 2016, 12 May 1949
63   Labour Party Conference Report, 1949, 189
64   Attlee, As It Happened, 172

65 House of Commons Debates, Vol 468, col 2204
66 The Royal Institute of International Affairs, Britain
     and Western Europe (A Report by a Study Group, London,
     1956), 8
67 House of Commons Debates, Vol 456, col 106
68 The New York Times, 13 July 1947
69 House of Commons Debates, Vol 469, col 2210
70 'Mr Bevin's Record', The Economist, 17 December 1949
71 Strang, Home and Abroad, 290
72 House of Commons Debates, Vol 456, col 106
73 Dalton Diary, 19 November 1948
74 Strang, Home and Abroad, 890
75 Brown, In My Way, 207
76 Dalton Papers, Letter from Ernest Bevin to Herbert
     Morrison, 22 January 1951
77 Dumaine, Quai d'Orsai 1945-1951, 497
78 Dean Acheson, Sketches From Life (New York, 1961),
     35-9
79 Cmd 7970 (1950), Anglo-French Discussions Regarding
     French Proposals for the European Coal, Iron and
     Steel Industries, May-June 1950
80 Vincent Auriol, Non Septennat 1947-1954, edited by
     Pierre Nora (Paris, Gallimard, 1960), 265
81 Cmd 7970, 13-14
82 In this he followed the advice of the British
     ambassador to Paris. Letter from Sir Oliver Harvey
     to Ernest Bevin, dated 10 June 1950 (copy in the
     Dalton Papers)
83 Anthony Nutting, Europe Will Not Wait (London, Hollis
     & Carter, 1960), 32
84 Kirkpatrick, Inner Circle, 240
85 House of Commons Debates, Vol 481, col 1173-4,
     29 November 1950
86 Arthur Bryant, Triumph in the West 1943-1946, based
     on the Diaries and Autobiographical Notes of Field
     Marshal the Viscount Alanbrooke (London, Collins,
     1959), 533
87 Williams, A Prime Minister Remembers, 176
88 Nadav Safran, From War to War (New York, Pegasus,
     1969), 99-100
89 Dalton, High Tide and After, 190
90 House of Commons Debates, Vol 419, col 1361-2,
     21 February 1946
91 Ibid, Vol 475, col 2083

92 Acheson, _Present at the Creation_, 329
93 Interview with Sir Kenneth Younger, 16 May 1975
94 For two perceptive discussions of these issues see
    Richard Rose, _The Relation of Socialist Principles_
    to British Labour's Foreign Policy 1945-1951
    (unpublished DPhil thesis, Oxford 1961) and
    M.R.Gordon, _Conflict and Consensus in Labour's_
    Foreign Policy (California, Stanford University
    Press, 1969)
95 Piers Dixon, _Double Diploma: The Life of Sir Pierson_
    Dixon (Londo, Hutchinson, 1968), 179
96 Strang, _Britain in World Affairs_, 338-9
97 In 1950, for example Bevin said: 'I tried from the
    day I took office until 1947 to be friends with
    Russia'. _Labour Party Conference Report_ (1950), 146

CHAPTER 3: HERBERT MORRISON

1   Herbert Morrison, An Autobiography (London, Odhams, 1960), 273. For more detailed and critical dis- cussion of Morrison's career, see B.Donoughue and G.E.Jones, Herbert Morrison: Portrait of a Politician (London, Weidenfeld & Nicolson, 1973)
2   Morrison, Autobiography, 164
3   C.R.Attlee, The Granada Historical Records Interview (London, Panther Record, 1967), 49
4   The full Labour delegation was: H.Morrison, H.Dalton, W.Whiteley (all members of the Government), Seymour Cocks, Aidan Crawley, Maurice Edelman, Peggy Herbison, Fred Lee, L.Ungoed-Thomas, T.Nally, and R.W.G.Mackay who was a leading supporter of the Harold Federalist cause in the Labour Party
5   Macmillan, Memoirs Vol 3: Tides of Fortune (London, Macmillan 1969) 169
6   Ibid 171
7   Dalton Papers: Strasbourg File. Letter from Dalton to Attlee, 10 September 1949
8   Macmillan, Tides of Fortune, 174
9   Ibid, 169
10 Council of Europe, Consultative Assembly Official Report (First Session; sixth sitting, 17 August 1949), Vol 1, 232
11 Ibid, 228
12 Macmillan, Tides of Fortune, 183
13 The Times, 10 March 1951
14 For details of the crisis, see B.Donoughue and G.Jones, Herbert Morrison, 84ff
15 House of Commons Debates, Vol 485, col 1059-60, (12 March 1951), and a week later, col 2095-9 and 2102-3
16 Ibid, Vol 487, col 1954 (May 1951)
17 Lord Gladwyn, Memoirs of Lord Gladwyn (London, Weidenfeld & Nicolson, 1972), 252
18 M.A.Fitzsimons, The Foreign Policy of the British Labour Government 1945-51 (Indiana, University of Notre Dame Press, 1953), 146
19 H.Nicolson, Diary with Letters (Vol 3: 1945-1962) edited by H.Nicolson (London, Fontana, 1971), 192-3 1 August 1951

20 Donoughue and Jones, Herbert Morrison, 498
21 Joseph Frankel, British Foreign Policy 1945-73
      (London, R.I.I.A. by Oxford U.P, 1975), 132;
      Morrison's statement to the House of Commons on
      20 June 1951; his speech in the debate the
      following day: House of Commons Debates, Vol 489
      col 519-26, col 822-32; and his performance in
      the debate on 11 July 1951: Ibid, Vol 450,
      col 424-8
22 Dean Acheson, Present at the Creation (London,
      Hamish Hamilton, 1969), 556f
23 Donoughue and Jones, Herbert Morrison, 503
24 House of Commons Debates, Vol 424, col 67-70
      (12 February 1951)
25 Dalton Papers: Miscellaneous 1951. Marginal note by
      Dalton on a letter to Attlee, dated 14 March 1951.
      The note was added some time after the letter was
      sent.
26 Germany No 10 (1952) Cmd. 8626. p3 quoted in
      F.S.Northedge, Descent from Power (London, Allen
      & Unwin, 1974), 157; and Saul Rose, 'The Labour
      Party and German Rearmament: A view from Transport
      House', Political Studies, Vol XIV, No 2 1966,
      133-44
27 House of Commons Debates, Vol 496, col 969-74
      (26 February 1952), also Harold Nicolson, Diary with
      Letters Vol 3, 205, 3 March 1953
28 Dalton Papers: Diary, 16 September 1951
29 Hugh Dalton, High Tide and After (London, Muller,
      1962), 360f
30 Lord Gladwyn, Memoirs, 251. Gladwyn expressed a
      preference for McNeil
31 Attlee, Granada Historical Records Interview, 55, 49
32 A.Husler, Contribution a l'etude de l'elaboration de
      la politique etranger brittanique, 1945-56 (Geneva,
      1961), p30, quoted in D.Vital, The Making of British
      Foreign Policy (London, Allen & Unwin, 1968), 70
33 Fitzsimons Foreign Policy 151
34 Quoted in Donoughue and Jones, Herbert Morrison, 498
35 Interview with Sir Kenneth Younger, 16 May 1975
36 Donoughue and Jones, Herbert Morrison, 514

CHAPTER 4: ANTHONY EDEN

1   Apart from Eden's own 1800-page account of his career
    and the flood of publications on inter-war and post-
    war British foreign policy in which he figures pro-
    minently, a considerable number of biographies and
    critical studies are devoted specifically to him:
    Dennis Bardens, Portrait of a Statesman: The
    Personal Life Story of Sir Anthony Eden (London,
    Fredrick Muller, 1955); Lewis Broad, Sir Anthony
    Eden: The Chronicles of a Career (London, Hutchinson,
    1955); Alan Campbell-Johnson, Sir Anthony Eden
    (London, Robert Hale, 1955); Randolph S.Churchill,
    The Rise and Fall of Sir Anthony Eden (London,
    MacGibbon & Kee, 1959); and Geoffrey McDermott,
    The Eden Legacy and the Decline of British Diplomacy
    (London, Leslie Frewin, 1969)
2   Winston S.Churchill, The Second World War, Vol IV:
    The Hinge of Fate (London, Cassell, 1951), 337
3   Anthony Eden, Foreign Affairs (London, Faber, 1939);
    Anthony Eden, Freedom and Order (London, Faber,
    1947); Anthony Eden, Days for Decision (London,
    Faber, 1949)
4   See, for example, Harold Macmillan, Tides of Fortune
    (London, Macmillan, 1969), 46, Lord Chandos, The
    Memoirs of Lord Chandos (London, The Bodley Head,
    1962), 291-2 and Herbert Morrison, An Autobiography
    (London, Odhams, 1960), 297-8
5   The Earl of Avon, The Eden Memoirs: Full Circle
    (London, Cassell, 1960), 247
6   Eden, Full Circle, 249
7   Valentine Lawford, 'Three Ministers', The Cornhill
    Magazine, No 169 (1956-8)
8   Lord Moran, Winston Churchill: The Struggle for
    Survival 1940-1965) (London, Constable, 1966), 576
9   Ibid, 592
10 Ibid, 556
11 Ibid, 627 and 559
12 Robert Rhodes James (ed), Chips: The Diaries of Sir
    Henry Channon (London, Weidenfeld & Nicolson, 1967),
    entry for 5 November 1952, 470

13 Moran, Winston Churchill, 501-2
14 Ibid, 710
15 Ibid, 724
16 The Earl of Kilmuir, Political Advanture (London, Weidenfeld & Nicolson, 1964), 193
17 Chandos, Memoirs, 291
18 Kilmuir, Political Adventure, 257
19 David Dilks (ed), The Diaries of Sir Alexander Cadogan (London, Cassell, 1971), 376
20 Moran, Winston Churchill, 592
21 Interview with Lord Gladwyn, 7 May 1975
22 Related in Moran, Winston Churchill, 627
23 Harold Nicolson, Diaries and Letters 1939-1945 (London, Fontana, 1970), 337
24 Ibid, 345
25 Sir Harold Nicolson, Diplomacy (London, Oxford University Press, 3rd ed, 1963), 52-4
26 Eden, Full Circle, 188
27 The Royal Institute of International Affairs, Documents on International Affairs 1951 (London, Oxford University Press, 1954), 34607
28 Eden, Days for Decision, 212
29 Ibid, 126
30 Quoted in Western European Co-operation: a Reference Handbook (London, Central Office of Information, November 1955), 14
31 The Earl of Avon, The Eden Memoirs: Facing the Dictators (London, Cassell, 1962), 351
32 Ibid, 597
33 Ibid, 367
34 The Royal Institute of International Affairs, Documents on International Affairs, 1952 (London, Oxford University Press, 1955), 41-2
35 Eden, Full Circle, 49
36 Alan Thompson, The Day Before Yesterday (London, Sidgwick & Jackson, 1971), 105
37 Anthony Eden, 'Britain in World Strategy', Foreign Affairs, Vol 29, No 3 (April 1951)
38 Dwight D.Eisenhower, The White House Years: Mandate for Change, 1953-1956 (London, Heinemann, 1963), 142
39 R.N.Rosencrance, Defence of the Realm: British Strategy in the Nuclear Epoch (New York, Columbia University Press, 1968), 199
40 House of Commons Debates, Vol 494, col 34, 19 November 1951

41 Dean Acheson, Present at the Creation: My Years in
   the State Department (London, Hamish Hamilton,
   1969), 630

42 House of Commons Debates, Vol 504, col 1709,
   31 July 1952

43 The full text of the Eden memorandum is given in the
   Department of State Bulletin, 8 February 1954,
   186-7

44 House of Commons Debates, Vol 524, col 401-16,
   24 February 1954

45 Lord Boothby, My Yesterday, Your Tomorrow (London,
   Hutchinson, 1962), 57; Kilmuir, Political Adventure,
   177

46 Thompson, Day Before Yesterday, 104

47 Documents on International Affairs 1952, pp 43-4

48 Kilmuir, Political Advanture, 186

49 Council of Europe, Consultative Assembly, Fourth
   Ordinary Session (First Part) 26th - 30th May 1952,
   Documents, Vol I, Document II, pp 288-90

50 Anthony Nutting, Europe Will Not Wait (London, Hollis
   & Carter, 1960), 44-5

51 House of Commons Debates, Vol 520, col 316,
   5 November 1953

52 Cmd 8562 (1952), Treaty between the United Kingdom
   and the member states of the European Defence
   Community

53 Eden, Full Circle, 33-4

54 Ibid, 165-6

55 Interview with Lord Gladwyn, 7 May 1975

56 Nicolson, Diaries and Letters 1945-1962, 237

57 House of Commons Debates, Vol 531, col 811,
   29 July 1954

58 Acheson, Present at the Creation, 511

59 Eden, Full Circle, 77

60 Ibid, 105

61 Anthony Eden, Towards Peace in Indo-China (Oxford
   University Press for Chatham House, 1966), p XI

62 Anthony Nutting, No End of a Lesson: The Story of
   Suez (London, Constable, 1967), 25

CHAPTER 5: HAROLD MACMILLAN

1   Earl of Kilmuir, Political Advanture (London,
    Weidenfeld & Nicolson, 1964), 243, 256
2   Harold Macmillan, Tides of Fortune (London, Macmillan,
    1969), 695
3   Kilmuir, Political Adventure 193
4   Lord Butler, The Art of the Possible (London, Hamish
    Hamilton, 1971), 181
5   Macmillan, Tides of Fortune, 638
6   Ibid, 696
7   Earl of Avon, Full Circle (London, Cassell, 1960)
8   Lord Butler records that Macmillan 'exploded' when he
    first learnt that Eden's doctor had advised him to
    leave the country for a complete rest during the
    Suez crisis (Butler, Art of the Possible, 194)
9   This was more clearly seen later in his failure as
    prime minister to give a more positive lead on
    Europe, and in another aspect in his celebrated mis-
    understanding with de Gaulle at Rambouillet in 1962.
    Cf J.R.Bevins, The Greasy Pole (London, Hodder &
    Stoughton, 1965), 32, 34
10 Eden, Full Circle, 336 and passim
11 See Chapter 6,
12 Macmillan, Tides of Fortune, 620
13 Ibid, 584. Cf Lord Gladwyn, Memoirs of Lord Gladwyn
    (London, Weidenfeld & Nicolson, 1972), 276
14 Cf Sir William Hayter, A Double Life (London, Hamish
    Hamilton, 1974), 174.
15 By the mid-sixties officials of the Turkish Foreign
    Office were describing it as 'a dead duck' (in con-
    versations with the author)
16 The Pact was signed and Britain adhered to it before
    Macmillan became foreign secretary, though Macmillan
    as defence minister was of course much concerned
    with it.
17 Macmillan, Tides of Fortune, 108
18 Ibid, 637
19 Harold Macmillan, Riding the Storm (London, Macmillan,
    1971), 82, 84
20 Ibid, 434, 435. See below, Chapter 6 on this issue

CHAPTER 6: SELWYN LLOYD

1   Evidence of a senior official (private information).
    But cf Earl of Avon, Full Circle (London, Cassell,
    1960), 166-7
2   Cf Avon, Full Circle, 318, 449, 488; H.Macmillan,
    Riding the Storm (London, Macmillan, 1971), 119,
    144-5, 169, 186, 472
3   Cf Avon, Full Circle, 274
4   The exception is Kilmuir Political Advanture, 312-13,
    But it is difficult to know how much the generally
    'vinegary' tone of Kilmuir's memoirs was affected by
    his still active resentment at his summary exclusion
    from the Cabinet in 1962
5   Rt Hon Lord Harlech, KCMG, in an interview with the
    author, 19 March 1975. Lord Harlech was parliamen-
    tary private secretary to Selwyn Lloyd as minister
    of state, later under-secretary at the Foreign Office
    1956-7, and himself minister of state 1957-61,
    Ambassador to Washington 1961-5
6   Lord Harlech to the author; cf Michael Howard
    Disengagement (London, Penguin, 1958); Lord Gladwyn,
    Memoirs (London, Weidenfeld, 1972), 176
7   Cf Gladwyn, Memoirs, 265. Also private information
    from a Minister in the Eden government
8   Evidence of a minister in the Eden government
    (private information)
    After serving more than one term as prime minister
    and foreign secretary of his native Belgium, M.Spaak
    became the second secretary-general of NATO in the
    late fifties cf P.H.Spaak, The Continuing Battle
    (London, Weidenfeld & Nicolson, 1971), 236-7
    Some significant conversations on these points with
    Monnet, the 'father' of the European idea, are re-
    corded by Lord Gladwyn, Memoirs, 349, Sir W.Hayter
    A Double Life (London, Hamish Hamilton, 1974), 91-2,
    and C.L.Sulzberger The Last of the Giants, (London,
    Weidenfeld, 1970), 854
9   A ministerial colleague of Lloyd's in a letter to the
    author (private information). Cf Hayter, Double
    Life, 91

10   Lloyd's attitude, however, was not hostile to the EEC.
     Lord Gladwyn, who was ambassador to France, records
     that the Foreign Office was 'indignant' at this
     suggestion that Britain might have the intention of
     'trying to sabotage the Common Market'. On the con-
     trary the idea was 'welcomed, if indeed it could be
     formed'. Gladwyn, Memoirs, 294
11   See above Chapter 5. Cf also Avon Full Circle, 343-4
     for a contrary view
12   Cf Gladwyn, Memoirs, 253
13   For Eden's view of Lloyd as a parliamentarian see
     Avon Full Circle, 318. This view is confirmed by
     colleagues to whom the author has spoken
14   For this point I am indebted to one of Lloyd's
     ministerial colleagues at the Foreign Office
15   Cf Hayter, Double Life, 156
16   It is generally thought that only Sir Walter Monckton
     (Viscount Monckton of Brenchley) had real reserva-
     tions on Suez, though it is believed that R.A.Butler
     and others had their doubts, particularly towards
     the end, Thomas Suez Affair, 81-2, 104-5, 181.
     Butler himself, while slightly enigmatic as is his
     wont, does not claim to have dissented, or to have
     spoken against the use of force, Butler, The Art of
     the Possible (London, Hamish Hamilton, 1971), 188-9.
     There were no resignations from the Cabinet on this
     issue. Cf also Lord Birkenhead, Walter Monckton
     (London, Weidenfeld & Nicolson, 1969), chapter 31
17   Avon, Full Circle, 481
18   Macmillan, Riding the Storm, 286, 472. Cf Kilmuir,
     Political Adventure, 312; A.Sampson, Macmillan
     (London, Penguin, 1967), 142
19   Macmillan, Riding the Storm, 186
20   Macmillan was on occasion subject to 'crises de nerf'
     - not surprisingly in view of the responsibility he
     carried - which made him sometimes physically ill;
     notably at the abortive 'U2' Summit in May 1960,
     when Khrushchev broke up the meeting with Macmillan,
     Eisenhower and de Gaulle after the American U2 plane
     had been shot down over Russia
21   Macmillan, Riding the Storm, 192. Macmillan's tribute
     to Zulueta's valuable contribution is confirmed by
     all the ministers and officials to whom the author
     has spoken.
22   Lord Harlech to the author

23 Lord Harlech to the author
24 Hon A.Nutting, minister of state, Foreign Office,
    1954-6, under-secretary, Foreign Office 1951-4.
    Nutting has told his side of the story in his book
    <u>No End of a Lesson</u> (London, Constable, 1967). On
    the 'official' reaction, see Lord Gore-Booth, <u>With</u>
    Great Truth and Respect, (London, Constable, 1974),
    229-33
25 Opinion expressed to the writer by a senior official
    of that period (private information)
26 Hayter, <u>Double Life</u>, 156
27 Opinions expressed to the writer by senior officials
    of that period (private information)
28 Thomas, <u>Suez Affair</u>, 127-8. Only the Permanent
    Under Secretary, Sir Ivone Kirkpatrick, the deputy
    under-secretary of state, Sir Patrick Dean and the
    secretary of the Cabinet, Sir Norman Brook, were
    early and fully informed, according to Thomas, who
    cites a Cabinet minister as his authority and also
    says that Kirkpatrick himself was 'dubious' about
    the proposed action.
29 It has been suggested by a recent unfavourable critic
    of the higher civil service that a minister's private
    secretary may put his loyalty to the service and to
    his permanent head before his loyalty to the minister
    M. Williams, <u>Inside No.10</u> (Weidenfeld & Nicolson,
    London, 1972), 199, 347-8. A good private secretary,
    however, would be able to reconcile these loyalties,
    and whatever may have been the case during the
    1964-70 Wilson government, there is no reason to
    doubt that Lloyd's secretaries did so.
30 Notably in recent years the late Iain Macleod and
    R.H.S.Crossman. Cf also J.R.Bevins, <u>The Greasy Pole</u>
    (London, Hodder & Stoughton, 1965), Chapters 6 and 7.
    Cf also Kenneth Harris, <u>Conversations</u> (London,
    Hodder & Stoughton, 1967), 270-1. A minor but inter-
    esting example is recorded in Leslie Smith, <u>Harold</u>
    <u>Wilson</u> (London, Fontana, 1964), 103-6. It illus-
    trates the point that even a very new and junior
    minister need not come off worse in such encounters.
31 Cf Thomas, <u>Suez Affair</u>, 47
32 Ibid
33 Ibid, Chapter 8, pp 69, 76, 80, 94, 149
34 Cf Gladwyn, <u>Memoirs</u>, 291-3

35 Opinion expressed to the writer by a senior Foreign
   Office official and a Cabinet minister of the period
   (private information)
36 Thomas, Suez Affair, 78, 86, 101, 107. Menzies always
   believed there was an outside chance of getting an
   acceptable settlement up to the moment when Eisenhower said the use of force was not contemplated.
   Cf Menzies' own account of the Suez crisis in his
   book Afternoon Light (London, Cassell, 1967),
   Chapter 8
37 Thomas, Suez Affair, 81, 113
38 Ibid, 181
39 Macmillan, Riding the Storm, 119. Avon, Full Circle,
   449, 488, 503, etc. Cf also K.Young, Sir Alec
   Douglas-Home (London, Dent, 1970), 95
40 A point made by two of Lloyd's ministerial colleagues
   to the author (private information)
41 Macmillan, Riding the Storm, 153, 169, 172; Lord
   Harlech to the author
42 Cf Avon, Full Circle, 63-4, 98-9, 332, 335-6
43 Macmillan, Riding the Storm, 282; Hayter, Double Life,
   156; Thomas, Suez Affair, 168; (confirmed by private
   information)
44 Cf Hayter, Double Life, 155
45 Ibid, 173-4; Gladwyn, Memoirs, 277
46 A view expressed to the author by a number of his
   former colleagues
47 Macmillan, Pointing the Way (London, Macmillan, 1972)
   63-5
48 Cf Macmillan, Riding the Storm, 432; Hayter, Double
   Life, 95; Sampson, Macmillan 256-7 and others record
   a 'leak' in the Washington Post in March 1960 of
   remarks hostile to the EEC supposed to have been
   made by Macmillan. Unfortunately one cannot be sure
   how reliable a 'leak' is as evidence. Macmillan was
   certainly apt to talk 'for effect' sometimes: but
   shortly after this he said in Parliament that Britain
   did not want to weaken the Six, or widen the gap in
   Europe
49 Macmillan, Pointing the Way, 51, 55-6
50 Dean Acheson, Present at the Creation (New York, 1970),
   583, 656, 701-5
51 Macmillan, Pointing the Way, 695; Avon, Full Circle,
   318

52 At this period the 'off-shore islands' of Quemoy and
    Matsu held by Chiang Kai-shek's Nationalists were
    being bombarded by the Chinese Communists. The US
    was committed to supporting Chiang Kai-shek

CHAPTER 7: LORD HOME

1   K.Young, <u>Sir Alec Douglas-Home</u> (London, Dent, 1970),
    121;   cf Harold Macmillan, <u>Pointing The Way</u>, 231;
2   Earl of Avon, <u>Full Circle</u> (London, Cassell, 1960)
    274
3   Lord Butler, <u>The Art of the Possible</u> (London, Hamish
    Hamilton, 1971), Young, <u>Douglas-Home</u>, 133. Lord
    Home's own views were expressed in an interview
    with the author, 6 March 1975;   they are shared by
    ministerial colleagues and officials to whom the
    author has spoken. Cf Lord Home, <u>The Way the Wind
    Blows</u>, (London, Collins, 1976) p 71
4   See Earl of Kilmuir, <u>Political Adventure</u> (London,
    Weidenfeld & Nicolson, 1962), 313;   Lord Hill of
    Luton, <u>Both Sides of the Hill</u> (London, Heinemann,
    1964), 243, 244;   Young, <u>Douglas-Home</u>, 85;
    Macmillan, <u>Pointing the Way</u>, 135, 230, 165 and
    <u>passim</u>. These opinions are confirmed by other
    colleagues to whom the author has spoken. It seems
    generally agreed that these qualities helped to
    make him a good man to work with
5   A quality particularly testified to by one of his
    senior officials to the author. Cf Young, <u>Douglas-
    Home</u>, 118-19
6   Lord Home to the author, cf Home, <u>The Way the Wind Blows</u>, 173-5
7   Lord Harlech to the author, 24 April 1975
8   Young, <u>Douglas-Home</u>, 103, 125, 150, 105 cf also Home,
    <u>The Way the Wind Blows</u>, 144-5, 148, 171 for his
    views on relations with the US and Russia
9   Lord Home to the author;   cf Young, <u>Douglas-Home</u>, 63
10 Cf Chapter 6 note 34 For Home's views on negotiating
    with the Russians, cf Home, <u>The Way the Wind Blows</u>, 157-8
11 Lord Home to the author. Cf Young, <u>Douglas-Home</u>,
    124;   Butler, <u>Art of the Possible</u>, 258
12 Private information
13 Kilmuir, <u>Political Adventure</u>, 313
14 Rt Hon J Godber (parliamentary under-secretary,
    Foreign Office, 1960-1, minister of state, Foreign
    Office, 1961-3 and 1970-2) in an interview with the
    author, 16 April 1975;   and Lord Harlech to the
    author

15 Cf Macmillan, Pointing the Way, 101, 107, 112–14,
    184–5
16 Young, Douglas-Home, 244 cf Home, The Way the Wind Blows, 46
17 Cf Macmillan, Pointing the Way, 449–51
18 The 'five principles', later extended by Harold Wilson
    to six, were first enunciated in talks between Home
    and Ian Smith, the Rhodesian premier, in September
    1964, (Young, Douglas-Home, 201); cf F.S.Northedge,
    Descent from Power (London, Allen & Unwin, 1974),
    224
19 A point particularly made by a minister in that gov-
    ernment to the author
20 Cf Harold Macmillan, At the End of the Day (London,
    Macmillan, 1973), 342–61
21 Hill, Both Sides of the Hill, 243; Lord Hill was a
    member of the Macmillan Cabinet 1957–62
22 Kilmuir, Political Advanture, 313
23 Lord Home to the author
24 Lord Home to the author; cf Home, The Way the Wind Blows, 71
25 For Macmillan's view on possible concessions over
    Berlin and Germany see Macmillan, Pointing the Way,
    408. President Kennedy himself and other American
    leaders were not unsympathetic, but the West German
    Chancellor, Adenauer, could not be moved on these
    points (Lord Harlech to the author; Rt Hon J.Godber
    to the author)
26 Rt Hon J.Godber to the author
27 Evidence of a minister in the Macmillan and Heath
    governments (private information)
28 Evidence of a minister in the Macmillan and Heath
    governments (private information)
29 Lord Home to the author, cf Home, The Way the Wind Blows ,241
30 Lord Home to the author
31 The views of senior officials, expressed to the author
    (private information)
32 Cf Young, Douglas-Home, 113–14, 143
33 Rt Hon J.Godber to the author
34 Lord Harlech to the author
35 Evidence of a minister in the Heath government
    (private information)
36 Northedge, Descent, 354
37 Cf Schlesinger, A Thousand Days (London, Mayflower,
    1967), 337, 356, and elsewhere
38 Macmillan, End of the Day, 336; Schlesinger,
    Thousand Days, 315–16

39 Lord Harlech to the author
40 Macmillan, End of the Day, 380-92
41 On Acheson's views, see Schlesinger, Thousand Days,
    315, 318-23. Acheson was one of Kennedy's unofficial
    advisers on foreign policy
42 Young, Douglas-Home, 132
43 Lord Harlech to the author
44 Young, Douglas-Home, 116. Young misrepresents Presi-
    dent Kennedy's views; the latter viewed the possi-
    bility of military intervention without enthusiasm.
    Cf Schlesinger, Thousand Days, 280-2; Macmillan,
    End of the Day, 337
45 Young, Douglas-Home, 332
46 Ibid, 337
47 Ibid, 127
48 Ibid
49 Lord Home to the author. Cf Home, The Way the Wind Blows, 169-70
50 Macmillan, End of the Day, 261-2
51 Rt Hon J.Godber to the author. Cf Schlesinger,
    Thousand Days, 458
52 Ibid, 458-9
53 Young, Douglas-Home, 135
54 In December 1961, and again in September 1962.
    Cf Macmillan, At the End of the Day, 284
55 Ibid, 276; see also Chapter 8, below p 179
56 Ibid, 258, 175-6. The US eventually came round to
    the British position on Malaysia (Schlesinger,
    Thousand Days, 428)
57 Lord Harlech to the author. Lord Harlech was ambassa-
    dor to Washington at the time. Cf Schlesinger,
    Thousand Days, 632, for Lord Harlech's part in the
    crisis. Some members of the British Cabinet, however,
    believed we had very little influence (Lord Duncan-
    Sandys to the author)
58 Young, Douglas-Home, 145. Cf Macmillan, End of the
    Day, 213-4. Lord Home to the author
59 These events are described in Young, Douglas-Home,
    chapters 16-26 and by Lord Home, The Way the Wind
    Blows,   chapters 13-16
60 Ibid, 283
61 Northedge, Descent, 268
62 For fuller accounts of this complex problem, see Young
    Douglas-Home, chapter 21; Lord Birkenhead, Walter
    Monckton (London, Weidenfeld & Nicolson, 1969), 343-4,
    358-9; Butler, Art of the Possible, Chapter 10;

Sir Roy Welensky, Welensky's 4000 Days (London, Collins, 1964) cf Home, The Way the Wind Blows, 251-8

63 Young, Douglas-Home, 236

64 Ibid, 271

65 Some of the crises of this period could hardly be discussed at manageable length, either verbally or on paper, without a considerable degree of 'oversimplification'. This applied for instance to the Laotion imbroglio, the case and plot of which resembled one of the more fanciful Gilbert and Sullivan operas.

66 Notably in a speech at Berwick in December 1961, delivered to a small audience, but which received wide publicity. Young, Douglas-Home,137-8; Home, The Way the Wind Blows, 160-5

67 Young, Douglas Home,197

CHAPTER 8: R A BUTLER

1   Harold Macmillan has given his account of these events
    in The End of the Day, Chapter 15, Butler in his
    memoir The Art of the Possible (London, Hamish
    Hamilton, 1971), Chapter 11. See also Randolph
    Churchill, The Fight for the Tory Leadership (London,
    Heinemann, 1964), and an article by Iain Mcleod in
    The Spectator (March 1964)
2   Cf The Earl of Kilmuir, Political Adventure (London,
    Weidenfeld, 1962), 191-2, 185-6; Lord Hill of Luton,
    Both Sides of the Hill, (London, Heinemann, 1964),
    283-40, 238-40. Kilmuir said Butler 'played his
    cards too close to his chest'. Lord Mcran,Churchill,
    The Struggle for Survival, (London, Sphere Books,
    1968), 473 says he had the reputation of 'backing
    his horses both ways'. These views may have been
    unfair, but they did Butler great harm.
3   Cf J.R.Bevins, The Greasy Pole (London, Hodder &
    Stoughton, 1965), 145;
4   Particularly with the permanent under-secretary, Sir
    Harold Caccia, a very able official (Lord Butler
    to the author, 13 May 1975)
5   Butler, Art of the Possible, 257. Carrington's
    valuable contribution was confirmed by Lord Butler
    in a recent letter to the author
6   Butler, Art of the Possible, 196, 231
7   Ibid, 249, citing the opinion of the then lord
    chancellor, Lord Dilhorne. Cf Bevins, Greasy Pole,
    145
8   Evidence of a ministerial colleague (private
    information)
9   A view strongly held by Lord Butler himself. (Lord
    Butler to the author)
10 Butler, Art of the Possible, 254-7. This passage
    contains a particularly good specimen of the non-
    ambiguous ambiguities at which Lord Butler is so
    adept.
11 Ibid, 252-3

12 Cf F.S.Northedge, <u>Descent from Power</u> (London, Allen
    & Unwin, 1974), 230-99;   Arthur M.Schlesinger, <u>A</u>
    <u>Thousand Days</u> (London, Mayflower, 1967), 427, 488;
    K.Young, <u>Sir Alec Douglas-Home</u> (London, Dent, 1970),
    197;   L.B.Johnson, <u>The Vantage Point</u> (London,
    Weidenfeld & Nicolson, 1971), 135
13 Harold Macmillan, <u>Pointing the Way</u>, (London, Macmillan,
    1972), 382;   <u>Tides of Fortune</u>, (London, Macmillan,
    1969), 641;   <u>At the End of the Day</u>, Chapter IX;
    Schlesinger, <u>Thousand Days</u>, 452;   Johnson, <u>Vantage</u>
    <u>Point</u>, 290
14 Butler, <u>Art of the Possible</u>, 257
15 Lord Butler to the author
16 Lord Butler to the author
17 Lord Butler to the author;   Young, <u>Douglas-Home</u>, 195;
    cf Ibid, 183-4
18 Butler, <u>Art of the Possible</u>, 253

CHAPTER 9: PATRICK GORDON-WALKER

1   N.Deakin (ed), Colour and the British General Election
    1964 (London, Pall Mall Press, 1965), 77-105
2   House of Commons Debates, Vol 701, col 70-1
    (3 November 1964)
3   Harold Wilson, The Labour Government 1964-70. A
    Personal Record (London, Weidenfela & Nicolson and
    Michael Joseph, 1972), 4
4   Interview with Patrick Gordon-Walker, 23 January 1975
5   The Times, 17 June 1964
6   'The New Britain', reprinted in The Times Book of the
    House of Commons 1964, (London, The Times, 1965),
    267-82
7   Ibid, 278
8   P.C.Gordon-Walker, 'The Labour Party's Foreign and
    Defence Policy', Foreign Affairs, Vol 42, No 3,
    391-8
9   Ibid, 393
10 Ibid
11 Wilson, Labour Government, 40
12 Ibid, 46
13 Ibid, 42
14 Interview with Gordon-Walker; see also Wilson,
    Labour Government, 46-50
15 Wilson, Labour Government, 51
16 Gordon-Walker, 'Foreign and Defence Policy', 395
17 Ibid
18 Ibid
19 Interview with Gordon-Walker
20 Wilson, Labour Government, 45
21 Richard Crossman, Diaries of a Cabinet Minister, Vol 1.
    Minister of Housing, 1964-66 (London, Hamish Hamilton
    and Jonathan Cape, 1975),68 (22 November 1964). This
    source should be regarded with some caution. The
    diary is rather gossipy in places and it is not clear
    how reliable a source it really is. However, it is
    valuable in so far as it gives one minister's impres-
    sion of his colleagues and of the events at the time.
22 Private information
23 Crossman, Diaries, Vol 1, 70 (24 November 1964), and
    137 (22 January 1965)

24 Patrick Gordon-Walker, <u>The Cabinet</u> (London, Fontana, revised edition 1972), 168

CHAPTER 10: MICHAEL STEWART

1   Anthony Shrimsley, The First Hundred Days of Harold
     Wilson (London, Weidenfeld & Nicolson, 1965), 16
2   Interview with Michael Stewart, 16 January 1975
3   Richard Crossman, Diaries of a Cabinet Minister,
     Vol 1 : Minister of Housing 1964-66 (London, Hamish
     Hamilton and Jonathan Cape, 1975), 136
4   Ibid
5   Harold Wilson, The Labour Government: A Personal
     Record (London, Weidenfeld & Nicolson and Michael
     Joseph, 1971), 66
6   Ibid,
7   Paul Gore-Booth, With Great Truth and Respect
     (London, Constable, 1974), 35
8   Ibid; see also William Wallace, The Foreign Policy
     Process in Britain (London, RIIA, 1975), 54
9   Interview with Michael Stewart
10   M.Stewart 'British Foreign Policy Today', Australian
     Outlook, Vol 20 (1966), 109-24
11   Paul Gore-Booth, Great Truth, 424
12   Geoffrey McDermott, The New Diplomacy and its
     apparatus (London, Plume Press and Ward Lock, 1973),
     48
13   Wilson, Labour Government, 272
14   For the detailed recommendations, see the Report of
     the Review Committee on Overseas Representation
     1968-1969 (London, HMSO, 1969), Cmd 4107. For
     comments see George Brown, In My Way (London, Penguin,
     1972),157; and articles in International Affairs:
     M.Donelan, 'The Trade of Diplomacy', Vol 45, No 4,
     605-16; F.S.Northedge, 'Britain as a Second Rank
     Power', Vol 45, No 1 37-47; and Andrew Shonfield (a
     member of the Duncan Committee), 'The Duncan
     Committee and its critics', Vol 46, No 2, 247-68
15   Interview with Michael Stewart
16   Wilson, Labour Government, 273
17   Crossman, Diaries, Vol 1, 442 (31 January 1966) and
     445 (3 February 1966)
18   Interview with Michael Stewart
19   Crossman, Diaries, Vol 1, 442 (31 January 1966)
20   Ibid

21 'The New Britain', reprinted in The Times Book of the
    House of Commons 1964, (London, The Times, 1964),
    278-9
22 'Time for Decision', reprinted in The Times Book of
    the House of Commons 1966 (London, The Times, 1966),
    283 (my emphasis)
23 Wilson, Labour Government, 218 (my emphasis)
24 Letter to author from Michael Stewart, 7 June 1975
25 Crossman, Diaries, Vol 1, 563, (7 July 1966)
26 See below, Chapter 11
27 Stewart, 'British Foreign Policy', 111-13
28 Gore-Booth, Great Truth, 336
29 For the part played by the prime minister in these
    attempts, see Wilson, Labour Government, passim
30 Ibid, 86
31 Gore-Booth, Great Truth, 337
32 Wilson, Labour Government, 204. Wilson adds that had
    he known he would 'not have agreed to a statement in
    those terms'. However, Stewart did give his appro-
    val for the statement because it was a quid pro quo
    for obtaining the bombing halt. Letter from Michael
    Stewart to the author, 4 June 1975
33 Letter from Michael Stewart to the author, 4 June 1975
    However, for a slightly different view, see Wilson,
    Labour Government, 609ff. It is possible that the
    two men are referring to slightly different incidents
34 Quoted in Robert Boardman and A.J.R.Groom (eds), The
    Management of Britain's External Relations (London
    Macmillan, 1973), 19; see also T.M.Franck & E.
    Weisband (eds), Secrecy and Foreign Policy (London,
    Oxford University Press, 1974)
35 'The New Britain', reprinted in The Times Book of the
    House of Commons 1964, 280
36 'Time for Decisions', reprinted in The Times Book of
    the House of Commons 1966, 282
37 Letter from Lord Gore-Booth to the author, 16 June
    1975. For details of Wilson's speech, see U.N.
    Chronicle, Vol 3, No 1 (January 1966), 73-5
38 Letter from Michael Stewart to the author, 4 June 1975
39 Interview with Michael Stewart; also from private
    information
40 See, for example, the resolutions carried at the 1968
    and 1969 Labour Party Annual Conference. The full
    text of the motions and the debate appear in Report
    of the 67th Annual Conference of the Labour Party,

Blackpool 1968 (London, The Labour Party 1969),
260ff; and _Report of the 68 Annual Conference of
the Labour Party, Brighton_ (London, The Labour Party,
1970), 212ff

41 Letter from Michael Stewart to the author, 4 June 1975.
For an earlier and similar reaction, see the discussion of the Congo crisis, in Chapter 7 above

42 See, for example, Stewart's speeches to the House of
Commons during most of his second period at the
Foreign Office

43 See, for example, a speech by Lord Shepherd (a junior
minister at the Foreign Office) to the party's
annual conference in 1968, _Report_, 262-3

44 Wilson, _Labour Government_, 744

45 Interview with Michael Stewart

46 Ibid

47 Ibid. See also _Keesing's Contemporary Archives_,
Vol XVII (1969-1970), col 24032-3 for an account of
the May 1970 NATO Foreign Ministers Meeting and
Stewart's remarks. _House of Commons Debates_,
Vol 768, col 1681-8 (July 18 1968 - one month _before_
the Czech crisis)

48 Interview with Michael Stewart

49 George Brown, _In My Way_ (London, Penguin, 1972), 139.
Also see below p 213

50 Crossman, _Diaries_, Vol 1, 203 (18 April 1965)

51 Gore-Booth _Great Truth_, 407

52 Wilson, _Labour Government_, 86

53 Letter from Lord Gore-Booth to the author, 16 June
1975

CHAPTER 11: GEORGE BROWN

1   See, for example, Anthony Lewis, 'Mr.Brown: An
     American View', _The Observer_, 15 January 1967. The
     opening paragraph records three allegedly typical
     George Brown anecdotes. However, this article and
     one the following week (22 January 1967) provide an
     interesting and probably fair assessment of Brown as
     seen by a distinguished American columnist
2   George Brown, _In My Way_ (London, Penguin Books, 1972)
3   For Brown's account, see _Ibid_, 65-9
4   _Ibid_, 117
5   Cf a similar incident involving Herbert Morrison;
     see above, p 77. For the effect of this and another
     incident involving a photographer at the party con-
     ference in Scarborough, see Marcia Williams, _Inside
     Number 10_ (London, Weidenfeld & Nicolson, 1972), 202.
6   Richard Crossman, _Diaries of a Cabinet Minister:
     Vol 2, _Lord President of the Council and Leader of
     the House of Commons, 1966-8_ (London, Hamish
     Hamilton and Cape, 1976), 29
7   Paul Gore-Booth, _With Great Truth and Respect_ (London,
     Constable, 1974), 347
8   George Brown (interviewed by Kenneth Harris), 'Why I
     am What I am', _The Observer_, 14 August 1966
9   Ibid (emphasis in the original)
10   Gore-Booth, _Great Truth_, 347
11   For the full text of the speech, see the _Report of the
     61st Annual Conference of the Labour Party held at
     Brighton_ (London, The Labour Party, 1963)
12   Robert McKenzie, _British Political Parties_ (London,
     Mercury Books, 2nd ed. 1963), 631
13   _The Observer_, 14 August 1967 (emphasis in original)
14   Brown, _In My Way_, 125
15   Gore-Booth, _Great Truth_, 349-50
16   Interview with Lord George-Brown, 28 January 1975
17   Brown, _In My Way_, 124-5
18   Quoted in Geoffrey McDermott, _The New Diplomacy and
     its Apparatus_ (London, Plume Press and Ward Lock,
     1973), 49
19   Letter from Lord Gore-Booth to the author, 16 June 1975
20   Brown, _In My Way_, 119

21 Interview with Lord George-Brown

22 Brown, In My Way, 163-7; Geoffrey Williams and Bruce
    Reed, Denis Healey and the Policies of Power (London
    Sidgwick & Jackson, 1971), 231-2

23 For the contrasting versions see Brown In My Way,
    163-7 and Harold Wilson, The Labour Government 1964-
    1970 A Personal Record (London, Weidenfeld & Nicolson
    and Michael Joseph, 1971), 469ff

24 See above, p 204

25 Brown, In My Way, 120

26 Ibid, 121

27 For Brown's comments on the Foreign Office, see Ibid,
    Chapters 7 and 8. For a staunch rebuttal of many of
    them, see Gore-Booth, Great Truth, 407ff

28 Interview with Lord George-Brown

29 Brown, In My Way, 76-7

30 See, for example, his speeches on foreign policy to
    the annual party conference in 1966 and 1967 and
    particularly his speech on the EEC application in
    1967. Also his speeches to the House of Commons on
    6 December 1966, 20 July 1967, 2 November 1967 and
    24 January 1968

31 Interview with Lord George-Brown

32 Ibid

33 Ibid

34 Brown, In My Way, 133

35 Nora Beloff, 'Getting Wilson to Market', The Observer,
    23 October 1966

36 Ibid

37 Brown, In My Way, 214-15

38 For a full account, see Wilson, Labour Government,
    Chapters 18, 20 and 21

39 Patrick Gordon-Walker, The Cabinet (London, Fontana,
    revised edition, 1972), 128-9

40 Report of the 65th Annual Conference of the Labour
    Party, held at Brighton (London, The Labour Party),
    271

41 Statement on Defence Estimates (Cmd 3203, London,
    HMSO, 1967)

42 Brown, In My Way, 133

43 Report of the 66th Annual Conference of the Labour
    Party, held at Scarborough (London, The Labour Party,
    1968), 234

44 Wilson, Labour Government, 243

45 The details can be obtained by reference to Wilson,
    Labour Government, Chapter 19; Brown, In My Way
    133-40; Gore-Booth, Great Truth, 355-62 and
    Chester L.Cooper, The Lost Crusade (London,
    MacGibbon & Key, 1971), 350-68
46 Wilson, Labour Government, 357
47 Brown,In My Way, 140
48 Ibid
49 Joseph Frankel, British Foreign Policy 1945-1973
    (London, Oxford University Press for the Royal
    Institute of International Affairs, 1975), 165
50 Brown, In My Way, 132. The account is based on
    Brown's memoirs, 129-32
51 Ibid, 128. Some of the detail of the criticism is
    disputed by Gore-Booth, Great Truth, 365. However,
    he adds that 'for all this I believe, and I believed
    at the time, that Mr.Brown is right in substance'
52 Brown, In My Way, 127
53 Ibid, 128-9
54 Wilson, Labour Government, 396-7
55 Gordon-Walker, Cabinet, 138-51. Also The Sunday
    Times, 9 April 1972
56 Frankel, British Foreign Policy, 138
57 Brown, In My Way, 127
58 Ibid, 126
59 Gordon-Walker, Cabinet, 93
60 Interview with Lord George-Brown; for the text of
    the resolution see Brown,In My Way, 270-1
61 Interview with Lord George-Brown
62 Brown, In My Way, 140ff
63 Gore-Booth, Great Truth, 379
64 Brown, In My Way, 157-8
65 Brian Lapping, The Labour Government 1964-70 (London
    Penguin Books, 1970), 65
66 F S.Northedge, 'Britain as a Second-Rank Power',
    International Affairs, Vol 46, No 1 (January 1970),
    40
67 Brown, In My Way, Chapter 9; Wilson, Labour Govern-
    ment, 506ff; Williams, Inside Number 10, 241-4;
    Crossman, Diaries, Vol 2, 712-4
68 Wilson, Labour Government, 272
69 McDermott, New Diplomacy, 48
70 Williams, Inside Number 10, 151
71 Frankel, British Foreign Policy, 103
72 Brown, In My Way, 158

73 William Wallace, <u>The Foreign Policy Process in</u>
     <u>Britain</u> (London, RIIA, 1975), 293
74 Wilson, <u>Labour Government</u>, p.512. See also a sympa-
     thetic assessment of Brown in Crossman, <u>Diaries</u>,Vol 2,
     714-16
75 <u>The Observer</u>, 14 August 1966
76 Interview with Lord George-Brown
77 Lord Gore-Booth to the author, 16 June 1975
78 Brown, <u>In My Way</u>, 121-4
79 Quoted in Ibid, 272
80 Wallace, <u>Foreign Policy Process</u>, 169
81 Crossman, <u>Diaries</u>, Vol 2, 57
82 Ibid, 110

POSTSCRIPT

1   Harold Wilson, The Labour Government 1964-70: A
    Personal Record (London, Weidenfeld & Nicolson and
    Michael Joseph, 1971), 511
2   Private information and Richard Crossman, Diaries of
    a Cabinet Minister, Vol 2 (London, Hamish Hamilton
    and Cape 1976), 649, 716-7, 719
3   See above, p 194-5
4   For the text of the speech see M.Stewart, 'British
    Foreign Policy Today', Australian Outlook, Vol 20
    (1966), 109-24
5   Ibid, 117-19
6   For a fuller discussion of British policy east of Suez,
    see Phillip Darby, British Defence Policy East of
    Suez, 1947-1968, (London, Oxford University Press,
    1973); Wilson, Labour Government; Geoffrey Williams
    and Bruce Reed, Denis Healey and the Policies of
    Power, (London, Sidgwick & Jackson, 1971); Patrick
    Gordon-Walker, The Cabinet (London, Fontana, 2nd ed,
    1972); and Brian Lapping, The Labour Government,
    1964-70 (London, Penguin Books, 1970). In 1972
    a Conservative cabinet minister, speaking to one of
    the authors, described the British contingent at
    Singapore as 'merely a token'
7   See above, p.170.

INDEX

Acheson, Dean, 54, 56, 62–3, 97, 142, 160–1
Aden, 166, 171, 178, 201, 216
Adenauer, Konrad, 97, 139, 161
Arabia, 175, 177–8
Atlantic Pact (NATO), 45, 48–52, 56, 68, 77, 91–2, 96–8, 101–2, 114, 178–9 185–6, 194–5, 203, 211
Attlee, Clement, 35–6, 42, 45–6, 50, 70, 77–9, 181, 192; relations with Bevin, 18, 29–31; relations with Morrison, 70, 74–9
Australia, 62, 131
Austria, 40, 116
Avon, Earl of, see Sir A. Eden

Baghdad Pact (CENTO), 95, 104, 114, 124, 137, 170
Bangladesh, 155, 168
Benelux, 47–50, 101–2
Berlin, 160–1, 163; crisis (1948–9), 139, 160; crisis (1958), 138–40, 147–8, 150, 153, 158–60; wall, 139, 161
Bermuda Conference (1957, 127, 136
Bevin, Ernest, Chapter 2 passim, 6, 9, 11, 17, 21, 25, 70, 72–5, 79, 88, 126, 206, 218; relations with

Attlee, 18, 29–31; early career, 27–8, 34; relations with colleagues, 30, 35, 64; personality, 27–8 31–2, 34, 36–7, 64–9; relations with officials, 32–8, 64; foreign office planning department, 34–5; view of Britain's role in the world, 36, 38; relations with Russia, 37, 39–46, 64; attitude to UN, 41–2; 'third force' idea, 42; relations with America 44–6, 48–51, 68; and ERP 44–7, 53, 68; and BTO, 46, 48–50; and NATO, 46, 48–50; and Western Union, 46–50, 67–8; and the Dunkirk Treaty, 47; attitude to Europe, 48–50, 51–6; attitude to Commonwealth, 51–2, 57–8; and German rearmament, 56; and middle east, 57–61, 65, 67; and far east, 57, 61–4; and 'socialist' foreign policy, 65–7; career assessed, 64–9
Biafra, 193, 202, 211
Boulding, Kenneth, 16
Brown, George, Chapter 11 passim, 6, 9, 11, 20, 31, 191, 193–6, 199, 201, 203–4, 222; relations with Wilson, 18, 206–8; 212–14

qualities, 205-6; early career, 205; relations with colleagues, 206, 209-210; relations with officials, 206-9, 215-16, 218-19; position in Labour Party, 206, 209; relations with Russia, 206; relations with Europe, 206, 209-212, 216-18; relations with Africa, 208; and middle east, 209, 211, 213-16; and a 'socialist' foreign policy, 210; and far east 212-13; view of Britain's role in the world, 217; relations with America, 217; attitude to Commonwealth, 217; resignation, 218; career assessed, 218-20

Brussels Treaty Organisation (BTO), 46, 48-50, 53, 101-102

Butler, R.A., Chapter 8 passim, 9, 11, 21, 87, 111, 113, 119, 157; early career, 174; qualities, 174-5; relations with colleagues, 175; relations with officials, 175-6; relations with America, 176-177, 179-80; relations with Russia, 176-7, 180; relations with Europe, 177, 180; and far east, 178, 180; and the middle east, 178; and Cyprus, 178-80; relations with Home 179; career assessed, 180.

Bulganin, N.A. 114, 205

Caccia, Lord, 9, 183, 192
Canada, 49, 92, 131, 158
Caradon, Lord, see Sir H.Foot

Central African Federation, 156, 174
Ceylon, 57, 61, 131
Chalfont, Lord, 183, 188, 200, 207
Chamberlain, N., 82, 146, 153, 174
Chinese People's Republic, 61-3, 79, 106, 158-9, 168, 177-8, 223
Churchill, W.S., 20, 28, 35, 40, 43, 55, 79, 82-3, 87, 91, 94-5, 99, 101, 103, 105-6, 113-14, 119, 121, 125, 127, 134, 146; relations with Eden, 18, 84-6, 94; concept of the 'interlocking circles', 50, 91-92, 133, 159, 184
Colombo Plan, 63
Colonial Office, 131-2, 156-157, 175
Commonwealth Office (CRO), 131-2, 144, 146, 150, 175, 189; merges with the foreign office, 17, 156-7, 193, 199, 201
Congo, 147, 151-2, 158-9, 164-5, 172
Conservative Party, 20, 23, 84, 91, 99, 104, 108, 124-5, 133, 135, 146, 168-9, 174-5, 185, 193
Cripps, Sir Stafford, 30, 35, 73
Cuba, 173; missile crisis, 148, 159, 162, 166-8
Cyprus, 131, 142, 159, 175, 177-9
Czechoslovakia, 48, 203

Dalton, Hugh, 28, 30, 36, 51, 61, 79
Disarmament, 138, 143, 158, 160, 203;Minister,129,184

Dulles, J.Foster, 89, 95–7, 101–2, 104–6, 114, 121, 133–9, 142, 162
Duncan Report, 25, 194
Dunkirk Treaty, 47–8

ECSC (Schuman Plan), 55–6, 79, 92, 100, 122–3
EDC (Pleven Plan), 56, 78–9, 96, 100–2, 108, 122
Eden, Sir Anthony, (Lord Avon), Chapter 4 passim, 6, 9, 11, 28, 66, 75, 110–112, 114, 118–21, 125–9, 134, 136, 142, 144, 146, 152–3, 221; relations with Churchill, 18, 84–6, 94; early career, 81–3; qualities, 83, 88–90, 93–4, 108–9; position in Conservative Party, 84, 104, 108; relations with officials 86–8; view of foreign affairs, 88–90; view of Britain's role in the world, 90–2, 109; attitude to Commonwealth, 91–2, 96; relations with Europe, 91, 99–102; relations with America, 91, 95–6; relations with Russia, 94–5, 98; relations with Dulles, 95–6; and the middle east, 95–6, 102–5; and the German problem, 96–8; and the far east, 105–7; health, 107; career asses assessed, 107–9.
EEC see European Community
EFTA 140–1, 187, 196
Egypt, 60, 74, 76, 78, 102–4, 111, 115, 124, 134, 136, 132, 170, 178, 214
Eisenhower, President D.D., 94–5, 103, 105, 113–14,

121, 133–4, 136, 138, 159–60, 162–3
ELDO, 211
ERP, see Marshall Plan
Euratom, 102
European Community (EEC),8, 18, 23, 102, 122–4, 140–1, 145, 150, 154, 167–8, 184–5, 187, 195–7, 199, 201, 204, 206, 209–12, 223–5

Foot, Sir Hugh (Lord Caradon), 156, 188, 200
Foreign Office (FCO), 7, 17, 19–21, 44, 64, 69; planning machinery, 34–5, 86, 210; under Bevin, 32–8; under Morrison, 74; under Eden, 86–8; under Macmillan, 113; under Lloyd, 117–18, 125–6, 128–30; under Home, 145, 149, 153–157, 171; under Butler, 175–6; under Gordon Walker, 183–4; under Stewart, 192–3; 202, 204, under Brown, 206–7, 215–19
Formosa, see Taiwan
Frankel, J., 213–18
France, 46–9, 53–6, 61, 93, 97, 101, 105, 113–14, 122–3, 134–6, 139–40, 150, 161, 168, 176, 194–5, 210–11

Gaitskell, Hugh, 74, 182, 206
de Gaulle, President, 124, 139–40, 150, 154, 161, 167, 177, 185, 195, 199, 211
Germany, 38–9, 41, 48–9, 54–5, 64, 76, 93, 96–8, 102, 114, 116, 121–2, 153,

158, 160–2, 167, 186, 195,
East, 139, 150, 160–2, 167;
rearmament in West, 56, 74,
78, 100–2, 122
Gibraltar, 200, 216
Gladwyn, Lord, (Gladwyn Jebb),
79, 101
Gordon Walker, Patrick,
Chapter 9 passim, 9, 11,
191–2, 203–4, 210, 212,
214–15; outside parlia-
ment, 181–3; early career,
181–2; relations with
colleagues, 182; and a
'socialist' foreign policy,
183; relations with
officials, 183–4, 189;
view of Britain's role in
the world, 184; attitude
to Commonwealth, 184, 187;
relations with America,
185–6; relations with
Europe, 184, 187; rela-
tions with Wilson, 188;
career assessed, 189–90
Gore-Booth, Lord, 9, 183–4,
207, 209, 216
Greece, 28, 43, 142, 178–9
Greenhill Lord, 9, 209

Hayter, Sir William, 32–3
Healey, Dennis, 32, 191, 208,
214, 222
Heath Edward, 145, 153–4,
159, 167–8, 171, 196, 224
Herter, Christian, 149, 159
Hitler, Adolf, 93–4
Hogg, Q. (Lord Hailsham),
117, 174
Home, Lord (Sir A.Douglas-
Home), Chapter 7, passim
9, 11, 87, 131, 174–5, 179,
183, 193, 221, 224; early
career 144–6; position as
a peer, 144–5, relations

with officials, 145–6,
149, 155–7, 171, qualities,
145–7, 151–2, 171–2, relations with America, 174,
150–1, 158–68, 224; atti-
tude to Commonwealth, 147,
154–6, 158, 168–9, view
of Britain's role in the
world, 147, 157–8, 165,
172; relations with
Russia, 148, 156, 160–4,
172; attitude to 'summits',
148–9; relations with
Europe, 150–1, 158–9,
167–8; and the middle
east, 150, 165–6, 170,
224; relations with
colleagues, 151–3, 106–7;
and 'bi-partisan' foreign
policy, 152; compared
with Eden, 152; relations
with Macmillan, 153–4;
relations with Heath, 154–
155, 168; and the far
east, 162–4, 166; reappointed foreign secretary, 167;
career assessed, 171–3;
Hungary, 46, 134
Hussein, King, 115, 137

India, 57–8, 61, 63, 104,
131, 154–5, 158–9, 168,
170
Indo-China, 90, 105–8, 162,
197
Indonesia, 61, 166, 177–8,
200–1
Iran, see Persia
Iraq, 58, 60, 104, 114–15,
137, 160
Israel, 60, 111, 115, 134,
152, 170, 214–15, 224
Italy, 55, 90, 101–2, 108,
112

Japan, 62, 77
Johnson, President L.B., 167,
  176-7, 186, 199, 223
Jordon, 60, 124, 137

Kennedy, PresidentJ.F., 154,
  158, 160-1, 163-7, 176
'Kennedy Round', 179
Khrushchev, N.S., 114, 127,
  139, 160-2, 176, 205
Kilmuir, Lord (Sir D.Maxwell-
  Fyfe), 86, 99, 110
Kirkpatrick, Sir I., 33, 35-
  36, 131
Kissinger, Henry, 9, 20, 149,
  159, 170, 215, 219
Korea, 40; war, 56, 63, 74,
  76, 79, 120
Kosygin, A., 213

Labour Party, 20, 23, 31, 33,
  50, 64-5, 79, 113, 125,
  133, 151, 181, 185, 187,
  193, 195, 197, 200, 203,
  212; national executive,
  55, 74; Parliamentary
  (PLP), 32, 73, 181-2, 191-
  192, 194, 206, 209
Laos, 106-7, 153, 159-60,
  162-4
Lloyd, Selwyn, Chapter, 6
  passim, 9, 11, 17, 88,
  145-6, 149-50, 178; early
  career, 117, 119-20; relations with Eden, 120-1,
  126-7; relations with
  America, 121-2, 125, 127,
  136-40; relations with
  Russia, 121-2, 124-5, 127,
  137-40; relations with
  Europe, 122-4, 140-2;
  attitude to the Common-
  wealth, 123, 131-2; and
  the middle east, 124, 130-
  131, 134-7; relations

with officials, 125-6,
  128-31, 141-2; relations
  with colleagues, 125-6
  128-9, 141; qualities,
  125,135, 141-3; relations
  with Macmillan, 126-8,
  142-3; view of Britain's
  role in the world 133;
  career assessed, 118-19,
  141-3
Lebanon, 137

Macmillan, Harold, Chapter
  5 passim, 6, 7, 9, 11, 29,
  46, 71, 88-9, 118-19,
  125-8, 136-41, 145-6, 150
  153-4, 156-61, 163-7, 171,
  174, 178, 183, 195; relations with Eden, 111;
  qualities, 112; early
  career, 112; relations
  with America, 112-14;
  relations with Europe,
  113, 115; attitude to
  Commonwealth, 113; relations with officials, 113;
  relations with Russia,
  113-14; attitude to
  'summits', 114; and the
  middle east, 114-5;
  career assessed, 110,
  115-16
Malaysia (Malaya), 61, 166,
  175, 177, 200-1
Marshall, General G., 43-4
  48-9, 52
Marshall Plan (ERP), 44-5,
  47, 53, 68
Molotov, V.M., 40-1, 44-5,
  98
Monnet, Jean, 54, 123
Morgenthau, Hans, 13
Morrison, Herbert, Chapter
  3, passim, 181, early
  career, 70, relations

with Attlee, 70; relations with Europe, 71-73, 78, position in Labour Party, 73-4; relations with officials, 74-5, 78-9; relations with colleagues, 77-9; contrasted with Bevin, 74-5; and the middle east, 76-8; attacked by Opposition, 78; possible replacements, 79; career assessed, 80
Multi-Lateral Force (MLF), 179, 185-6, 188
de Murville, C., 149, 176-7
Mussolini, B., 82, 93-4

Nassau (Polaris) Agreement, 164, 186
Nasser, President G.A., 104, 134-5, 178, 214,216
NATO, see Atlantic Alliance
Nigeria, 201-2, 211, 233
Non Proliferation Treaty, 176, 200
Northedge, F.S., 9, 24
Nuri-es-Said, 104, 137
Nutting, Sir, A., 94, 100, 103, 108, 129

OEEC, 52, 140

Pakistan, 57, 104, 131, 154-155, 158-9, 168, 170
Palestine, 58, 60
Parliamentary control of foreign affairs, 19, 23, 189, 219
Persia, (Iran), 104-5, 170; Gulf, 58, 124, 166, 170-1, 178, 216; oil, 74, 76-8, 105, 108
Pleven Plan, see EDC
Plowden Report, 175, 193

Poland, 39, 46, 160
Pompidou, President, G., 167-8, 211
Portugal, 151, 172, 202
Prime Minister's role in foreign policy process, 18, 128, 189

Rhodesia, 151-2, 155, 167-170, 197, 199-202, 208, 214; UDI, 169, 199; UN Sanctions, 170, 216; Pearce Commission, 169-70
Rusk, Dean, 149, 159-60, 186
Russia, see USSR

Salisbury, Lord, 87, 144
Saudi Arabia, 115, 150, 171, 178
Schuman Plan, see ECSC
SEATO, 163, 166
Smith, Ian, 169, 223
Snyder, Bruck and Sapin approach to foreign policy analysis, 14
Soames, Sir C., 199, 219
South Africa, 147, 158, 168-70, 172-3, 202; arms sales, 154, 156, 208; Simonstown agreement, 150
Spaak, P-H, 100, 123
Spain, 147, 172-3
Sprout, H & M, 16
Stalin, J.V., 39-40, 94
Stewart, Michael, Chapter 10 passim, 9, 11, 209-11, 221-3; early career 191-192; relations with colleagues, 192, 222; relations with officials, 192-3, 202, 204; view of Britain's role in the world, 192-4; qualities, 193; relations with

Wilson, 194–5;   attitude
to Commonwealth, 194–7,
199–200; relations with
America, 194, 197–9, 203–
204;   relations with
Russia, 195, 204;   rela-
tions with Europe, 195–6,
201, 204;   and the 'third
world', 200;   reappointed
foreign secretary, 201,
222;   and the far east,
223;   career assessed,
203–4

Strang, Lord, 33, 66–7

Suez, 58, 60;   crisis, 23,
107, 117–19, 123, 125,
127–30, 133–6, 142, 150,
155, 158, 174, 214;   canal,
104, 108, 124, 159, 170,
208;   canal users' asso-
ciation, 127, 134;   'east
of Suez' policy, 150, 194,
212–13, 223

Sukarno, President, 166, 177

Taiwan (Formosa), 63, 143,
159, 168

Test Ban Treaty, 138, 154,
160–1, 164, 176

Thorneycroft, Peter, 117,
152

Truman, President H.S., 39,
43, 49, 59;   Doctrine,
44–5

Turkey, 40, 43, 46, 114, 137,
142, 178–9

UN, 39, 41–2, 46, 52, 59–60,
63, 78, 119, 129, 131,
134–5, 151, 156, 158, 164,
169, 172, 188, 194, 196,
200, 209, 216, 223;   security council, 41, 164, 215;
secretary general, 42, 214,
216;   general assembly,

90, 120–1, 200;   force in
the Congo, 164–5;   sanc-
tions against Rhodesia,
170, 200, 223;   force in
Cyprus, 179;   force in
Sinai, 214

USA, 38, 41–6, 48–51, 53,
56, 59–60, 62–3, 65, 68,
77, 91–2, 95–7, 99, 101–3,
112–15, 118, 121, 125,
127, 132–9, 143, 147,
150–3, 158–68, 177–9,
185–6, 194, 197–9, 203,
213;   Congress, 19, 49,
106

USSR, 37–47, 49–50, 62–4,
67–8, 91, 93–4, 96–8,
104, 106, 111, 113–16,
118, 120–2, 124–5, 134,
136, 138–9, 143, 148,
150–1, 158, 160–5, 167,
170–2, 176–8, 195, 202,
213–14

Vietminh, 105–6

Vietnam, 106, 134, 164, 186,
197–9, 201, 203, 209, 213,
223–4

Vital, David, 17

Walker, P.G., see P.Gordon-
Walker

Wallace, William, 19

WEU, 102, 212

Wilson, Harold, 171, 181–3,
186, 189, 191, 193–4,
198–200, 209, 211, 213–15,
218, 222;   relations with
Brown, 18, 106–8, 213–14;
relations with Gordon
Walker, 188;   relations
with Stewart, 194–5

Yemen, 137, 166, 171, 178

Younger, Sir Kenneth, 9, 22,

75
Yugoslavia, 90, 108